D0368683

UPRISING

ALSO BY SALLY ARMSTRONG

NONFICTION

Bitter Roots, Tender Shoots:
The Uncertain Fate of Afghanistan's Women

Veiled Threat: The Hidden Power of the Women of Afghanistan

FICTION

The Nine Lives of Charlotte Taylor

UPRISING

A New Age Is Dawning for Every Mother's Daughter

SALLY ARMSTRONG

THOMAS DUNNE BOOKS

ST. MARTIN'S PRESS ☒ NEW YORK

THOMAS DUNNE BOOKS.
An imprint of St. Martin's Press.

UPRISING. Copyright © 2013, 2014 by Sally Armstrong. All rights
reserved. Printed in the United States of America. For information, address
St. Martin's Press, 175 Fifth Avenue, New York, NY 10010.

www.thomasdunnebooks.com
www.stmartins.com

Library of Congress Cataloging-in-Publication Data

Armstrong, Sally, 1943–
Uprising : a new age is dawning for every mother's daughter / by Sally
Armstrong. — First U.S. edition.
    pages cm
  Includes bibliographical references and index.
  ISBN 978-1-250-04528-7 (hardcover)
  ISBN 978-1-4668-4398-1 (e-book)
  1. Women political activists—Biography.   2. Women—Social conditions—21st
century.   3. Women—Economic conditions—21st century.   4. Social justice.
5. Human rights.   6. Leadership.   I. Title.
  HQ1236.A757 2014
  305.4009'05—dc23

                                                    2013046337

St. Martin's Press books may be purchased for educational, business,
or promotional use. For information on bulk purchases, please contact
Macmillan Corporate and Premium Sales Department at 1-800-221-7945,
extension 5442, or write specialmarkets@macmillan.com.

A different version of this book was previously published under the title
Ascent of Women by Random House Canada.

First U.S. Edition: March 2014

10 9 8 7 6 5 4 3 2 1

For Malala Yousafzai,
who spoke up for girls' education in Pakistan:

"I want to say to the world that you must try to get
education, because it is very important . . . it is also important that
we should say no to wrong. And if there is something
going wrong we must have the confidence to say that this thing
is going wrong, and we must raise our voice."

And for everyone dedicated to making such education
happen, especially Sally Wales Goodrich (1942–2010),
a mother, mentor, friend, and wife. Sally's son was a
passenger on the second plane to hit the World Trade Center on
9/11, yet she turned that evil into goodness, devoting the rest of
her life to the education of Afghan students.

Contents

The Making of a Revolution

The earth is shifting. A new age is dawning. From Kabul and Cairo to Cape Town and New York, women are claiming their space at home, at work, and in the public square. They are propelling changes so immense, they're likely to affect intractable issues such as poverty, interstate conflict, culture, and religion, and the power brokers are finally listening.

The new wave of change isn't about giving the "little woman" a fair shake or even about pushing reluctant regimes to adhere to hard-won international laws relating to women. It is based on the notion that the world can no longer afford to oppress half its population. The economist Jeffrey Sachs, spearheading the United Nations Millennium Project, claims that the status of women is directly related to the economy: when one is flourishing, so is the other; when one is in the ditch, so is the other. The World Bank asserts that if women and girls are treated fairly, the economy of a village will improve.

Those who monitor the state of the world's women are speaking out as never before. There's this, from Isobel Coleman, senior fellow for U.S. foreign policy at the Council on Foreign Relations in New York: "Countries that oppress their women are doomed to be failed states."

And this, from Farida Shaheed of Pakistan, United Nations Independent Expert in the Field of Cultural Rights: "More women are enjoying more rights and more spaces than ever before."

And this: "Together men and women are the two wings of a bird—both wings have to be not wounded, not broken, in order to push the bird forward." That's from Sima Samar, chair of the Afghanistan Independent Human Rights Commission.

And Canada's Marilou McPhedran, director of the Institute for International Women's Rights, says, "Change does not occur because we want it to occur or because it's fair for a just society. Change occurs because people engage in the process."

One of the most vocal leaders of the new age of women is Hillary Clinton, who had plenty to say while U.S. secretary of state: "Recent history shows that agreements that exclude women and ignore their concerns usually fail. . . . In country after country, we have seen women help push peace agreements to the finish line. Where women are excluded, too often the agreements that result are disconnected from ground-truth and less likely to be successful and enjoy popular support."

Now, at last, is the time for women.

Most Western women thought that our time had come with the second wave of the women's movement during the 1960s and '70s (the first wave being the fight for the right to vote led by suffragettes in Australia, New Zealand, the United Kingdom, the United States, and Canada more than half a century earlier). Although much was accomplished, the finish line when it came to equality still eluded many women in the West; in the rest of the world it remained a seemingly unattainable dream. Not anymore. The catalysts of change today are women from the East as well as the West, and Africa too. And they have powerful backing from mainstream economists, policy gurus, and political figures who have realized that educating and otherwise advancing the opportunities and rights of women and girls is the way forward.

Two unlikely factors have contributed to the dawning of this new age: distortion and disease. The rise of Islamism in the late-twentieth century spurred women in Asia and the Middle East to resist what they saw as the extremist hijacking of their religion. In Africa, the HIV/AIDS pandemic brought women together as never before when they realized they would die if they didn't take action against the sexual improvidence of men. In the West, the information-based society that burst on the scene with the turn of the century moved a woman's style of management into the mainstream: networks rather than hierarchies and shared leadership rather than top-down management became new touchstones in the corporate world.

And Facebook, Twitter, e-mail, and blogging brought women the world over together. Women wearing blue jeans discovered that women in hijabs were not subjugated, voiceless victims. Women wearing hijabs found out that contrary to what the fundamentalists said, women in blue jeans were not whores and infidels. Together they learned that the impunity and power of opportunistic men were holding all of them back, hurting their children, making the future bleak. And they knew it was time for systemic change. Today women are becoming a force so powerful that everyone from presidents to pollsters is beginning to see us in a new light—as the way to end poverty and conflict, as the means of improving the economy. It's a change in attitude that centuries of women have worked toward.

A new cohort of savvy game-changers has emerged. They represent millions of women who've been trapped in religious dogma, suffocating in cultural contradictions. Until recently they had been bullied into silence by extremists who claim, "This is our culture, our religion, and none of your business." Now women have found their voices and told the rest of the world that it *is* our business, that cultural traditions are no excuse for criminal behavior.

After a flurry of changes in the West in the sixties, seventies, and eighties, it seemed that an unsettling quiet prevailed. Some said feminism was dead. But early into the 2000s the aspirations of young people in war-torn regions like Afghanistan and disease-ravaged Africa were bubbling beneath the surface. They wanted to shed the parts of the past that choked their dreams. Like participants in the women's movement that had gone before, the new wave of young people challenged taboos. They tackled unmentionable topics such as female genital mutilation. They started asking questions they had never asked before, about why men decided whether women would go to school, work outside the home, own property. The temperature rose and the lid on the pot began to rattle.

Young women began to sneer at old men with old customs. Women who hadn't dared to speak up started denouncing cultural practices and bogus religious claims that had survived for centuries. The biggest fear for extremists, misogynists, and chauvinists today is that women in Asia and Africa and the Americas are finding common ground.

In 2001, women throughout the world were riveted to the fate of the burqa-clad women of Afghanistan who'd been denied education, jobs, and health care under the Taliban. Ten years later, in 2011, there was Tahrir Square; women around the world cheered for their sisters who were helping to topple Egypt's dictatorial regime. During the decade in between, Pakistan's hated Hudood Ordinance, which demanded that a raped woman have four male witnesses to prove she hadn't caused the rape, were brought down; the personal status laws in Egypt that deny women rights in marriage were challenged for the first time; women in Kabul found the courage to march in the street; Liberian women surrounded the men at a peace conference and barricaded the building, saying they wouldn't leave until a peace accord was struck and held a "sex strike" to make their point. In Swaziland, grandmothers from twenty-five African countries plus Canada gathered to demand action and turn the tide on HIV/AIDS. In the United States in 2012, women finally spoke back to the religious right en masse in defense of *Roe v. Wade*, the court case that gave American women abortion rights in 1973. And in Canada, Aboriginal women, who had accused the government of failing to take action on the file of their missing and likely murdered sisters, aunts, daughters, and mothers, called for outside help from the United Nations and got it, giving the government an embarrassing black eye.

None of these events would have happened without the change that women had begun to lead. For example, Malala Yousafzai, sixteen, has become the voice of girls throughout the world. She is the epitome of the change that is sweeping nation after nation today. Only a few years ago, we would likely never have heard her story. When the cowardly Taliban shot her in the head on October 9, 2012, for daring to go to school and speaking up for girls' education, it wouldn't have been surprising if the people living in the Swat Valley, Pakistan, dismissed the news—"So what? She's a girl." Elsewhere, had we heard the story, we would have tut-tutted and said, "How dreadful, but it's the way they treat their girls; there's nothing we can do."

Instead, Malala's story made every newspaper in the world and every radio and television broadcast; people stayed tuned as news spread about where she was being treated and when she was being transferred first to Islamabad and then to London, England. In February we saw or read about all the details of the reconstruction cranial surgery and the cochlear implant the doctors would use to repair the damage to her skull and restore some of her hearing. I was in Victoria, British Columbia, when I had a call from a news agency. "Hurry to the studio," they said. "We need a news hit— Malala just got out of the hospital." Then in early March she was in the news again. Sporting a little pink backpack, Malala was returning to school. And on July 12, 2013, her sixteenth birthday, she stood in front of the UN and spoke like a seasoned advocate about girls' education.

She had become the world's daughter. It was as though the citizens of the world had lifted a curtain and suddenly saw the extraordinary stupidity of refusing to educate girls and the consequences of kow-towing to the extremists who claim they are acting in the name of God when they shoot teenage girls in the head for wanting to learn to read. Ban Ki-moon, Secretary General of the United Nations, said, "By targeting Malala, extremists showed what they feared most: a girl with a book."

Malala has that elusive "it" factor—the one that combines strength and sweetness, resolve and vision. She wore the late Benazir Bhut-to's scarf and brilliantly combined the prophet Muhammad with Jesus Christ, Martin Luther King Jr., Nelson Mandela, and Gandhi when she spoke in her straightforward, from-the-heart style at the UN.

She put the world on alert that July 12 when she said, "There was a time when women social activists asked men to stand up for their rights. But this time we will do it by ourselves." And she announced the way forward for women: "They thought that the bullet would silence us, but they failed. And out of that silence came thousands of voices. . . . Weakness, fear, and hopelessness died; strength, power, and courage [were] born."

It's not just the newfound leaders like Malala who are driving change. The foot soldiers in this war against oppressors of women and girls are also marching. In India, when Jyoti Singh Pandey was raped to death by a bunch of hooligans in a bus, a curtain also was raised. Her legacy is that the brutal story ripped the lid off fifty years of secrecy about the status of women in India. As it turns out, the fastest-growing democracy in the world and the hottest economy needs to change the way it treats 50 percent of its population. Now the women of India are on the street, demanding change. And the world is watching from a different lens.

"Thousands of people have been killed by the terrorists and millions have been injured. I'm just one of them," said Malala. "So here I stand, one girl among many. I speak not for myself, but [so that] those without [a] voice can be heard. . . . One child, one teacher, one book, and one pen can change the world."

Like a modern-day Joan of Arc, this sixteen-year-old kid recovering from a bullet wound to the head got the attention of the world. She has the platform, and the world is listening.

This new commitment to the education of girls is a major shift. For example, in Afghanistan, the women refer to their illiteracy as blindness. When I asked them what they meant by that, one woman explained: "I couldn't read, so I couldn't see what was going on." In fewer than a dozen words, she described a system that men in power have relied on for centuries—keep women uneducated so they won't know what's going on.

The upsurge in education is changing the way women and girls live their lives. In Saudi Arabia, enrollment in primary and secondary schools for girls has been rising by 8.3 percent a year. The women who in 2011 and 2012 protested the ban against females' driving were dentists and professors and IT specialists. These women and their daughters are no longer willing to ask permission of male guardians to move about freely on their own in their home country, travel abroad, or have a medical procedure. What's more, the birthrate in Saudi Arabia is falling to European levels, and customs such as marrying a first cousin are falling out of favor. Farida Shaheed says, "The more options women have, the less they are under the thumb of their husbands, fathers, priests, and mullahs."

The changes I describe in this book are not about the triumph of women over men, Western values over Eastern, or one religion over another. They're aimed at solving the world's most intractable problems—poverty, conflict, and violence. This new manifesto for women is being written in mud-brick houses in Afghanistan and in Cairo's Tahrir Square; in the forests of Congo even as women hide from roaming militias; and in a shelter in northern Kenya where 160 girls between the ages of three and seventeen launched a precedent-setting lawsuit against their government for failing to protect them from rape.

Women revolutionaries and visionaries in cities and villages the world over are making history. Leading the way are women like Gloria Steinem, Hillary Clinton, and Isobel Coleman from the United States; Sima Samar from Afghanistan; Farida Shaheed from Pakistan; Shirin Ebadi from Iran; and Ellen Johnson Sirleaf from Liberia. The list of game-changers also includes Luz Méndez from Guatemala, Siphiwe Hlophe from Swaziland, and Mary Eberts, Fiona Sampson, and Margot Franssen from Canada, as well as women from every far-flung corner of the planet who have marched and petitioned and stood in solidarity to eradicate religiously or culturally sanctioned acts of violence against women and children.

Supporters are jumping on this bandwagon like born-again believers in the power of women. The philanthropist Bill Gates says, "The past decade has seen more progress against inequality than any of the previous five." Doug Saunders, a columnist for *The Globe and Mail*, writes, "The most potent forces in the world right now . . . are all centered around the mythic figure of the teenage girl," commenting on a campaign by the charity Plan International, Because I Am a Girl, which recognizes that the fate of girls and young women is precisely the fate of their countries and communities. Britain's royal family ended a thousand years of tradition in 2011 by reversing a primogeniture rule that favored males for succession to the throne; females now have the same rights to the throne as men. The writer Naomi Wolf says, "Once you educate women, democratic agitation is likely to accompany the massive cultural shift that follows." And Harvard psychologist Steven Pinker, author of the recently published examination of human violence *The Better Angels of Our Nature*, states unequivocally that the world would be more peaceful if women were in charge. "Over the long sweep of history, women have been, and will be, a pacifying force. Traditional war is a man's game: tribal women never band together and raid neighboring villages." For women, security means more than the absence of war. It means that they can get medical attention when they are giving birth; it means that their children can go to school safely. It means that they can farm the land without fear of land mines and find water without fear of being raped and killed on the path from the village to the well.

The United Nations Security Council unanimously adopted Resolution 1325 on October 31, 2000—the first time the Security Council addressed the disproportionate and unique impact of armed conflict on women; recognized the undervalued and underutilized contributions that women make to conflict prevention, peacekeeping, conflict resolution, and peace building; and at the same time stressed the importance of women's equal and full participation as active agents in peace and security. Nice words, but the fact is, more than a decade later, women still have to fight their way to the negotiating table and are often not included. Says Hillary Clinton, "If we want to make progress toward settling the world's most intractable conflicts, let's enlist women."

The idea isn't new. A dozen years ago, in 2001, Jane Jacobs explained the far-reaching effects of well-managed economies and the vital role that women play in them in her book *The Nature of Economies.* Using the form of a platonic dialogue—a conversation over coffee among five fictional friends—Jacobs put these words in the mouth of one of her characters: "This is why societies that are oppressive to women and contemptuous of their work are so backward economically. Half their populations, doing economically important kinds of work, such as cooking and food processing, cleaning and laundering, making garments and concocting home remedies, are excluded from taking initiatives to develop all that work—and nobody else does either. No wonder macho societies typically have pitiful, weak economies."

Since Jacobs wrote that passage, the concept of improving the economy and reducing poverty and violence by empowering women has taken flight. It's been a long time coming. The journey to get to this place has been a perilous one for women through thousands of years of oppression and trickery. Women were burned alive at the stake for daring to have opinions. They were beheaded for failing to produce a male heir. They suffered foot binding to create dainty, useless feet to please their men (feet so tiny, deformed, and painful that the women could barely walk, let alone run away). They continue to be subjected to female genital mutilation and honor killing and forced marriage. They're still jailed for being raped in places like Afghanistan. Some clerics and religious leaders have described women as whores, harlots, and jezebels; as brainless and even soulless. Women's story of change is one of stunning courage, tenacity, and wit.

Women such as Christine de Pizan were proclaiming women's rights in the 1400s in France. Mary Wollstonecraft was doing the same in England in 1792 when she wrote *A Vindication of the Rights of Woman*. Between those historical points, Isabella of Castile, Elizabeth I of England, Christina of Sweden, and Catherine the Great of Russia all reigned as monarchs, and each in her position embodied some form of female emancipation. Women led the bread riots in England and France in the 1500s, marched to protest the salt shortages in the colonies of New England in the 1700s, and made sorties into the world of equality rights as long as four and five centuries ago. The suffragettes and the Famous Five from Canada agitated for change early in the twentieth century. And the beginning of the second wave of the feminist movement in the sixties made women such as Betty Friedan and Doris Anderson famous. Helen Reddy's "I am woman, hear me roar" sounded like a call to arms when she first sang it in 1972. But in the past, the gains women made were often modified, and women themselves were cast back into their historical roles as mother, wife, caregiver, or temptress.

For the past five decades, the second wave of the women's movement has struggled to alter the law, change the status quo, and improve the lives of women. In a push-me, pull-you process, women have scored significant victories (writing gender equality into constitutions) and suffered serious losses (failing to get enough women elected to alter the culture of politics in Canada, the United States, and the countries of the European Union). Even in places that have established quotas for women in parliament, like Rwanda and Afghanistan, there's been an obdurate resistance to the ideas and goals that women bring to the table. But now the threads required for serious progress on human rights have started to weave themselves together into a tapestry of change. You want a better economy? Put the women to work. Your health system is lagging? Improve maternal and infant health care. War is your problem? Bring women to the negotiating table. Is poverty stubbornly stuck at unacceptable levels? Ask your women to make the budget.

It's a sweeping generalization, but my experience writing about women in zones of conflict as well as in developing and developed countries tells me that women are more interested in fair policy than in power, in peace than in a piece of the turf. And women leaders have long asserted that a sense of community is far more valuable than a sense of control. The information age is altering the grip of top-down power, giving rise to the less confrontational leadership style that women prefer. Gloria Steinem, who is perhaps the best-known contemporary feminist in the world, predicted that the switch would take time when she said a decade ago, "One day an army of gray-haired women may quietly take over the Earth."

As a journalist, I have been telling women's stories for twenty-five years. Until recently the oppression and abuse and second-class citizenship that we endured were seen as women's immutable lot in life, dictated by culture and religion. Now that treatment is seen as symptomatic of a failed economy, the consequences of sidelining half of the world's population.

Scenes still play like YouTube videos on the back of my eyelids: The woman in Croatia who was gang-raped in 1991 because she lived in a village that the belligerents wanted. The women of Malicounda Bambara in Senegal who banded together in 1997 and swore a public oath, "Never again, not my daughter," and eradicated female genital cutting there. The girl on the Shomali Plains in Afghanistan who couldn't read or write and didn't know how old she was when she became the sole guardian of her six younger brothers and sisters after the Taliban killed her parents and grandmother in 2000, who told me, "I will go to school and learn to read and I'll take them with me." The women in Nairobi who held a public meeting in 2010 to announce that they would make marital rape a crime, proclaiming, "We were there in the room the day that signaled the beginning of the end of violence." The woman in Canada who grew up in a polygamous family and was forced into a polygamous marriage and had sister wives, eight children, seventy-six stepchildren, forty-seven brothers and sisters. When she broke away, she used one of her best assets, her sense of humor, to sum up the absurdity of that polygamous sect: "I'd become my own step-great-grandmother."

I also still see the thugs in the lives of these women, who get away with denying the girls an education, with refusing to let the women go to work; the rapists and warlords who see women and girls as pawns or worse; the so-called men of God whose misogyny knows no bounds. They're all on notice now. Diplomats and activists are no longer silenced by men who claim they are acting in the name of God and that no one outside their culture or faith can point out the error of their ways. Claiming violence is "none of your business" has become an oxymoron. Violence is everyone's business.

The World Bank has issued reports every five years since 1985 to say that if attention is paid to the girl child—educating her, taking care of her health, feeding her—the economy of the village will improve. Why? Because she will marry later and have fewer children, and those children will be healthier. But it's more than that: in many places, women's intelligence is an untapped resource. If you foster it, the benefits spill over from the domestic sphere into public life. Research conducted by Plan International has found that the level of poverty reduction and economic growth in a country is directly correlated to the levels of education attained by the women—more than any other factor. Studies done in 2010 by MIT and Carnegie Mellon University on collective intelligence found that if you add females to a group, its collective intelligence improves.

There was a time when people were not chastised for making gross presumptions about women: that raped women asked for it and women who were beaten by their husbands liked it. No one would dare to talk that way now in countries where women have achieved emancipation. In 1994, an Alberta judge claimed that a young woman had "not presented herself . . . in a bonnet and crinolines" when she applied for a job in a trailer at a construction site and was raped. He implied that it was her own fault and said, "A well-chosen expletive, a slap in the face or . . . a well-directed knee would have been a better response than charging the offender." He was removed from the bench.

When the Canadian MP Margaret Mitchell presented the idea of a sweeping reform of the judiciary to the House of Commons in 1982—reform that included criminalizing marital rape and making sexual assault, including wife abuse, child abuse, and incest, a crime— her fellow members of parliament laughed! When the new sexual assault bill passed in 1983, nobody was laughing. Now similar changes are being demanded elsewhere in the world. Honor killing, female genital mutilation, forced marriage, and a litany of assaults against women and girls are being named for what they are. They aren't cultural, they're criminal. Until recently there has been a taboo against speaking out on issues pertaining to sex and abuse. But if you can't talk about it, you can't change it. Now the women are talking, and their conversation is life altering.

I remember being in Bangladesh on assignment in 2002 to research abuses against women that were increasing in frequency as well as severity. Women had been beaten by their spouses, had had their joints dislocated, had had acid tossed in their faces; one had been tied to a railway track and rescued moments before a train roared by. While I was walking to a village with Rita Adhikary, who was working for the nongovernmental organization World

Vision, a young woman who was trying to hide at the side of the road beckoned to me. When I got close enough, I saw that she had been badly burned. Blistered skin was hanging from the underside of her breasts, from her arms and her face. One of her eyes was bulging out of its socket after an apparent beating. When I asked her what had happened, the men who had gathered on the street to watch us all claimed that she was a stupid woman who had spilled boiling water on herself.

Rita spoke up and said, "Spilled water doesn't burn the underside of your breast. Thrown water does. Who did it?" She chased down the facts by asking women who were standing nearby what had happened, then she called the police and gave them the details and the name of the man who had assaulted the woman, and finally she told the woman where she could find help and shelter. When I wrote the story for *Homemaker's* magazine, the publisher was concerned about using the photos I had taken, which explicitly displayed the woman's injuries. They were too hard to look at, the reality too upsetting. So other photos were used. Whose sensibilities were being protected by shielding the awful truth? Why is it that the shame of assault lies with victims rather than the perpetrators?

In 2011, though, a similar story won an Academy Award for filmmaker Sharmeen Obaid-Chinoy. In her documentary *Saving Face,* she chronicled the ghastly wounds that Pakistani women suffer when men throw acid in their faces. She riveted attention on a hideous crime that nobody wanted to talk about. In just ten years, the screen that filters public awareness has been lifted, and the silence has been broken in Pakistan and elsewhere. Talking is the antidote for oppression and injustice. The first result when women share stories of victimization is realizing that other people don't live that way. For the women of Afghanistan, that realization began when they understood that their religion had been manipulated by political opportunists: despite what the fundamentalist mullahs said, there was scant evidence in the Quran to support the actions of the extremists. The second result of telling our stories is overcoming the personally perturbing question of who we will be if we change the way we are.

In 1997, women in Senegal told me that they spent months discussing their plan to stop female genital cutting with the village chiefs and imams, as it felt so daunting at first to attempt to bring an end to a cultural practice that was two thousand years old. Like other women who tackle the status quo, the Senegalese women wondered if changing an ancient custom would change who they are. But once those initial steps have been taken, achieving change is more about effort and patience.

The Arab Spring was the result of a collection of gatherings at the barricades, conversations at the well, and petitions to rulers. But it took an unexpected reaction to oppression and corruption to trigger the revolution that raced through the Middle East and North Africa: the self-immolation of Mohamed Bouazizi in Tunisia on December 17, 2010. History has taught us that the barrier to change doesn't come down with the first assault. But each renewed strike will weaken the opposition and ultimately destroy it. The late Canadian journalist and social activist June Callwood put it this way: "The first thing to get out of the way is expectation that virtue always triumphs; in truth, most attempts to confront and defeat misdeeds are only partially successful or else seem to be outright failures. It doesn't matter; nothing is wasted in the universe. Even an effort that apparently goes nowhere will influence the future. Though the system looks untouched, it has a fatal crack in it. The next assault, or the one after that, will bring it down. At the very least, someone, somewhere, has learned a lesson and will be more thoughtful."

The people of Poland and Czechoslovakia and other former Soviet republics followed that strategy. Citizens in Tunisia, Egypt, Yemen, Syria, Libya, and the rest of North Africa and the Middle East are doing the same today. Women invariably join these protests, exhibiting tenacity and daring. But as much as they stand at the barricades with men, their fight for emancipation extends way beyond deposing a despot. During the two intifadas (the Palestinian uprisings against Israeli occupation in 1987 and again in 2000), Dr. Salwa Al-Najjab, an obstetrician and gynecologist in Ramallah on the West Bank, and her colleagues found that the number of honor killings in the Palestinian Territories fell dramatically. "During the intifada, women were seen as partners," she says. "The young women and men passed out pamphlets, threw stones, and worked on the street together. At that time, the killing of women decreased. But when there was no change in the political situation, the women went back to their houses. Then they were seen as women, not as partners, and the rate of femicide increased [once more]."

The women of Egypt were similarly shocked when they marched on International Women's Day in 2011, just weeks after the historic events on Tahrir Square, and were attacked by the men in the crowd as well as by the military. Some of them were subjected to virginity tests—in other words, they were raped—and told to go home. But the old threats failed to cow them. They created a Web site called HarassMap, a brilliant method of plotting each incident of groping, catcalling, ogling, sexual commentary, stalking, obscene phone calling, indecent exposure, sexual invitation, intimidating facial expressions, rape, and sexual assault on city maps. The site is also stuffed with reports, accusations, and physical descriptions. It's a clever new style of naming and shaming, a show-and-tell of harassment. The site also has a Get Help link to legal and psychological counseling. These women have been to the barricades, and they aren't going home again.

It's as though the centuries-old jig is suddenly up. The abuse of women and girls is being revealed as a bully tactic by out-of-date males who are trying to cling to power. A decade ago, policies began to change so funding for a program—be it education, health, or small-business building—required a gender component to it. Now governments boast about supporting initiatives that promote education and health care for girls. Even corporate boards are fretting about attracting more women because the economic sages claim profits and productivity increase in relation to the rise in numbers of women appointed to boards of directors. And increasingly, newspapers are publishing stories about the emancipation of women in some of the most ancient, traditionally oppressive countries on the planet.

This book is the story of the revolution in women's lives. One of the stories is about a young Afghan, Noorjahan Akbar, who along with her friend Anita Haidary founded Young Women for Change (YWC), an organization that is as modern as it is provocative. And they have done this in one of the world's capitals of female oppression: Kabul. Their aim is to reshape the emotional landscape of Afghanistan.

When I met her in 2012, Akbar was just twenty-one years old and barely over five feet tall. But she's the face of the new Afghanistan. "I want to mobilize the youth," she told me. "Sixty-five percent of the population of Afghanistan is under the age of thirty. We have never fought a war. We have new ideas. And we want to get rid of those old customs that nobody wants."

She moved on to another organization that seeks emancipation for women through poetry in 2013, but in 2011, when she founded Young Women for Change, she was a sophomore at Dickinson College in Pennsylvania. Akbar came home to Kabul on all her school holidays and with Haidary set up projects to bring change to Afghanistan. They began by building a tennis court for young people and starting literacy classes for children. But, Akbar says, "We wanted to work with issues that are our passion. As women growing up in Afghanistan, we faced a lot of discrimination. We are the witnesses of injustices like forced marriage, underage marriage, sexual harassment, and physical beatings." They felt they couldn't wait any longer for those who had promised change—the Karzai government, the UN, the rest of the international community—to deliver.

Akbar told a few friends that she would hold a meeting at a restaurant and invited them to come. She hoped five might turn up.

Seventy arrived, and the restaurant owner found the idea of hosting a meeting demanding women's rights so unnerving that he kicked them all out. So they located an office space and began holding their meetings there. Since then, they've handed the tennis and literacy programs off to others and have concentrated on holding art exhibits about women's rights, a series of monthly lectures to increase awareness, and a protest walk to end harassment of women on the street, and in the spring of 2012, they opened an Internet café for women. In the process, they also brought young men into the movement.

"At first we didn't think we needed the men, and considering that some women aren't allowed to communicate with men, we needed to make sure everyone was comfortable," Akbar said. "But there is so much segregation in our society—by tribe and gender—that keeps us apart. We don't want to do that anymore, so we felt we needed men who would be role models, men who would be outspoken about violence against women. Although there is a powerful backlash against men who speak up for women and against violence, young people will get a better picture when they see men and women from different ethnic groups standing together [in public]."

In the meantime, she is still pressing a lot of very reactionary buttons. If a man harasses her in the street—speculates on her virginity, comments on her breasts, or calls her a prostitute for being on the street without a male escort, which is all too common in Afghanistan—she stops and asks him, "Why did you say that?" If a man gropes her, which is also not at all unusual, she'll say, "What's your problem? These streets are mine too. I have the right to walk freely in my city." She wants to make the men stop behaving in a way that she finds ridiculous. "If they harass me physically, I hit them with my backpack. When I ask them what they're trying to do, I feel I am planting a seed of doubt in their hearts, and that's valuable. The next time they might think before speaking or acting. When you start to question the injustices you've put up with all your life, that's very empowering."

She even walked down the main street in Kārte Seh—the neighborhood where YWC is located—with a recording device hidden in her head scarf and gathered evidence of the truly revolting things men say to women on the street. Then she delivered the recording to ABC News, which sent it to radio and television stations in Kabul to play for their viewers and listeners. She feels she and her collaborators have nothing to lose. "Afghan women have been sent to jail for being raped, killed for giving birth to a girl, kept from going to school, harassed our whole lives." She honors the example of the mothers of Afghanistan who suffered ongoing abuse but fought to educate daughters like her. "We've seen what men can do for the last thirty years," she says. "Let's see what women can do."

Once in a very long while, maybe a lifetime, you get to tell a story about how lives can be altered. The process of change is usually daring, certainly time-consuming, invariably costly, and occasionally heartbreaking but eventually an exercise so rewarding that it becomes the stuff of legends. But as with all movements and most periods of change, there are false starts and setbacks. Change is fueled by anger and disappointment, as well as by inspiration and patience. What is happening today is the culmination of all the waves of women's efforts that went before. Once change like this begins in earnest, once it has lifted off, the momentum picks up and it becomes unstoppable.

Lots of people remain pessimistic. They suggest that soon the Taliban will return to power and Afghan women will be thrown back into the dark ages. Others say the women of the Arab Spring are a one-off, that the draconian personal-status laws that govern family life, marriage, divorce, and inheritance will keep them subservient.

I don't believe either prediction is true, and neither do the women I interviewed for this book.

I

The Shame Isn't Ours, It's Yours

The first corner turning was realizing we weren't crazy.
The system was crazy. —GLORIA STEINEM

Rape is hardly the first thing I would want to mention after delivering the uplifting news that women have reached a tipping point in the fight for emancipation. But as much as major corporations now want women on their boards, and the women of the Arab Spring have flexed their might in overthrowing dictators, and the women of Afghanistan and elsewhere are prepared to go to the barricades to alter their status, sexual violence still stalks them. It doesn't stop women from reforming justice systems, opening schools, and establishing health care. It doesn't eliminate them from leadership roles or prevent them from acting as mentors and role models. But rape continues to be the ugly foundation of women's story of change. Burying the terrible truth is as ineffective as wishing it hadn't happened. Naming the horror of sexual violence is a crucial part of the change cycle.

Rape as punishment or as a means of control still lurks in the lives of women. Marital rape is an old story. Date rape is relatively new. In many households, husbands still claim that they own their wives and have the right to sex on demand. Defenseless children

are sexually abused by fathers, uncles, and brothers; in some countries, men think that having sex with a virgin girl child will cure
HIV/AIDS. The impunity of men when it comes to rape consti-
tutes a centuries-old record of disgrace. For women, sexual violence has been a life sentence.

I've spoken to women in Africa and Europe, in Asia and North
America about the role of rape in their lives. Some of the stories they
told me made me gasp in near disbelief at the extent of the horror
inflicted on them. Others made me cheer for the awe-inspiring courage they showed in demanding justice. They all described perpetrators who banked on the silence of society and the shame of the
victims to protect them from consequences. But they also spoke of
the fearlessness and tenacity it takes to end this scourge.

Some people think you shouldn't talk about rape. If it happens
to you, be quiet, don't tell, because the stigma could prevent you
from getting a job, making new friends, finding a partner. People
say, "Put it behind you. There is no good in rehashing the past."
Others still dare to say, "She asked for it. She was dressed like a
whore." Or worse, "She needed to be taught a lesson." And too
many people refuse to accept the statistics. They don't want to believe that one human being could be so brutal to another human
being, so they dismiss the topic as not fit for polite conversation.
People who don't intervene when something is wrong give tacit
permission for injustice to continue, proving that there's no such
thing as an innocent bystander.

Rape has always been a silent crime. The victim doesn't want to
admit what happened to her lest she be dismissed or rejected. The
rest of the world would prefer to either believe rape doesn't happen
or stick to the foolish idea that silence is the best response.

Today the taboo around talking about sexual violence has been
breached. Women from Bosnia, Rwanda, and the Democratic Republic of the Congo have blown the whistle about rape camps and
mass rapes and even re-rape, a word coined by women in Congo to
describe the condition of being raped by members of one militia

and raped again when another swaggers into their village. Instead of being hushed up, cases such as that of Mukhtar Mai, the Pakistani girl who was gang-raped by village men who wanted to punish her for walking with a boy from an upper caste, have made headlines around the world. And the raping of an unconscious girl in Steubenville, Ohio, in 2012 got everyone's attention, mostly because some of the media reported that the "poor boys who raped her were going to jail and their lives were over." An outraged public responded with a conversation that went viral: "If you're so worried about your high marks and your great 'rep' and your football scholarship, don't go around raping unconscious girls and posting the photos on YouTube."

The causes and consequences of rape are at last being debated at the United Nations. The International Criminal Court in The Hague declared rape a war crime in 1998. The UN Security Council decided that rape was a strategy of war and therefore a security issue in 2007. The announcement was welcome news to the activists, but most people asked what the Security Council could or would actually do with their newly forged resolution, which called for the immediate and complete cessation by all parties to armed conflict of all acts of sexual violence against civilians. The resolution also called for states to provide more protection for women and to eliminate the impunity of men. Getting traction on a UN resolution is like hoping for rain in the middle of a drought. Women are fed up with waiting for action. Eve Ensler, the award-winning playwright, author of *The Vagina Monologues*, and founder of V-Day, the global activism movement to end violence against women and girls, had an idea. What if 1 billion women around the world stood up on the same day and sang the same song and danced the same dance? What if together they claimed their own space, raised their own voices, took back the night? Would that send a message that 50 percent of the population has had it with violence against women? The naysayers said it could never be done. But the naysayers hadn't asked the world's women.

On February 14, 2013, 1 billion women from India and the Philippines to the United States, the United Kingdom, and Germany danced, sang, and reclaimed their own bodies. On February 14, 2014, they did it again. Thousands of pairs of feet stomping, hands clapping; little kids and grannies, businesswomen and teenagers flooded into public squares in 207 countries. They danced, raised their arms skyward, and sang in a victory chant that was heard all over the world.

> *I dance 'cause I love,*
> *Dance 'cause I dream,*
> *Dance 'cause I've had enough,*
> *Dance to stop the screams*
> *Dance to break the rules*
> *Dance to stop the pain*
> *Dance to turn it upside down*
> *It's time to break the chain*

They were taking part in One Billion Rising, which was the largest global action in history to end violence against women. Like a rising tide, the decision to stop the oppression, the abuse, the second-class citizenship of women was already surging in Asia, in Africa, in North America and Europe. When Eve Ensler did the math, she made a startling announcement: "One in three women on the planet will be raped or beaten in her lifetime. One billion women violated is an atrocity. One billion women dancing is a revolution."

The idea came to her when she returned to the Democratic Republic of Congo—to Bukavu and the City of Joy she had built with the women who had suffered the worst and likely most depraved abuse the world had ever known. It was a bald and thin Eve Ensler who had just stumbled out of the fog and fear of uterine cancer treatment who fell into the welcoming arms of the women she had worked with in what had come to be known as the rape capital of the world. Eve linked her own cancer to the cancer of cruelty that these women knew. In her new book, *In the Body of the World*, she describes "the cancer from the stress of not achieving, the cancer of buried trauma" and the epiphany she had that "cancer was the alchemist, an agent of change": "I am particularly grateful for the women of Congo whose strength, beauty, and joy in the midst of horror insisted I rise above my self-pity."

It was there she imagined the dance. "It could transform suffering into action and pain into power. We could call on all women to dance, to take back the spaces, put their feet on the earth, reclaim their bodies." The idea spread like wildfire: urban and rural women, farmers and fishers, artists and teachers all said they would dance.

Eve Ensler says, "Dancing is a genius form of protest. You can do it together or alone, it gives you energy, makes you feel you own the street. Corporations can't control it." She lists dozens of events that made up One Billion Rising: a flash mob in the European Parliament, more than forty events in New York City, participation by cell phone in Tehran, a human chain in Dhaka, Bangladesh, and acid attack survivors in that country who rallied and danced. Fifteen city blocks in Manila had to be closed to accommodate more than a million women dancing. Two hundred women and men marched in front of the parliament in Afghanistan. There was the first-ever flash dance in Mogadishu, Somalia, and more than two hundred events in the United Kingdom. Hollywood actors like Anne Hathaway rose up. So did the Dalai Lama and politicians and CEOs. Eve says the participation was beyond her wildest dreams. She's on a mission to stop the violence that she calls "the methodology of oppression" once and for all. Her goal was to find the right steps to end violence "so it's not perpetual Groundhog Day."

One Billion Rising was the wind needed to blow on the coals so the fire would ignite. And now she wants the international community to step up and keep stoking the fire. "Our time has come," she says. "This is the moment to trust what you know, trust your instinct, move knowledge into wisdom. Now is the moment to stop waiting for permission. Stand up for your truth." She calls women the people of the second wind and calls on all of us to keep rising.

One Billion Rising isn't a single assault on violence against women. It's part of a collection of volleys against sexism and oppression that is gaining in strength around the world today.

One of the most stunning examples comes from Kenya, where in 2011 there was a watershed moment everyone had been waiting for. In the northern city of Meru, 160 girls between the ages of three and seventeen sued the government for failing to protect them from being raped. Their legal action was crafted in Canada, another country where women successfully sued the government for failing to protect them. Everyone from high court judges and magistrates in Kenya to researchers and law-school professors in Canada believed these girls would win and that the victory would set a precedent that would alter the status of women in Kenya and maybe all of Africa.

These are grand claims for redressing a crime as old as Methuselah, but the researchers and lawyers working on the case insisted that the evidence was on their side.

The suit was the brainchild of Fiona Sampson, winner of the 2014 New York Bar Association Award for Distinction in International Law. She is the project director of the Equality Effect, a nonprofit organization that uses international human rights law to improve the lives of girls and women. It came about by way of a touch of serendipity and a lot of tenacity. Sampson was doing a master's degree at Osgoode Hall Law School in Toronto in 2002 when she met fellow students Winifred Kamau, a lecturer from the University of Nairobi Law School, and Elizabeth Archampong, vice dean at the Faculty of Law at Kwame Nkrumah University in Ghana, who had come to Canada to study international law. Their mutual interest in equality rights drew the women together. A few years later, when Seodi White, a lawyer from Malawi, was a visiting scholar at the Center for Women's Studies at the University of Toronto, the trio became a foursome. When the African women wondered if the model used in Canada in the early eighties to reform the law around sexual assault—in which legal activists successfully lobbied to rewrite the law, educate the judiciary, and raise awareness with the public—could work in Africa, Sampson started thinking about ways to tackle the entrenched violence against women in countries like Kenya, Malawi, and Ghana.

Eight years after their initial meeting, the quartet gathered in Nairobi in 2010 with the pick of the human rights legal crop from Canada and Africa for the historic launch of Three to Be Free, a program that targets three countries, Kenya, Malawi, and Ghana, with three strategies—litigation, policy reform, and legal education—over three years in order to alter the status of women. Their intention was to tackle marital rape and make it a crime. But when the lawyers returned home and started their research, another serendipitous meeting took place. A woman named Mercy Chidi was in Toronto taking a course at the Women's Human Rights Education Institute at the University of Toronto. One of the lawyers working on the marital rape case, Mary Eberts, was teaching the course and heard Chidi's story. She called Sampson and suggested she meet Chidi, who was the director of a nongovernmental organization called The Ripples International Brenda Boone Hope Centre (which is known locally in Meru as Tumaini—the Swahili word for "hope"). First a word about Brenda Boone, the Washington-based executive whom the shelter is named for. She met Mercy in 2006 when Mercy was in Washington raising money to rescue kids with AIDS who'd been abandoned. "I invited Mercy and her husband to come to my house—they arrived in full African attire in my Capital Hill home that was full of antiques and Victorian furniture." Brenda asked how she could help, and when they asked her for a computer, she provided one immediately, along with a check for $5,000. A year later, Mercy was back in Washington to receive the International Peace Award. Brenda invited the Chidis back to her home—"I served them fried chicken because it was Sunday and I'm Southern"—and

Mercy explained that they had made a business plan and decided to open a shelter for girls who had been raped. "That pierced my heart," says Brenda. "I gave them another check, this time for $25,000, and committed to financing everything to get the place going." Brenda knew the missing piece was the legal action required to stop the raping of girls.

A few years later, when Mercy met Fiona Sampson and told her about the shelter and about the girls who can't go home because the men who raped them are still at large, they both knew it was time to tackle the root of the problem—the impunity of rapists and the failure of the justice system to convict them.

Sampson admits it was her own sense of urgency that made the concept take flight. "I am the last thalidomide child to be born in Canada," she explains, referring to the anti-morning-sickness drug whose side effects in utero had affected the development of her hands and arms. (The drug was banned in 1962.) "There was a culture of impunity in the testing of drugs at that time," she explains, "so I'm consumed with the desire to seek justice in the face of impunity."

Kenya has laws on its books designed to protect girls from rape, or "defilement." The state is responsible for the police and the way police enforce existing laws. Since the police in Kenya failed to arrest the perpetrators and fail on an ongoing basis to provide the protection girls need, the lawyers filed notice that the state is responsible for the breakdown in the system. Sampson said at the time, "We will argue that the failure to protect the girls from rape is actually a human rights violation, that it's a violation of the equality provisions of the Kenyan constitution. It's the Kenyan state that signed on to international, regional, and domestic equality provisions and it's therefore their obligation to protect the girls. Only the state can provide the remedies we're looking for, which is the safety and security of the girls."

Sampson and other human rights lawyers in Canada have done this successfully for approximately twenty-five years since the introduction of Section 15, the equality provision of the Charter of

Rights and Freedoms. Their track record includes considerable success with precedent-setting cases that establish the state's responsibility to protect the rights of Canadian women. One of them was a case in Toronto in 1986 involving a woman raped by a man referred to as the Balcony Rapist, who was targeting the women of one downtown neighborhood, gaining access to their bedrooms by breaking in through second- and third-floor balconies in the dark of night. The woman, who called herself Jane Doe, sued the police, claiming it was their responsibility to warn the potential targets of the Balcony Rapist and thereby protect them. The police tried to have her case dismissed using the argument that if they had warned the potential targets, it would have tipped off the rapist. But Jane Doe argued that the Toronto police used her as bait to draw out the predator. Her courage and dogged determination turned her case into a cause célèbre. In 1998, she won.

Mary Eberts, who is working on the Kenyan girls' suit, explains the connection between the two cases: "The police knew about this guy, they knew about his method of operation, and they knew where in the city the women he liked to target would be living, but they did not warn those women about the potential danger they were in. Jane Doe was raped by this guy, as the police might have predicted. She brought this case, which we are using as a precedent in the 160 girls' litigation, to say there is a duty on the part of the police to enforce the law—that's why the law is there. And if the police do not enforce the law, if the government does not enforce the law, then they are guilty of violating a person's equality."

Eberts knows that the stars need to be aligned for precedent-setting cases to work. Her colleague Winnie Kamau says a case like this couldn't have happened even a few years ago. "I think the timing was actually quite perfect, particularly in the Kenyan context," Kamau says. "We have a new constitution that was enacted in August 2010, and in the last half dozen years we have had some very progressive laws passed in our country. Five years ago it would have been difficult to bring everybody together, but the timing now I believe is right. There's also a lot more awareness among African women about their rights, and they have the feeling, the sense that they need to change. We can harness these energies."

The new Kenyan constitution contains powerful provisions that provide for increased equality for women and girls, provisions that have not yet been interpreted by the country's courts. This is precisely where the Canadian courts were twenty-five years ago when the Charter of Rights and Freedoms was enacted. New laws must be tested and interpreted in the courts. Reflecting on their own experience with charter challenges, the Canadian lawyers see this case as an opportunity to ensure that the courts interpret and apply constitutional provisions in ways that guarantee the human rights of women and girls. The process is time-consuming and expensive, but it's the best way to establish precedents that the courts can rely on for future cases. The Three to Be Free activists plan to take similar action in Malawi and Ghana once this case is won.

Historically, when you alter the status of one woman, you alter the status of her family. When a girl is confident and knows what her rights are, she knows what she can claim from the state and that the state owes her certain things by virtue of the fact that she's a citizen of that state. She can claim an education, livelihood, and shelter. She can claim that she has the right not to be marginalized. Once the state is held accountable for its obligation to promote women's human rights and to protect women and girls from violence, a climate of intolerance for violence against women follows. There's more likelihood that people who talk casually about violating women and girls will be censured by their friends and that women themselves will speak out, bring charges, demand justice.

It's a four-hour drive from Nairobi to Meru (population 1 million) and the shelter where the Kenyan girls are staying. We drive through banana farms and tea plantations, past dark umbrella-like acacia trees, inhaling the dry scent of the savannah. Bleating goats and signs declaring JESUS SAVES dot the landscape. Mango trees and roadsides drenched in pink, orange, and red bougainvillea smack up against fluorescent green billboards advertising Safari, the country's cell phone provider. When we cross the equator on the way to Meru, the heat intensifies but the traffic remains the same—heavy and fast, a series of near misses for both vehicles and pedestrians.

The rutted red dirt road into the Ripples International shelter is shaded by a canopy of lush trees that offer refuge from the heat of the equatorial sun. Hedges of purple azalea and yellow hibiscus camouflage the fence that keeps intruders away from this bucolic place that is a refuge for the 160 girls who are poised to cut off the head of the snake that is sexual assault.

I'd been briefed in Nairobi about what to expect when I met the girls whose cases have been selected for the lawsuit. The first one I'm introduced to is Emily. The size of the child takes my breath away. Emily is barely four and a half feet tall, her tiny shoulders scarcely twelve inches across. But when she sits down to tell her story, her husky eleven-year-old voice is charged with determination. "My grandfather asked me to fetch the torch," she explains. But when she brought it to him, it wasn't a flashlight he wanted. "He took me by force and warned me not to scream or he would cut me up." Along with thousands of men in Kenya and indeed throughout sub-Saharan Africa, Emily's grandfather believes that having sex with a girl child will cure HIV/AIDS, a belief that led him to rape his own granddaughter to presumably heal himself. What's worse, men believe that the younger the child is, the stronger the cure will be. Now she is taking the old man to the high court in Nairobi. Even Emily knows the case is likely to be history making. This little kid, along with the other 159 plaintiffs, knows that she may be the one who strengthens the status of women and girls not only in Kenya but in all of Africa.

"These men will learn they cannot do this to small girls," says

Emily, who, like the other girls I met, balances the victim label with the newfound empowerment that has come to her from the decision to sue.

Charity is also eleven and her sister Susan only six. Their mother is dead. Their father raped them—first Charity, then Susan—after they came home from school one day during the winter months. Charity says, "I want my father to go to the jail." Her sister is so traumatized that she won't leave Charity's side and only eats, sleeps, and speaks when Charity tells her it's okay to do so. Perpetual Kimanze, who takes care of these girls and coordinates their counseling and therapy, keeps a close eye on Susan when the little girl begins to talk to me in a barely audible voice, uttering each word with an agonizing pause between, and says, "My . . . father . . . put . . . his . . . penis . . . between . . . my . . . legs . . . and . . . he . . . hurt . . . me."

It's been six days since Emily was raped; she still complains of stomach pain. She can't sleep. She says in her native Kiswahili (a local dialect of Swahili), "Nasikia uchungu sana nikienda choo, kukojoa." It hurts to go to the bathroom.

Doreen, fifteen, has a four-month-old baby as a result of being raped by her cousin. Her mother is mentally ill. Her father left them years ago, and they had moved in with her mother's sister. When Doreen realized she was pregnant, her aunt told her to have an abortion; when her uncle found out, he beat her and threw her out of the house. She was considering suicide when she heard about Ripples and came to their Tumaini Centre.

In Kenya a girl child is raped every thirty minutes; some are as young as three months old. If a girl doesn't die of her injuries, she faces abandonment; families don't want anything to do with girls who have been sexually assaulted. She almost certainly loses the chance to get an education. Some can't go to school anymore because they've been raped by the teacher. Others are prohibited by the stigma; the girls are doubly victimized by being ostracized. They often become HIV positive as a result of rape, so their health is compromised. Urinary tract infections and sexually transmitted diseases plague them. Without an education, with poor health and no means of financial support, the girls drift into poverty. Their childhood is over and they become the face the world expects of Africa—poor, unhealthy, and destitute.

Twenty-five percent of Kenyan girls aged twelve to twenty-four lose their virginity due to rape. An estimated 70 percent never report it to the authorities, and only one-third of the reported cases wind up in court. If the prosecutor can prove that a girl was under the age of fifteen when she was assaulted, the rapist's sentence is life in prison. But there's the rub. The laws are not enforced, and rape is on the rise. More than 90 percent know their assailant: fathers, grandfathers, uncles, teachers, priests—the very people assigned the task of keeping vulnerable children safe. And raping little girls as a way of cleansing themselves from HIV/AIDS isn't the only reason they act. Says Hedaya Atupelye, a social worker I met at the shelter run by the Women's Rights Awareness Program in Nairobi, "Men think having sex with a little girl is a sign of being wealthy and stylish. Some of these men are educated beyond the graduate level, but they want to be the first to break the flower so they seek out young girls."

If it's the breadwinner who's guilty, the family will go hungry if he's sent to jail, so even a child's mother will choose to remain silent. "It's our African culture," says Kimanze. "No one wants to associate with one who's been raped or who's lived in a shelter. We need to stand up and say the shame isn't ours, it's yours."

In Kenya, people can pay to have their police charges disappear. Or they can bribe a police officer and no charges will be brought. If the case is taken seriously, statements are taken, the child is sent to a doctor for examination, and the file with the doctor's report is returned to the police. "This is also where money changes hands," says Atupelye. "If a girl, or for that matter a woman, goes to the police on her own, she is usually ridiculed and harassed. It was suggested half a dozen years ago that the police create a gender desk where a female would be safe in reporting the crime, but invariably the gender desk isn't manned and is covered with dust."

"One of the challenges is that our culture doesn't allow us to speak out about sexual things," says Mercy Chidi. "My only advice from my mother when I got my period was 'Don't play with boys; you'll get pregnant.' My own uncle tried to rape me, and to this day I have not told my mother. We have to break this silence." When the girls arrive at the shelter, she says, they are severely traumatized and don't want to talk to anyone. Some are frightened, others aggressive. They tend to pick on one another. And as much as they come around and begin to heal, Mercy says that they never completely overcome the trauma. "It's like tearing a paper into many pieces. No matter how carefully you try to put the pieces together again, the paper will never be the same. That's what sexual assault does." One little girl at the shelter begins to cry every night when it starts to get dark and the curtains are drawn. "It's the hour when her father used to come and rape her," Chidi says.

In the program at Tumaini Centre, the girls stay for six weeks; they receive prophylaxis drugs to prevent HIV/AIDS and pregnancy as soon as they arrive and medical care and counseling for the duration. If it isn't safe for them to return home, they go to a boarding school or stay on in the residence at the center. Those who go home come back once a month for six months and then every three months for ongoing counseling and support. When I visited, there were eleven girls in residence.

One of them, a fifteen-year-old called Luckline, had been raped by a neighbor. She was thirty-nine weeks pregnant when we met. When she talked about what had happened to her, she didn't sound like a victim. She sounded like a girl who wanted to get even, to make a change. She said, "This happened to me on May 13, 2010. I will make sure this never happens to my sister." When I asked what she would do after the baby was born, she said she wanted to return to school because she planned to become a poet. With little prompting, she read me one of her poems.

Here I come
Walking down through history to eternity
From paradise to the city of goods
Victorious, glorious, serious, and pious
Elegant, full of grace and truth
The centerpiece and the masterpiece of literature
Glowing, growing, and flowing
Here, there, everywhere
Cheering millions every day
The book of books that I am.

This from a teenager who is disadvantaged in every imaginable way. Yet she was preparing to sue her government for failing to protect her. This is how change happens. But it takes commitment and colossal personal strength for a girl to tackle the status quo and claim a better future for herself.

Back in Nairobi, I visit with Nano, a magistrate in the children's court. She insisted that her full name not be used, as she must be seen as totally impartial both to the children and to the system that she criticizes. "The difficulty," she said, "is that the police lack knowledge of the law. Not all but most need training and sensitization around sexual assault." And, she said, "It's hard to get evidence from children; they need psychologists and counselors to talk to them, and the Kenyan legal system simply doesn't have that resource. Even some magistrates lack training and knowledge of the Sexual Offences Act." Of the few cases that have made it to the court, she said, "The difficulty is, they come without the information I need to convict. The girls block it out or don't turn up. There are all kinds of judicial tools I can use: CEDAW [the Convention on the Elimination of all Forms of Discrimination against Women], the children's convention, even the new Sexual Offences Act legislation in Kenya. The investigating officer needs to tell the court what has been found, the charge sheets have to be drafted correctly, and the child needs to be able to tell the officer what happened; if she can, she needs to identify the man who defiled her and say, 'He is the one who did this to me.' The children have to be prepared for this. Without it, I cannot convict."

After that conversation with the magistrate, I sat in on the meeting that the team of lawyers was holding in a hotel across town. While diesel-belching buses and the traffic chaos in Nairobi created cacophony outside, the lawyers hunkered over their files at a long narrow table, creating a strategy for the case. They debated the wording, parsing every sentence, nitpicking the legal clauses, testing the jurisprudence. They knew it would take collaboration between lawyers, doctors, and academics, experts in human rights law as well as international law, to be successful. They also needed to protect the girls and make sure they weren't revictimized by the process. Once the child's story has been documented by an officer, the lawyer can make the accusation in court, thus preventing the girls from being further traumatized.

For five long days, they argued over how best to make the case. There were three choices: a civil claim, a criminal claim, or a constitutional claim. Finally they decided that a constitutional challenge was the way to go. The Kenyan constitution guarantees equality rights for citizens. It promises protection for men and women. It governs the laws that deliver that protection. The lawyers decided to argue that the state failed to execute the constitutional rights of the girls. Then they set their sights on a court date. The journey they were on together is about girls who dared to break the taboo on speaking out about sexual assault. It's about women lawyers from two sides of the world supporting these youngsters in their quest for justice. It's about the kids who were told they had no rights but insist that they do. It's the push-back reaction that every woman and girl in the world has been waiting for. "This case is the beginning," said Chidi. "It'll be a long journey, but now it has begun." The feeling as they prepared to go to court was if they won, the victory would be a success for every girl and woman in Africa, maybe even the world.

On October 11, 2012, when the case went to court in Meru, the lawyers marched through the streets from the shelter where the girls had been staying to the courthouse. The kids wanted to march as well but were told their identity needed to be protected and they must stay back at the shelter. Nothing doing, they said. They marched beside their advocates to the courthouse chanting, "Haki yangu," the Kiswahili words for "I demand my rights." With all the hullaballoo on the street, the police at the court panicked and slammed the gates shut as the girls approached. Nothing would stop them now. They climbed onto the fence still calling, "Haki yangu," and then they looked at one another and started to laugh at the reversal in roles being played out in front of them. "Look," they called to each other, "these men who hurt us and made us ashamed are scared of us now." Soon enough the gates were opened and the girls and their lawyers entered the court to begin the proceedings that would alter their future.

There was something deliciously serendipitous about the power going off in northern Kenya seven months later on May 27, 2013, just as Judge J. A. Makau read his much-anticipated decision about this case that put rape in a glaring spotlight, a case that could alter the status of women and girls in Kenya and maybe all of Africa. When the lights came on, the judge in the high court in Meru, Kenya, stated: "By failing to enforce existing defilement [rape] laws, the police have contributed to the development of a culture of tolerance for pervasive sexual violence against girl children and impunity."

Guilty.

The earth shifted under the rights of girls and women that day; the girls secured access to justice for themselves and legal protection from rape for all 10 million girls and women in Kenya.

Within forty-eight hours of the court decision, Fiona Sampson had heard from half a dozen other countries that want the same action. But "the win is only as good as the justice each girl gets," says Marcia Cardamore, whose PeopleSense Foundation was the major funder of the court case. She underscores the need for close follow-up when she says, "We sent a letter to the court to give three months' notice to the police that we need to see results or we'll take more action, put more legal pressure on them. Without due process, we haven't won anything."

Marcia is part of a new generation of women philanthropists who are determined to make changes. She belongs to an organization called Women Moving Millions that was founded in 2005 by Helen LaKelly Hunt and her sister, former U.S. ambassador to Austria Swanee Hunt, who understood that moving the bar for women's equality rights meant raising the financial stakes. "I get the sense I am not an outlier and there are other women in the world who want to overcome these injustices," says Marcia. Like everyone else involved with this case, she's watching and ready to act if justice is not forthcoming.

The road they travel was paved by women who went before: those who were willing to cry foul rather than be silenced by shame; those who worked tirelessly to make the world understand that rape is not the right of men; those who insist rape is not the "fault" of women but a control issue among men who have failed to grasp the consequences of scarring a woman's mind by assaulting her body.

Like so many issues that have reached a turning point for women, rape has gone from being the crime no one wants to talk about, to making headlines, to being a prominent subject in courts, in newly published books, and in award-winning films. Among the first to go public on a world stage were the extraordinarily brave women from Bosnia who went to the International Criminal Court in The Hague in 1998; despite the very real possibility that they would be forever rejected by their families, they testified about what had happened to them: they had been rounded up, taken to enemy camps, and gang-raped.

Their story of sexual violence actually began when the USSR

collapsed in 1991 and its sister state Yugoslavia (created at the end of the First World War from seven independent nations) erupted in a civil war in the Balkans so virulent that former neighbors, old friends, and business partners attacked one another in a ferocious bloodbath that riveted the world's attention. I began covering the story soon after that, which is how I came to meet some of the women who had been gang-raped. But getting their story published was a story in itself.

In the fall of 1992, I was in Sarajevo to cover the effect of war on children. The siege of Sarajevo was like nothing I had ever seen before. Snipers and soldiers were waging a war against civilians. Targets of the shelling were hospitals, schools, and playgrounds. Explosives made in the shape of children's toys were maiming kids who picked them up. Families were forced to live in basements while soldiers took over the rest of the house. And all this was happening in a breathtaking setting, in a city that had played host to the Olympic Games, in a region that was picture-postcard beautiful. The towns had names that sound like songs. White stucco houses with red clay roofs dotted the landscape.

The sun cast a glow on ancient hills that turned purple at dusk and glowed buttery yellow at dawn. But the streets were rife with the Devil's work, and there was peril at every corner.

The day before I was to leave Sarajevo, I began to hear rumors about Bosnian Serb soldiers who were rounding up Bosnian Muslim women and dragging them off to rape camps. Every journalist knows that one of the first casualties of war is the truth, and I thought that what I was hearing was propaganda. This was two years before the horror of Rwanda, before Darfur, before Congo. But as the day progressed, I kept hearing about the rape camps from more and more credible sources. At that time, I was the editor in chief of a magazine, and magazines have a much longer lead time than newspapers. If this story was true, it was breaking news that needed to be published immediately; it couldn't wait the three months it would take to get it to my magazine readers.

I gathered everything I could—cell phone numbers, names, details about Muslim wives and sisters and daughters being gang-raped eight and ten times a day. When I flew back to Canada, I went straight to a media outlet and handed over the file to an editor I knew. I said, "This is a horrendous story. Give it to one of your reporters." I went back to my office and waited for the headline. Nothing. I waited another week and another—still nothing. Seven weeks later, I saw a four-line blurb in *Newsweek* magazine about soldiers gang-raping women in the Balkans. I called the editor I'd given the package to.

As soon as he heard my voice, he started to giggle—nervously. "Oh, I knew you'd be calling me today," he said.

"What happened?" I wanted to know.

"Well, Sally," he said, "it was a good story, but, you know, I got busy and, you know, I was on deadline and, you know, I forgot."

I was astounded. I said, "More than twenty thousand women were gang-raped, some of them eight years old, some of them eighty years old—and you forgot?"

I hung up and called my staff together and told them what had happened. We decided to do the story ourselves. I was on a plane back to the war zone two days later.

Six women who were refugees in Zagreb, Croatia, were willing to be interviewed, but they were reluctant to have their names used as they knew they'd be rejected by their families if word of the rapes got out. While most women did not become pregnant, some did. Of those who were pregnant, some managed to get abortions; some had been kept in prison until abortion was impossible. And still others had escaped but couldn't find medical help in time for an abortion. Many who gave birth left the newborns at the hospital. Mostly I talked to frightened women who badly needed health care and counseling and were too traumatized to share their stories. I worried about asking a woman to relive the horror and began to wonder how to best tell a story that most preferred to be silent about.

Then I met Dr. Mladen Loncar, a psychiatrist at the University of Zagreb, who told me about a woman who was furious with the silence around this atrocity and had plenty to say. He promised to call her and ask for an interview on my behalf, and when he did, Eva Penavic said yes, she would talk to me. Getting to her was a problem, though, as she was living as a refugee on the eastern border between Bosnia and Croatia, near the city of Vukovar. The area was being shelled day and night.

The photographer I drove with accelerated through towns where buildings were still smoking from being hit by rocket-propelled grenades (and turned up the volume on a Pavarotti CD to block out the sound of grenades exploding in the distance). We finally arrived late in the afternoon at the four-room house Eva was sharing with her extended family of seventeen. For the next seven hours, I listened while she described the hideous ordeal she'd survived.

Eva told me that she thought the men pounding at her door in the little eastern Croatian village of Berak in November 1991 had come to kill her. Rape was the furthest thing from her mind when they shot off the hinges of her door. After all, she was regarded as a leader in this village of eight hundred people. She was forty-eight years old. She had five grandchildren.

Eva was a wise woman who knew that her sex didn't guarantee her safety. She was the child of a widow who had to leave home and find work in another village. She was the niece of an abusive man who tried to force her into an arranged marriage when she was sixteen. But despite all her girlhood experiences, she could never have imagined the horror she'd be subjected to during the brutal conflict in the former Yugoslavia.

Eva was one of the civil war's first victims of mass gang rape. The crime committed against her was part of a plan, a cruel adjunct to the campaign known as "ethnic cleansing"—a phrase as foul to language as the act is annihilating to its victims. An estimated twenty thousand to fifty thousand women, mostly in Bosnia and some in Croatia, shared Eva's fate.

Historians claim that what happened there was worse than the rapes of opportunity and triumph usually associated with war. This was rape that was organized, visible, ritualistic. It was calculated to scorch the emotional earth of the victim, her family, her community, her ethnic group. In many cases, the victim's husband, children, cousins, and neighbors were forced to watch.

In other cases, victims heard the screams of their sisters or daughters or mothers as one after another was dragged away to be raped in another room.

Eva was canning tomatoes in a little stone pantry at the back of her house when her door splintered open and twelve men rushed in, subdued her, and blindfolded her. Hissing profanities in her ear, they bullied her out the door and beat her about her legs as she stumbled along a path to a neighboring house, which an extremist Serbian group known as the White Eagles had moved into just the week before.

Born of Croatian parents, Eva knew every house in her home village, every garden, the configuration of the town center, every bend of the creek that flowed around it. Her lifelong best friend, Mira (her name has been changed), was Serbian. As children, they spent their days chasing geese through the middle of town to the Savak Creek. The game was always the same, the kids shrieking wildly as they chased baby geese, with the big geese in hot pursuit of the kids. Eva became a sprinter of such caliber that she was selected to represent first her village, then her district in regional track meets.

As a young woman, she fell in love with a man named Bartol Penavic, and on November 17, 1958, they were married. Together they raised three children, saw them married and settled, and in time became grandparents. Life was good.

The countryside surrounding the village resembles a mural crayoned by children—a clutch of clay-colored houses here, a barn there. On one side of the village stretches a patchwork of rolling hills and thick oak forest so green and purple and yellow that the colors could have been splashed there by rainbows; on the opposite side is flat black farmland with hedgerows of venerable old trees. The town itself is an antique treasure, a three-hundred-year-old tableau of muted colors and softly worn edges—as unlikely a setting for ugliness as could be imagined.

By the time spring began to blossom in 1991, Croatia had declared its independence from Yugoslavia and there were rumblings of trouble. But no one paid much attention. Eva said, "We'd lived together—Croats and Serbs and Muslims—for fifty years. How could anyone change that?" Bartol had told her, "Now is the time for us. Our children are settled. It's time for us to enjoy life." They'd had their share of grief: Eva's father had been killed during the Second World War, and the uncle who assumed charge of her was appalled that she dared to choose the man she would marry. Bartol's family saw Eva as a peasant, hardly a match for the son of the biggest landowner in the surrounding villages. Despite the odds against them, their thirty-three-year marriage had been rich with the promise of happily-ever-after.

Then in the fall, barricades appeared on the street. As a precaution, they sent their daughter and two daughters-in-law away with the grandchildren to a safer place. Soon enough, the village was under siege. Their sons managed to escape as tanks rolled into town. Most villagers ran away; those who didn't, including Eva and Bartol, were rounded up and kept in detention. The interrogations and beatings began. Bartol was beaten to death. Eva was sent home by the commander and told to stay in the pantry at the back of the house.

Then the men came for her. They said they were taking her to another village for interrogation, but she knew precisely where they were going—to the nearby house where the White Eagles were headquartered. At the door, her captors announced to the others, "Open up—we bring you the lioness." Once she was inside, they attacked her like a pack of jackals. Six men stripped her, then raped her by turns, orally and vaginally. They urinated into her mouth.

They screamed that she was an old woman and if she was dry they'd cut her vagina with knives and use her blood to make her wet. She was choking on semen and urine and couldn't breathe. The noise was horrendous as the six men kept shrieking at her that there were twenty more men waiting their turn and calling out, "Who's next?" She was paralyzed with fear and with excruciating pain. The assault continued relentlessly for three hours.

When they were finished, they cleaned themselves off with her underwear and stuffed the fouled garments into her mouth, demanding she eat them. Then they marched her outside into the garden. She could hear the village dogs barking. She knew exactly where she was and she knew that the cornfield they were pushing her toward was mined. Still blindfolded, she was thrust into the field and told to run away. She stumbled through the slushy snow and sharp cornstalks, and when she was far enough away from the house, she ripped the blindfold off. Injuries from the rape slowed her down, but she was fast all the same. Then she slipped in the muddy field and fell, and at exactly that moment, bullets ripped over her head. She flattened herself into the mud as she heard the cheers of the terrorists, who thought they had bagged another kill. She waited a long time before getting to her feet and staggering on, and then wandered for three more hours, trying to focus, to think of a way to survive. Finally she stumbled into her neighbor's garden.

Mira had been waiting by the window all night, knowing her childhood friend had been taken away. When she heard the rustle in the garden, she rushed outside with her husband, and together they gathered up their battered friend. Mira bathed Eva, made her strong tea, and cradled her head while she vomited the wretched contents of her stomach and then collapsed. The next morning, Eva left the village. She didn't come back until the conflict was over.

I visited her again during the war and after the war was over, as well. Although she had reunited with her family and together they returned to Berak, the men responsible for the crime were still roaming the streets of her village, still gloating when Eva walked by.

The last time I saw her, in 2005, she told me she still wonders why she was spared. Cradling a new grandchild in her arms, she repeated the comment she'd made when I left her in 1991: "I've always wondered why God didn't take me when he took my Bartol. I think I must have been left here to be the witness for the women."

It took me the usual three months to get the story to our readers. But after it was published, they took up the torch for these women, and in the form of thousands of letters to the editor, they demanded that the United Nations do something about it.

This was rape as a form of genocide. In the rape camps, many Bosnian women were assaulted until they became pregnant. The Serbian soldiers, known as Chetniks, viewed systematic rape as a way of planting Serbian seeds into Bosnian women and therefore destroying their ethnicity and culture. It wasn't enough that the women felt their families would reject them because they had been raped, a shame to Islam. The women's suffering was twofold, just like that of the women of Rwanda and Congo in the years that would follow.

I often wondered what made Eva tell her story when others were too afraid to speak. She told me that in her opinion, the vanquished need a face and a name. Atrocities need a date and a time. Telling the truth is the only way to heal. "It's not enough to say, 'You raped me,'" she said. "When I say it happened, where it happened, and what my name is, it makes the rape something to be responsible for."

But even with worldwide attention on the mass rape of women in the Balkans, and the enormous pity for them and fury for the perpetrators that resulted, the stigma of being raped stuck to those women. One of the problems with stopping the scourge of rape in zones of conflict is eradicating that stigma. What everyone needs to understand is that these women and girls are just like everybody's mothers and daughters. They are women who had jobs to go to, mortgages to pay; their children, just like the children of their rapists, just like our children, also got croup and forgot to do their homework or ducked out of doing family chores. They had friends over for dinner, took holidays, went to the park, watched over their kids on the swings, the seesaws, the jungle gyms.

But somehow when we hear stories like Eva's or stories about the women in Rwanda or Congo, we turn the victims and their attackers into "others." We listen to foolish remarks such as "They've been at this for centuries; let them kill each other." Or "They always treat their women like this; it's not my business." Perhaps it's a way of separating ourselves from something we feel powerless to stop. But we do have power. We can write letters to the United Nations to demand action. We can speak up when others dismiss these atrocities as cultural or religious or worse—none of our business. It took a brave collection of women from Bosnia to do something about rape. They took their dreadful stories to the International Criminal Court in The Hague. They risked being rejected by their families by telling their stories to the world. But they gave the international tribunal the tools to do what courts and governments have avoided throughout history. It made rape a war crime. In 1998, the Yugoslavia War Crimes Tribunal, also in The Hague, made rape and sexual enslavement in the time of war a crime against humanity. Only genocide is considered a more serious crime.

I believe the shift in thinking about the role of women and the issues that women deal with in the first decade of the third millennium will go down in history as a turning point for civilization. Issues such as sexual assault that had been buried, denied, and ignored suddenly began to be explored in groundbreaking research papers and to figure in legislative reform.

Two books published in the spring of 2011 brought facts to light that might have put the international community on alert against the mass rape in Bosnia, Rwanda, and Congo. In one of them, *At the Dark End of the Street,* Danielle McGuire exposed a secret that had been held for sixty-five years. It's the story of the iconic Rosa Parks, the tiny, stubborn woman who defied the Jim Crow segregation rules in Montgomery, Alabama, when she refused to comply with a white man's order to move to the back of the bus. That solitary act of defiance was the catalyst that in 1955 gave rise to the civil rights movement. But McGuire's research brings out a more astonishing piece of the story. For ten years prior to her famous bus boycott, Rosa Parks was an antirape activist.

Parks began investigating rape in 1944, collecting evidence that exposed a ritualized history of sexual assault against black women. That evidence was ignored. All these decades later, McGuire is the first to tell what she calls "the real story—that the civil rights movement is also rooted in African-American women's long struggle against sexual violence." And she argues that given the role rape played in the lives of women—that it was ongoing, that it fueled the anger and powered the movement as much as the Jim Crow laws did—the history of the civil rights movement needs to be rewritten. She sees the infamous Montgomery bus incident as an event that was as much about women's rights as about civil rights. As McGuire eloquently writes, "It was a women's movement for dignity, respect and bodily integrity."

Gloria Steinem agrees. In a review of McGuire's book, Steinem wrote, "Rosa Parks' bus boycott was the end of a long process that is now being taken seriously. What Rosa Parks did was expose [to the leaders of the civil rights movement] the truth about sexual assault as well as the widespread ugliness of rape as a tool to repress, punish and control women during the civil rights movement. Her work was meant to be a call for change in America. And yet until the fall of 2011, hardly anyone even knew about it." Why didn't we know this before? Why has so much history involving women been either ignored or suppressed? How is it that the stunning facts Rosa Parks gathered were never published at the time? And would the world have changed had the information been available sooner?

The rape of black women as an everyday practice of white supremacy wasn't the only revelation in 2011. The other book, *Sexual Violence against Jewish Women during the Holocaust,* is a collection of essays edited by Sonja Hedgepeth, a professor at Middle Tennessee State University, and Rochelle Saidel, executive director of the U.S.-based Remember the Women Institute. As I read the book, I had to put it down from time to time to catch my breath. With all the documentation and literature of the Holocaust, all the memorials and reminders, how can it be that this appalling information about the gang-raping and sexual abuse of Jewish women has been left out until now? No one knows how many women and girls were sexually assaulted while they were isolated in ghettos or incarcerated in concentration camps, and no one ever will. Some women were murdered, and others chose to remain silent, as rape carries a stigma even in the chambers of death: even though a woman was raped, she was "having sex" with the enemy. The authors refer to this kind of shame as the most effective of all social weapons. And they say that women caught in war zones invariably face "a dilemma of fatal inclusion or unbearable ostracism."

The men who raped these women in Nazi concentration camps were obsessive about keeping records—of inhuman medical experiments performed, of the elimination of men, women, and children in the gas chambers or by shooting or hanging. But they kept no list of who was raped. There is not a word in the vast accountings of the Nazi regime about the sexual assault of women and girls. The story is simply missing. Seen as sexual objects as well as a biological danger by the Nazis, Jewish women were the target of sexual depravity and rape. And yet their story was suppressed. As the essays in this important book show, the survivors shared details before the trials at Nuremburg, but not a word was spoken during the trials.

In an interview with me, Gloria Steinem said, "The judges at Nuremberg didn't want crying women in the courtroom. And some Jewish historians didn't want to admit their women had been sexually assaulted and/or denied it had happened. It's taken sixty years for that to come out." She believes that the floodgates began to open when rape became a war crime and told me that women owe a debt of gratitude to Navi Pillay, the judge who made that historic ruling at the International Criminal Court. Because of her, and the recent work of other scholars and activists in the public sphere, the crime of rape is no longer seen as either inevitable or the fault of women.

"Think about Bosnia, Rwanda, and Congo," Steinem said. "If we had acknowledged what happened to Jewish women in the Holocaust or black women in the civil rights movement, we'd have been better prepared for what happened in Bosnia, Rwanda, and Congo. It's not about war, it's about genocide. To make the right sperm occupy the wrong womb is an inevitable part of genocide. The publication of these books is a warning to the world that sexual violence is a keystone to genocide, and they make it clear that today there's a shift in the sense that rape is now noticed and even taken seriously. That wasn't true before."

As the researcher Brigitte Halbmayr points out in *Sexual Violence against Jewish Women during the Holocaust*, "Unlike the cases in Rwanda and former Yugoslavia, where rape was used as a strategy of war, sexualized violence was not an inherent part of the genocidal process during the Holocaust. Instead, it was part of the continuum of violence that resulted from genocide. Rape was not an instrument of genocide, but was the byproduct of intentional annihilation."

Like the judges at Nuremburg, film directors and publishers have hesitated to expose the brutal truth about rape. But that too is changing. Lynn Nottage was awarded the 2009 Pulitzer Prize for Drama for her play, aptly titled *Ruined,* which chronicles the plight of women in the Democratic Republic of the Congo. The Pulitzer citation hailed *Ruined* as "a searing drama set in chaotic Congo that compels audiences to face the horror of wartime rape and brutality while still finding affirmation of life and hope amid hopelessness." The play tells the story of Mama Nadi, the proprietor of a local establishment that acts both as a shelter for women who've been damaged or "ruined" by the civil war and a bar/brothel for the nationalist and rebel soldiers who keep it raging on. Always the shrewd businesswoman, Nadi sides neither with the women she shelters nor with her militant patrons until the war outside closes in and there are choices to make and truths to face.

Two years later, a film called *Incendies* (Scorched) became another example of the new truth-telling. Adapted from a play by Wajdi Mouawad, a Lebanese-Canadian writer, and directed by the Quebec filmmaker Denis Villeneuve, it was nominated for an Academy Award for Best Foreign Language Film in 2011, even though it takes the audience where few have dared to go before with a story in which twins fulfill their mother's dying wish. They travel to the Middle East, where they discover they were born of rape by the man who ran the prison where their mother was incarcerated. That man turns out to be their brother as well as their father. It is a searing and courageous tale of the humiliation of rape, the will to survive, and the scorched-earth patterns of rapists.

Whether committed inside or outside a war zone, rape punishes women twice. First they suffer the physical abuse and then the never-ending memory and shame, which threaten and retreat like tidal surges throughout the rest of their lives. Justice can only come from acknowledgment and the conviction of the perpetrator.

That's what the girls in Kenya were counting on. And when the judge vindicated them in May 2013, magistrates from around the world were buffeted by the hot winds of change that blew out of Africa.

2

⊸—

Scriptured Oppression

Religion has been misused politically not only in Afghanistan but in every other part of the world. — DR. SIMA SAMAR, CHAIR OF THE AFGHANISTAN INDEPENDENT HUMAN RIGHTS COMMISSION

Do you remember at what point in your life you realized that something was amiss, and that society played a huge, mostly negative, role in reinforcing gender bias?

I remember the late, great Norma Scarborough, founder of the Canadian Abortion Rights Action League, telling a story about the exact moment when she realized there was an unfair playing field for women. There was a contest in her community—a spelling bee, if I recall correctly. Norma was nine years old, smart as a whip and something of a tomboy. She won the contest and then watched the contest organizer switch the prizes for first and second places so that she would get the doll carriage and the boy who came in second would get the bike. "I wanted the bike," she'd roar every time she told the story, to the delighted recognition of her audience. That was the event that introduced her to the thorny topic of sexual equality.

I experienced a similar aha moment. I was ten or eleven years old, picking through the mail scattered on my mother's kitchen

table. Christmas was just around the corner, so most of the enve-
lopes contained holiday greeting cards. I read each one, often having to decipher the grown-up handwriting conveying Christmas
wishes. In some cases, there was a family photo tucked into the
card; in others, the face of the card itself featured the family. It was
fun to see kids I knew, all dressed up and grinning for the ubiquitous
family portrait. But about halfway through the pile, I came across
a card that stopped me. What was going on here? In the photo on the
front of the card, the father was sitting in a big comfortable arm-
chair, leaning back, holding a pipe in one hand and looking totally
relaxed and self-satisfied. The mother was sitting on the edge of the
sofa across from him, leaning forward, as though she were ready for
flight. She was flanked by young boys in the same pose. Another
boy, standing behind the sofa, was leaning forward too. All of them
were staring at the man in the easy chair as though he were some
sort of deity: the adoring family gazing at the patriarch. It shouted
male power and female subservience, the father's benevolence, the
mother's angelic devotion. To be fair, it was the style in the 1950s to
create family portraits in *Father Knows Best* fashion.

The Christmas card was supposed to express feelings of peace
on earth. It didn't for me. Instead it raised a red flag that has been
flying in my consciousness ever since. I still have that card tucked
away with my late mother's keepsakes. I look at it from time to time
just to remind myself where women have been and how much further
we have to go. As Agnes Macphail, the first woman to be elected to
the Canadian House of Commons, declared in parliament on February 26, 1925, "I do not want to be the angel of any home. I want for
myself what I want for other women—absolute equality. After that
is secured, then men and women can take turns at being angels."

To "love, honor, and obey" was the mantra for most North
American women at the time that Christmas photo was taken. Historically, women had to accept various religiously or culturally
sanctioned acts all over the world—marital rape, female genital mutilation, foot binding, honor killing, polygamy, and a dozen other

miseries that defined their status. Women everywhere existed in financial purdah, and when their husbands died or otherwise abandoned them, they realized they had no right to the man's income. Even today, a conservative estimate suggests that 30 percent of the women who dwell on this earth are subjected to daily violence and are forbidden to work or leave their homes without a husband, brother, or son to escort them, or go to school or wear what they want to wear or dance the way they want to dance or speak up the way they want to speak up. Half of the population in places like Pakistan, Congo, Afghanistan, Saudi Arabia—and numerous other countries—is still subjected to state-sanctioned, culturally condoned misogyny.

How did women become second-class citizens in the first place? Why is it that the international community still excuses the abuse of women and denies them equality rights in the name of culture and religion? And how is it that women continue to step boldly forward in one instance and slide two steps backward in the next?

Many fine minds have turned to the question, particularly during the second wave of feminism, picking up on the work of thinkers such as Simone de Beauvoir, who shed light on the dark roots of women's presumed inferiority.

The theory that biology is destiny belongs to Beauvoir and comes from the blockbuster book she wrote in 1949, *The Second Sex*. Her meticulously researched argument suggests that men fundamentally oppress women by characterizing them as "the other." Man sees himself as the subject of life and woman as the object: he's essential, she's not. Women's inferiority is taken for granted. Although Beauvoir writes that biology is not enough in itself to explain how women became "the other," it does account for the fact that women and men have never shared the world in terms of equality. She accuses men of creating a false aura of sanctity around women as an excuse to organize society without them, preserving them in the domestic sphere. And she writes that the religions invented by men reflect this wish for domination.

Although they were rarely included in the mid-twentieth-century discussions about women's oppression, Middle Eastern women were also contributing to the debate. At about the same time as Beauvoir published *The Second Sex,* Doria Shafiq was challenging the legal, social, and cultural barriers for women in Egypt. A feminist, poet, and political activist, Shafiq called for a woman's right to vote and to run for political office when she founded the Daughters of the Nile Union in 1948. When she was refused a job at Cairo University because she was a woman, she became editor of *The New Woman* magazine, which gave her a platform for the reforms she wanted for women. She led a paramilitary force of Egyptian women to resist the British at the Suez Canal and called for a boycott of Barclays Bank when it refused to let women open bank accounts. But Egypt in the 1950s was no place for gender reform. In 1957, Shafiq was placed under house arrest by President Gamal Abdel Nasser's regime. For eighteen years she was forbidden to leave her home; her magazines were closed, her name was banned from the media, and her Egyptian writings were destroyed. In 1975, she committed suicide. By then there was hardly a trace left of the work she'd done. Women in Egypt are trying to resurrect her story today.

Betty Friedan created a stir in 1963 when she published *The Feminine Mystique,* referring to the malaise women in America suffered as "the problem that has no name." Rather than being arrested as Shafiq was, Friedan became a household name when she exploded the myth of domestic bliss. Her words were like balm to millions of frustrated women who'd been told they could find happiness and fulfillment vicariously through their husbands and children.

Germaine Greer, the Australian scholar and journalist, followed in 1970 with *The Female Eunuch,* a book that called on women to reject their traditional roles in the home and break the mold that society had imposed on them, to question traditional authority figures such as doctors, psychiatrists, and the clergy and to explore their own sexuality.

The triumvirate of blockbusters from Beauvoir, Friedan, and Greer led the way for women such as the American history professor Gerda Lerner. In her 1986 book *The Creation of Patriarchy,* Lerner argued that in the Neolithic period, women were valued as a resource because they could have children to add to the workforce and help produce food surpluses. But the status was short-lived; as she points out, by the second millennium BCE, in Mesopotamian societies, the daughters of the poor were being sold into marriage or into prostitution to advance the economic interest of the family.

I asked the Canadian feminist writer Michele Landsberg, whose 2011 book *Writing the Revolution* chronicles the history of change for women in Canada, what she thought about how women became oppressed in the first place. "All feminists brood from time to time about why it is that men in every nation, in every culture, at every time in human history—with very few exceptions—have sought to dominate and control women," she said, "especially seeking to dictate rules about our bodies, sex, and reproduction. Figures like the Venus of Willendorf suggest that prehistoric people must have been in awe of female reproductive power. Creating life must have seemed a great and even fearsome mystery. It strikes me that men invented religion in order to meet and overmatch women's awesome powers. All religions, after all, have at their core the will to control and dominate women's sexuality and reproduction while elevating men's dominion over women."

Indeed, a deity invariably played a role in the status of women. At times the consequences in the lives of women have been deadly.

On March 11, 2002, a fire broke out at a girls' boarding school in Mecca, Saudi Arabia. The blaze was reported to have started on the top floor at Makkah Intermediate School No. 31 at about eight in the morning. Firefighters said it was caused by "an unattended cigarette." There were eight hundred girls registered at the school, most of them from Saudi Arabia, but also international students from Egypt, Chad, Guinea, Niger, and Nigeria. The school was overcrowded, and it didn't have required safety features and equipment such as emergency exits, fire extinguishers, and alarms. The flames spread quickly, and the school filled with smoke. The girls, most of them still in their rooms getting ready for breakfast and morning classes, raced to the exits, but the guards posted there refused to unlock the gates so that they could escape. Why? In their haste to leave the burning building, the girls had not dressed properly—they were not wearing head scarves—and their male relatives were not there to receive them on the street. The girls were screaming to be let out, and passersby stopped to help as the school turned into an inferno.

Then the Mutawa'een, or religious police—officially known as the Committee for the Propagation of Virtue and the Prevention of Vice—turned up and beat back the crowd, reminding them that the girls would be committing a sin if they came out of the school without covering their heads. According to eyewitness accounts, they told the incredulous crowd, which now included parents of some of the girls, that they (the religious police) did not want physical contact to take place between the girls and the firefighters for fear of sexual enticement. Some reporters claimed that the few girls who got out were pushed back into the burning building by the guards and the Mutawa'een. When the firefighters rushed inside to rescue the girls, they were also admonished by the religious police.

In its report, Human Rights Watch quoted one of the firefighters, who said, "Whenever the girls got out through the main gate, these people forced them to return via another. Instead of extending a helping hand for the rescue work, they were using their hands to beat us."

Fourteen girls died in the fire. More than fifty were injured. The news leaped into cyberspace and quickly moved around the world. The story made headlines in the Saudi newspapers for days. The vice and virtue squad of Saudi Arabia was thrashed in editorials in leading newspapers, which asked what sort of barbarism was at work when innocent girls were forbidden to escape from a burning building. Saudi Arabia is a discreet place when it comes to its draconian rules for women and girls. The religious police are almost always safe from criticism. When Saudi princes sit down with presidents and prime ministers to discuss oil revenue, no one brings up the lives of Saudi girls and women. But this time the royal family could not hide behind the veil of silence.

Hanny Megally, the executive director of the Middle East and North Africa division of Human Rights Watch at the time, said, "Women and girls may have died unnecessarily because of extreme interpretations of the Islamic dress code. State authorities with direct and indirect responsibility for this tragedy must be held accountable."

There was action—not justice, but action. An inquiry was launched by the Saudi government. Prince Naif, minister of the interior, promised that those responsible for the deaths of the girls would be held accountable. The vice and virtue squad was given a public dressing-down. So was the General Presidency for Girls' Education. The cleric in charge of the school was fired and the school was taken over by the ministry of education. As it turns out, the Saudi people didn't like the fact that girls' schools were controlled by the conservative religious establishment, and they had tried before to bring the schools into the public realm. This time they succeeded.

However, in an about-face, Prince Naif refused to blame the Mutawa'een for the deaths of the girls. He claimed that the deaths hadn't happened because the girls hadn't been allowed to flee the fire but because of the stampede to escape. He acknowledged the presence of the Mutawa'een and said that they went there to prevent "mistreatment" of the girls. But he asserted that they hadn't interfered with the rescue efforts and only arrived after everyone had left the building. Eyewitnesses begged to differ.

The inquiry reported its conclusion on March 25, 2002: the fire was caused by a stray cigarette; the religious educational authorities responsible for the school had neglected the safety of the pupils; the clerics had ignored warnings about overcrowding that had led to the fatal stampede. Allegations that the Mutawa'een had prevented the girls from fleeing were dismissed.

In the wake of the report, the International Secretariat of Amnesty International issued a statement:

Amnesty International is gravely concerned at reports that 14 girls have lost their lives and dozens of others were injured following a fire at their school in Mecca on 11 March 2002 after the religious police (Mutawa'een) prevented them from escaping from the fire because they were not wearing headscarves and their male relatives were not there to receive them. The religious police are also reported to have prevented rescuers from entering the school because they were males and therefore not permitted to mix with females.

If these reports are true, this is a tragic illustration of how gender discrimination can have lethal consequences.

When state policies on segregation of sexes are implemented at the expense of human life, urgent steps are needed at the highest level. Policies and practices through which the lives of women and girls are devalued must be changed. . . .

Saudi Arabia must take urgent measures to end all forms of discrimination against women in accordance with CEDAW (Convention on the Elimination of All Forms of Discrimination against Women), to which Saudi Arabia is a state party.

As appalling as this story is, it is not a singular example of the blatant abuse of the rights of women and girls. The oldest atrocity, the one invariably mentioned in association with Islam, dates back to the pre-Islamic era called jahiliyah, the time of ignorance before Muhammad. That travesty is honor killing. Arab men of the time thought they should bury their infant daughters alive to avoid the possibility that they would grow up to dishonor the family. The prophet moved to eradicate that practice.

Infant girls were killed in other parts of the world because they were seen as worthless. In ancient Greece, after a baby was born, the wife would show the infant to her husband. If he decided to keep the baby, it would live. If he refused, the baby would be abandoned to die of hunger or exposure to the elements.

The practice was also prevalent in ancient Rome. An interpretation of a letter from a Roman citizen to his wife, dating from 1 BCE, demonstrates the casual nature with which infanticide was viewed: "I am still in Alexandria . . . if (good fortune to you!) you give birth, if it is a boy, let it live; if it is a girl, expose it."

So where did these ideas—that baby girls are worthless, that women can bring shame to the family—come from? Many presume the oppression of women began with the holy texts. While every one of them—the Bible, the Torah, and the Quran—is patriarchal and contains passages that denigrate women, they also represent some of the earliest records of women's lives and offer clues as to their treatment. Even before recorded history, we know that societies were either matriarchal or patriarchal, so at least in some places, women were leaders. Although modern scholars of the New Testament claim that women had leadership roles during the first thirty or forty years of Christianity, and in the early days of the Roman Empire, women (presuming they survived birth, given that infanticide wasn't outlawed until 374 CE) could own property and businesses and run their own households, those rights were stripped from them in 381 CE, when the Roman Empire became Christian.

As male leaders took over, they reinforced the scriptures of the Old Testament that suggested that the ills of humanity derive from women. Christians, Jews, and Muslims all look to the Old Testament as the original document. Judaism came first in about 900 BCE, then about a thousand years later Christianity developed, followed in 600 CE by Islam. So these three world religions are rooted in scriptures that denigrate women. Despite the endless scholarly debates by rabbis, priests, and Islamic religious leaders about what the holy texts say and don't say, most agree that in the Bible, the Torah, and the Quran, women are not blessed with equal rights. For example, the Old Testament says in Ecclesiastics 30:3, "The birth of a daughter is a loss." And in Ecclesiastics 26: 10–11, "Keep a strict watch on her shameless eye; do not be surprised if she disgraces you."

The Old Testament also serves up the Adam and Eve story featuring the snake and the apple. Depending on the religious analysis of that story and the modernization of the text, women have borne the taint of Eve in churches, synagogues, and mosques ever since.

But it's the New Testament that seals the social destiny of women in Christianity. For example, the sentiment "Wives, submit yourselves unto your own husbands, as it is fit in the Lord" is included not just once but three times in three different books (Colossians 3:18, 1 Peter 3:1, and Ephesians 5:22). Paul's letter to the Corinthians says, "It is disgraceful for a woman to speak in the church" (1 Corinthians 14: 34–35). Timothy 2:8 says, "I permit no woman to teach or have authority over a man; she is to keep silent."

The Quran and Torah have similarly discriminatory injunctions that forbid women to inherit or own property. The tone is also noteworthy. This passage from the Talmud, for instance, is derisive in the extreme; you can practically hear the contempt: "How can a woman have anything; whatever is hers belongs to her husband. What is his is his and what is hers is also his" (Sanhedrin, 71a; Gittin, 62a).

Once religion took a male-dominated stand, it nurtured the oppression of women. Augustine of Hippo, who would become St. Augustine, said, "What is the difference whether it is in a wife or a mother, it is still Eve, the temptress, that we must beware of in any woman. I fail to see what use woman can be to man, if one excludes the function of bearing children."

In twelfth-century Baghdad, the home of Islam, women were doctors and owned businesses. What's more, Islam was the only religion of the time that allowed people to practice any other religion, and its leader, the prophet Muhammad, had a working wife. So why do so many of today's mullahs and imams interpret the Quran in ways that oppress women, such as allowing the beating of a woman or claiming that her voice carries half the weight of a man's in court or that the father is the legal and only guardian of children? The Quran was written one hundred years after the prophet died; its suras and hadiths (the interpretation of the prophet's words) reflect the times more than they do the holy man.

By the mid-thirteenth century, Thomas Aquinas was teaching Christians that women were defective men, that they were imperfect in body and soul. In his *Summa Theologiæ*, the unfinished work he wrote as the sacred doctrine of the church, he asserts, "The inferiority of women lies not just in bodily strength but in the force of her intellect." He was influenced by Aristotle's reproductive biology, which claimed that women were born of defective sperm. The Canon Laws that followed laid out church rules and specified that women could not be witnesses in disputes or criminal proceedings, could not practice law or medicine or hold public office, and suffered from the same disability of intellect as children and imbeciles. Those laws would stick to women the way barnacles attach themselves to ships until the late 1900s.

Both Catholic and Protestant women felt the weight of the church and the edicts of men like Aquinas, and after him Martin Luther, who said, "A woman should stay at home." A woman's life was at the disposal of men and became embedded in the power of men. Her husband or father could deny her, beat her, even kill her; she was not a human being with rights, she was chattel. The institution of marriage was included in coverture, a legal doctrine that declared that a wife's rights were subsumed in those of her husband. Sir William Blackstone, known as "the codifier" because he wrote commentaries that refined the laws in England in the 1780s—the same Blackstone who created the "rule of thumb," which decreed that the width of the switch used to beat a wife or a child could be no wider than a man's thumb—penned the principles of coverture: a husband and wife were one person under the law, and that person was the husband. A married woman could not own property, sign legal documents or enter into a contract, obtain an education against her husband's wishes, or keep money for herself. If a wife was permitted to work, she was required to surrender her wages to her husband. In certain cases, a woman did not have individual legal liability for her misdeeds, since it was legally assumed that she was acting under the orders of her husband; generally, a husband and wife were not allowed to testify either for or against each other.

It was brilliant social commentators such as Charles Dickens who began to poke holes in religious laws and lay bare the consequences of both church and state decrees. In *Oliver Twist,* when Mr. Bumble is informed that "the law supposes that your wife acts under your direction," Dickens coined a famous phrase with Mr. Bumble's reply: "If the law supposes that, the law is a ass—a idiot."

The practice by which a woman adopts her husband's name as her own (i.e., when Mary Smith marries John Thompson, she becomes Mrs. John Thompson) is another example of coverture, and another sample of the way that laws that privileged men still cling to women's lives. Mary Eberts says, "The doctrine of coverture is the source of many injustices [now] done away with: i.e., the right of the husband to control the wife's property and her earnings; the exclusive right of the father to child custody; the incapacity of the wife to testify against her husband in court; et cetera. Women and their allies have been fighting these laws since the 1780s."

The church, whether Catholic or Protestant, had always been quick to denounce women who dared to express intelligent thought and analysis. For most of its history, women largely responded to canon law not by attacking it but by delivering their views as mystic pronouncements, as had Catherine of Siena (1347–1380) and Teresa of Ávila (1515–1582). Many scholars suggest that this metaphysical response to the church's views about women led to accusations of witchcraft—that women must be dealing with the Devil if they were speaking against the doctrines of the church. During the sixteenth and seventeenth centuries, women accused of practicing witchcraft were found guilty of consulting evil spirits and were burned alive in fires lit on hills so the entire village could watch.

The religious scholar Kim Murray of Salt Spring Island in British Columbia says that there was a plausible explanation for the rise in the execution of women as witches. A collection of world events had come together like a catalyst for economic and social change: the discovery of the New World, the finding of precious metals, the development of agriculture to feature crops that could be overwintered, plows that could open up the soil to create greater yields and improved animal husbandry. All of it was good news and led to increased prosperity, food abundance, and a birthrate that grew dramatically. But, says Murray, these changes also led to a Devil's brew of reaction when crops failed or were diseased. "And that's when people seeking to placate divinity in the face of disaster flock to the churches. There needed to be a scapegoat; that dubious distinction went to women." He points to two defining incidents. The first was a weather event known as the Little Ice Age, which struck Northern Europe between 1540 and 1660; during those years it was five to seven degrees cooler than it had been, and crops failed dramatically. The second event was an outbreak of ergot poisoning that occurred throughout Europe and in the American colonies, as well. "There's a fungus associated with grain called ergot," Murray explains. "It invariably turns up during a bad crop year. If consumed, it causes two things: spontaneous abortions and hallucinations. Women who suffered ergot poisoning were accused of intentionally aborting babies and conduct that was seen as demonic, so they were burned alive at the stake." The behavioral scientist Linda Caporael is a professor at the Rensselaer Polytechnic Institute in Troy, New York. Her work in analyzing the causes of witch burning led her to conclude that women were more affected by ergot poisoning than men, that pregnant women were most affected, and that mental symptoms from the poisoning included mania, melancholia, psychosis, and delirium, which were presumed by religious leaders to be symptomatic of demonic possession.

Unmarried women didn't fare any better than married women in the eyes of the church. They were their fathers' property and could be used or abused as their fathers saw fit. Like their married sisters, they were forbidden entrance to the professions and to all but a few trades. In 1588, Pope Sixtus V forbade them to appear on the public stage within his dominions, which soon led to a ban of actresses and female singers across Christendom.

It wasn't until well into the twentieth century that women would begin to shed the shackles of religious-based laws that had kept them away from professions, off juries, and out of the paid workforce. Although women have yet to achieve equality in any religion, including Hinduism and Buddhism, there are some Christians, Jews, and Muslims who still live by fundamentalist laws that oppress women and have hardly budged in a thousand years.

Modern interpretations have altered the original views of the authors of the various holy books, but modern fundamentalists in every religion are still draconian in enforcing old rules.

Dr. Sima Samar knows a thing or two about directives to women coming in the guise of a message from God. She is the woman who defied the Taliban and kept open her schools for girls and her health clinics for women in Afghanistan even when the Taliban threatened to kill her if she didn't shut them down. She says, "Religion has been misused politically, not only in Afghanistan but in every other part of the world. It's a question of education. If you don't know what's in the Quran, or you don't understand the meaning of the words, you are liable to misinterpret religion and use it against women's rights."

She views most of the edicts promulgated by mullahs in Afghanistan as misguided. The language of the Quran is Arabic. In Afghanistan, people speak Dari and Farsi. Not only that, but 85 percent of Afghan women and about 75 percent of Afghan men, including mullahs, are illiterate and so can't read the Arabic text anyway. It's not surprising that women in Afghanistan describe their illiteracy as a form of blindness.

It's the increase in literacy as well as the fact that women are becoming more confident and learning about tools to defend their rights that's bringing change to places like Afghanistan, despite its being home to some of the worst extremists.

Farida Shaheed, the prominent Pakistani women's rights activist, says, "Women are affected by religion throughout the world. Religion has not withered away. It is back and has increased in power, even in Eastern Europe [after the fall of the Soviet Union]. The issue is who does the interpretation of what religion means: religion as faith is the least problematic; as custom, it's a bigger problem; but as politics, it becomes the most problematic. Religion is being harnessed to further political agendas."

The research that Shaheed has conducted in Chile, the United States, Serbia, Mexico, Poland, Pakistan, Iran, India, Nigeria, and Turkey shows some interesting trends. "It's often not just religious groups who use religion for power," she says. "It's used for alliances across the board of very conservative agendas." Many of those agendas are written in the government offices of Muslim countries, not in the mosques.

Isobel Coleman, the foreign policy specialist and also the author of *Paradise Beneath Her Feet: How Women Are Transforming the Middle East*, sees extraordinary effort by both women and men to promote greater rights for women within the framework of Islam. "In many of these countries, some of the worst violations of women's rights are done in the name of Islam, but the new generation says, 'That's not the way we read it.'" Throughout the Middle East and in Pakistan, Afghanistan, Saudi Arabia, Iraq, and Iran, women and girls have told her that they insist on a greater role for women based on a more progressive reading of the Quran. And they see women taking more of the lead in pushing the boundaries.

The example that Coleman cites is Musawah (which means "equality" in Arabic), a movement launched in 2009 by Sisters in Islam, an NGO that seeks equality within the Muslim family and promotes women's rights within a religious framework. Its leader,

Zainah Anwar, says, "At the heart of Islamic feminism is the con-
tention that Muslim women will no longer be shut up by some verse
in the Quran." She refers to the family life of Muslims, which is
mostly based on what the Quran says about the role of women.
Coleman says, "It's very prescriptive, not always amenable to equality for women." Active in more than fifty countries in Africa, Asia,
the Middle East, Europe, North America, and Australia, Musawah
is a global movement calling for equality, nondiscrimination, and
dignity as the basis of all human relations; full and equal citizenship for every individual; and marriage and family relations based
on principles of equality, with men and women sharing equal rights
and responsibilities. The principles of Musawah are taken straight
from the seventh century CE, when Islam arrived in Arabia:

I am equal before the eyes of God
I have the right to my own property
I have the right to inherit property
I can sign my own contracts
I can choose my own husband
I can't be forced to marry against my will
I can write a marriage contract and impose conditions on my
    husband-to-be
I have the right to divorce my husband
I am entitled to dignity and respect
I am entitled to an education
I have the right to think for myself
I have the right to lead my people to the right path.

Musawah has been embraced by men and women as well as
secularists who usually keep their distance from religious organizations. But taking on the power brokers in the business of religion
is still a sometimes dangerous and always baffling task. Consider
the remarks of a senior academic in Saudi Arabia, Kamal Subhi,
who in response to the increasing demand of women in the king-

dom to be allowed to drive reported to the Saudi legislative assembly that allowing women to drive would spell the end of virginity in the kingdom. Or this from one of the leaders of the Christian right in the United States, the Reverend Pat Robertson: "The Feminist agenda is not about equal rights for women. It is about a socialist, anti-family political movement that encourages women to leave their husbands, kill their children, practice witchcraft, destroy capitalism, and become lesbians."

Women have challenged religious zealots in earlier eras, but there has generally been a reluctance to bring legal action against them. That has changed. Rebecca Cook, a professor at the University of Toronto's law school, is acclaimed for the academic work she has done for women, health, and human rights. Recently she stood as a witness in a Canadian court reference case that is bound to have international implications. The practice of polygamy among members of a religious sect called the Fundamentalist Church of Jesus Christ of Latter-Day Saints (FLDS) in a place called Bountiful, British Columbia, was on trial.

Getting the case to court was an ordeal that had been ongoing since 1904, when the Mormon Church issued a manifesto telling its followers to abandon the practice of polygamy. A splinter group that believed polygamy was ordained by God and was their ticket to heaven broke away and formed the FLDS. The followers, today estimated at about ten thousand, reside in Utah, Arizona, Texas, Colorado, South Dakota, Alberta, and British Columbia. Their activities went largely unnoticed (except for the occasional accusation from neighbors about child brides and multiple wives) until 1988, when a woman named Debbie Palmer escaped from the Bountiful community and went public with the disturbing facts of her life in a polygamous marriage. Her convoluted family tree contains so many branches that, as she says, she is her own step-great-grandmother. Palmer has eight children, seventy-six stepchildren, forty-seven brothers and sisters, and three ex-husbands. You need a calculator to do the matrimonial math and a user's guide to Canada's criminal code to follow the sad, often brutal, story of Palmer and the other women who have left the FLDS.

Palmer's parents moved to Bountiful when she was two years old. At fifteen, she was given in marriage to a man who was fifty-five. He had five other wives and thirty children, some of them older than Palmer. He died two years after they married, and she was given to another man, also fifty-five, who had four other wives and twenty-seven children. When he was deemed to be abusive by the sect's leader at the time, she was sent off to a third husband, who already had two wives and twelve children. That husband was accused and later convicted in a B.C. court of sexually assaulting and abusing Palmer.

By age thirty-four, she had been beaten, humiliated, and raped with a fist, with a stick, and anally by various men in the community. That was the year she finally packed her kids into an old van and drove out of Bountiful forever. She's been unpacking the emotional baggage ever since.

The criticism she leveled at the church leaders was shocking: she told of plural marriages in which men had as many as twenty-five wives, of marriages in which fifteen-year-old girls were wed to sixty-five-year-old men. She told of "lost boys" who were excommunicated to ensure plenty of wives for the community elders. She told of welfare fraud in which the first wife is the so-called legal spouse, making the rest single moms who apply for and get welfare. She disclosed the secret rituals of the sect and also described a community of white supremacists.

Adherents believe that the Second Coming of Christ will see everyone from outside their colony burned alive, while the men with their multiple wives and children are saved in a "lifting-up" that will literally raise their colonies above the fire. Then they will become gods of new planets. At least that's how they interpret this religious teaching: "As man is, God once was. As God is, man may become." Many FLDS rituals support this dogma.

At a wedding or "celestial marriage," the woman and man create the Sure Sign of the Nail, which means their middle fingers touch each other's wrists on the place Christ was nailed to the cross. And there's the Law of Chastity, which says a woman can have sex only when she's ovulating. Any other sex is considered adultery. "It's not about sex for salvation," says Palmer. "It's sex for breeding cheap labor."

If the road to heaven is multiple marriages, the way to hell is criticizing the leader. One of the laws of the FLDS is Blood Atonement. It states that if members have committed certain sins, such as complaining about the prophet (every leader is a prophet), they can be forgiven only if they have their "blood spilt upon the ground." Although the member winds up dead from the process, which can also involve being disemboweled and burned alive, she or he can gain entry to heaven despite the sin.

From the moment she fled with her children in 1992, Palmer appealed to every provincial attorney general in B.C. to investigate Bountiful. For years, nothing happened. In fact, Palmer had directed so many petitions and letters to B.C. attorney general Geoff Plant that when I arrived for an interview at his constituency office in Richmond, B.C., in 2004, his assistant sighed and said, "Will this result in another flood of letters?"

One attorney general after another refused to take Bountiful on, as they feared the constitutional right to freedom of religion would trump any criminal charges related to trafficking in child brides, underage marriage, and sex with minors. Furthermore, Bountiful's leader, Winston Blackmore, made sure his own idyllic interpretation of the sect was well understood by the Royal Canadian Mounted Police, who had been asked to investigate by women from the nearby town of Creston. Blackmore sent a parade of contented female followers to talk to the cops; the RCMP didn't bring any charges.

After CBC's *The Fifth Estate* aired a documentary on Blackmore called "The Bishop of Bountiful" in 2003, newspaper stories followed. Oprah Winfrey did a show about the religious shenanigans in Bountiful. A few days after that telecast, a letter was posted on her Web site from B.C.'s premier, Gordon Campbell. The letter claimed that prosecuting would "require significant police resources," that only a few witnesses had come forward, and that, furthermore, it was the fault of the federal government for not amending the criminal code regarding polygamy. Debbie Palmer kept the facts about polygamy flowing at conferences about violence against women and in letters to politicians. But still nothing changed. In jargon-filled apologias from both federal and provincial ministers of justice, Palmer was basically told to get lost.

I went to Bountiful to investigate the allegations in the spring of 2004. What I found was trouble in the so-called paradise. Fifteen-year-old girls were having babies with fifty-year-old men and were supposed to smile sweetly about it because it was God's will.

From a distance, the place looked like the Garden of Eden. Nestled beneath British Columbia's East Kootenay Mountains, in a temperate valley of rich topsoil, the community of Bountiful seemed like a land of peace and prosperity. As I drove closer to this colony of a thousand people, I could see children playing in the fields. Teenage girls in pastel ankle-length dresses and long braided hair waved a greeting, looking as though they'd come out of another century, one that valued plain living and family ties.

Inside the colony, a different story unfolded. There used to be a collection of nine rocks on the ground at the entrance, each one with a letter on it, spelling out "Keep Sweet"—the sect's dictum to its women. Recently someone had flipped the rocks over and written a different set of letters: "Fuck you!!" The plot where the rocks were displayed was gone and the ground was bare. The long-held secrets of Bountiful were leaking like the battered oil cans that littered the place. They revealed incest and deception, sexual abuse, cross-border trafficking of brides, the breeding if young girls like cattle, tax fraud, and white supremacy. Not your average Canadian tale.

A power struggle had broken out in 2002, when the U.S.–based leader of the cult, Rulon Jeffs, died. His son Warren presumed he'd succeed his father, but Winston Blackmore, the bishop of Bountiful, felt that role was rightfully his. By the time I got there in 2004, the pressure within the community was explosive. One woman living inside the colony said, "It could boil over—it could get perilous here." Women outside the colony rallied to rescue those who wanted to leave and were determined to use the leadership chaos to expose the sect's seamy truths.

Linda Price, from the neighboring town of Creston, told me, "It was knowing that young girls are having babies against their will that moved me to action." She and other neighbors already had been questioning their town's live-and-let-live philosophy toward Bountiful, but Winston Blackmore was wealthy, with half a dozen of his businesses providing income for the town—a good reason not to rock the boat. Then Price's own adult daughters called her after seeing the CBC documentary. "How can you live in a community where women are being abused?" they asked her. "How can Dad play hockey with those men?"

The women in Creston organized a province-wide protest, as well as a secret safe house where the women and girls of Bountiful could find shelter and advice. It operated like an underground railway, shuttling the frightened souls of Bountiful to a world they'd never known—a world that their church claimed would lead to their being burned alive with the nonbelievers. But mostly the Creston women were working on getting criminal charges brought.

When I spoke to Winston Blackmore on the phone, he wouldn't confirm that he had twenty-eight wives and eighty-some children, but his followers claimed that was the case. Basing their gospel on a literal interpretation of the Book of Mormon, members of the FLDS believe the only way to survive the apocalypse is through plural marriage. So a man should gather as many wives as he can—preferably the prettiest, smartest, and youngest women available—and produce an abundance of children.

Although most men in the sect have only three or four wives to service in the name of God, those with more require breeding charts to record each woman's ovulation date. This way, a wife knows who is getting bedded by her shared husband on which night. It's hard to imagine a thirteen-, fourteen-, or fifteen-year-old child having her cycle marked on such a chart. Yet some of the girls believe that to carry the child of a man like Blackmore is a guarantee of admittance to heaven.

Blackmore's religious Waterloo came about because of another extreme: the Blood Atonement law. Vanessa Rohbock, a young woman from Colorado City, had been found guilty of sinning in the eyes of the American sect leader Warren Jeffs, and before she could be made to "atone," she fled to Canada, where she was sheltered by Blackmore. "The blood thing has nothing to do with the fundamentals of our religion," Blackmore said. "The girl is [now] safe and sound and happily married to a fine man." His actions helped Rohbock, but they were seen by Jeffs as blasphemy. He stormed into Bountiful and tried to discredit Blackmore in front of the Canadian followers. Some chose to obey Jeffs, but others defied him. Ever since Jeffs's father, the revered ninety-three-year-old Rulon, had died, the battle for the souls and the million-dollar property at Bountiful was on.

Although he refused to meet me in person, Blackmore consented to several e-mail exchanges and a few phone calls. He claimed that he didn't know what Warren Jeffs was up to: "He has several people convinced that he talks with his [dead] father, our past presidents, and God on a daily basis. A gigantic claim, but one that holds the imagination of the masses." (Blackmore's steadfast followers also claimed he talked to God.) Regarding the split in the colony at Bountiful, Blackmore said that before the leadership struggle began, a woman would never speak out against her husband or family. "Today, every woman among them would leave her husband and hate him in a minute if Warren directed that she do so. Children spy on parents and without notice. It is over for their families."

Barry Beyerstein, a cult expert at Simon Fraser University in

British Columbia, told me that the power struggle in Bountiful wasn't unusual. "Cults tend to implode due to internal contradictions, jealousies, slights," he explained. "But when they tie that to the end of the world being near, danger is also near." His international research shows that when cults reach that stage, most split and start new and smaller colonies. Others turn into Waco and Jonestown and self-destruct with a vengeance.

Preventing the consequences of hyperreligious behavior means using the law. In the case of the religious sect at Bountiful, the law is clear: it is illegal to practice polygamy in Canada. Cross-border trafficking in girls is also illegal—but it's happening in order to broaden the gene pool in Bountiful and its sister colony in Colorado City. A man setting up each of his polygamous wives as single mothers so they can get a child tax benefit for all their children is also illegal, but it's a money-making scheme for Bountiful.

Audrey Vance, who has lived in Creston for forty-two years, was also moved after seeing Winston Blackmore's first wife, Jane, on *The Fifth Estate*. "She had the courage to go on national TV and tell her story about being the [community's] midwife, about listening to a fifteen-year-old girl crying while she delivered her baby because she didn't want to be married or to be pregnant." The fifteen-year-old was the daughter of one of Blackmore's other wives. As Jane recounted, when she raised her concerns with her husband, Blackmore said, "Well, Mother, I want you to mind your own business because you are not the bishop."

After Jane Blackmore's stunning account of underage sex, coercion, and sexual abuse, all the people I talked to, including Jane, told me they presumed the attorney general would subpoena the birth records she'd kept as a midwife. But her phone never rang, and a search warrant was never served.

Since the justice system continued to ignore the polygamy issue, the women in Creston decided to hook their protest to the Education Act instead. They sent letters to the editors of major B.C. newspapers claiming that the Bountiful Elementary Secondary School

(BESS) was receiving an annual government grant of $460,826. Vance, a former school trustee in Creston, wanted to know why a polygamist school funded with taxpayers' money was left alone to teach a cult lifestyle to school-age children.

Vance's information came from women inside Bountiful, who could not be named for fear of repercussions. They had told her that the department of education routinely gave the school several weeks' notice before an inspection—time enough for the school staff to remove all the white-supremacist slogans that had been posted on the classroom walls. Inspectors apparently were fooled, but Vance thinks they should have been wise to the fact that the teachers were never able to explain why the school had hardly any graduates. The reason, of course, was that the girls left school to be married, and many of the boys were sent away. Only a few students were allowed to finish high school. But that information was never shared with inspectors, and it seems they never did ask for it.

The new complaint from the women of Creston didn't spark any action, either. In the meantime, then attorney general Geoff Plant explained to me somewhat impatiently, "Under the Charter of Rights and Freedoms, they are protected by freedom of religion. I cannot prosecute because it could result in a charter challenge."

One of the authors of the gender-equality guarantee in the Canadian Charter of Rights and Freedoms, the lawyer Marilou McPhedran, saw this as "flimsy reasoning from a high-ranking representative of the people in a free and democratic society." She was surprised that Plant would justify his inaction because of speculation that the criminal code prohibition of polygamy might be trumped by the charter's guarantee of freedom of religion. "There are no absolute rights or freedoms in Canada," she explained. She pointed to the Supreme Court case of the Jehovah's Witness family who refused a blood transfusion for their sick child—their right to freedom of religion was overruled in favor of the safety and health of the child.

"In the Bountiful case," said McPhedran, "the excuse that women and girls have consented to their treatment would likely collapse when measured with the criminal code prohibition of polygamy and equality rights of women and girls in sections 15 and 28 of the charter."

So why were government officials dithering?

Doug Barron, a corporal in the Creston RCMP, told me they would investigate a complaint but hadn't received one. When I reminded him that the daily news was full of RCMP investigations into other criminal activities where no one had made a complaint, such as terrorist cells and biker gangs, he had no comment.

As for Plant, he replied curtly, "My only source of knowledge about Bountiful is the media. Most of what I say is misrepresented by the media, so why should I believe what they say about others?" He took the same line as the RCMP. "If people think there's been an offense, they need to go to the police. It concerns me when people think I have some responsibility for this."

The women of British Columbia disagreed. They saw the inaction as morally bankrupt and a failure to protect Canadian citizens, and they launched three protests in April and May 2004. One was the letter from the Creston women regarding the Education Act; another came from the Western Women's Committee of the Canada Employment and Immigration Union (CEIU), who sent a letter to Geoff Plant, copying it to every other level of government and minister that seemed to be responsible, including Prime Minister Paul Martin, asking that the laws governing polygamy, statutory rape, incest, and provincial and federal tax fraud be enforced in Bountiful. And a third came from a group of women, including Debbie Palmer, who filed a complaint with the B.C. Human Rights Tribunal.

Debbie Palmer was living in Prince Albert, Saskatchewan, with her three school-age children and one grandchild when I interviewed her for the magazine story. She could have papered the walls of her four-bedroom duplex with the petitions and letters she'd sent to authorities in Canada. She had already written a book and kept up-to-date data on the goings-on within the cult. She also provided help for those who left. "There's nothing for these women," she said. "They have little education, absolutely no financial support, and no status on the outside as a married woman."

The emotional turmoil the apostates suffer is immense. "We don't know how to deal with flashbacks and post-traumatic stress," Palmer said. "We've been raised to always be sweet, to love the person you're assigned to and to believe that you are safe in a community, apart from the world and its sins." Of the ugly goings-on inside the colony—things like rape, molestation, and abuse—she said, "We didn't have names for that."

Winston Blackmore, who is Palmer's stepgrandson, brother-in-law, and nephew, told me that he too is upset with any form of abuse: "As a long-time bishop, husband, and father, I have been especially saddened when I see it among plural families." But he also wrote that monogamists don't have bragging rights on good behavior. "When you monogamists can show us a system that is without abuse, divorce, infidelity, neglect, jealousy, or any of the other things that you love to gasp at us over, then and only then should there be a story written about us."

As I drove out of Bountiful, a thunderstorm was brewing over the mountains. One woman, whose identity had to be protected, matched the mood of the mounting storm. "What's happening in there is pure evil," she said.

Later in 2004, Plant said he had encouraged police to reopen the Bountiful file. He claimed that he had also begun looking into the school's funding and the overall welfare of the young girls in the community. "It has reached a point where there is enough concern in the public that we'd better be doing something about it, as opposed to standing by and doing nothing."

Eventually, after a maddening collection of false starts and after much stomping and denying and accusing, a charge of practicing polygamy was finally made in January 2009 against the two most prominent men of the Bountiful community, Winston Blackmore and James Oler. But the prosecution failed to convict them, and the charges were dropped. Crown prosecutors were reluctant to try again because of that same old fear that charges would be declared unconstitutional on the basis of religious freedom.

By then there was another new attorney general of British Columbia, Wally Opal, who decided that the situation could not be sustained. On October 22, 2009, the B.C. government asked the provincial court for clarification—a process known as a reference—of whether Canada's 121-year-old law against polygamy is consistent with the Canadian Charter of Rights and Freedoms.

As the case began, Rebecca Cook explained: "The polygamy reference case being heard in Vancouver is extremely important, not only for issues here but in different parts of the world. The documents that come out of this case will be important to other groups in other parts of the world by raising awareness about how these cases can be brought to court." The gathering of expert testimony from around the world was fascinating, too, in illustrating the different ways that women's groups were addressing polygamy. Cook said, "One way to try to eliminate it is to criminally prohibit it. Another way is to limit it: for example, in Indonesia a man needs the permission of his first wife to take a second wife." She examined what the law in each jurisdiction actually says and found that though in one place all the wives must agree if a man is to take another wife, in others they don't have to. Similarly, some jurisdictions say women must inherit equally regardless of the type of marriage they are in. Others claim that women in polygamous marriages cannot inherit at all.

Cook wondered whether there was any instance where women could freely choose a discriminatory structure of marriage. The question she posed is this: Should the state sanction an unequal form of marriage that is unfair to women? "The reference case in B.C. is important in terms of how the court sees women's equality versus men's equality: the inherent role of unequal structure, how it stereotypes women particularly in the case of Bountiful into childbearing-service roles, having sex at certain times, maximizing the chances of childbearing and being trained to be sweet. The wrong is the unfair structure: it allows a man to marry multiple spouses but not women. It denies women sexual exclusivity and it stereotypes them in childbearing roles."

When the reference case began, all sides lined up to have their day in court. The judge, Chief Justice Robert Bauman, listened to months of testimony, called on dozens of witnesses, and ultimately made his lengthy and careful judgment. He ruled that though the ban on the practice of polygamy infringed on some sections of the charter, polygamy remained illegal in Canada. He wrote that "the harms associated with the practice are endemic; they are inherent," and that the harms found in polygamous societies "are not simply the product of individual misconduct; they arise inevitably out of the practice." He further stated, "There is no such thing as so-called good polygamy."

His judgment was in keeping with attitude changes the world over: the oppression of women not only hurts individuals but also hinders economies and holds back progress. A judgment impossible to imagine even a decade earlier now seemed inevitable.

His comprehensive legal opinion is the first in the world to fully expose the effects of polygamy. In his conclusion he listed harms done, an itemization worth quoting at length:.

(a) It creates a pool of unmarried men with the attendant increase in crime and anti-social behaviour;

(b) The increased competition for women creates pressure to recruit increasingly younger brides into the marriage market;

(c) This competition causes men (as fathers, husbands and brothers) to seek to exercise more control over the choices of women, increasing gender inequality and undermining female autonomy and rights. This is exacerbated by larger age disparities between husbands and wives in *both* polygynous and monogamous relationships; and

(d) Men reduce investment in wives and offspring as they spread their resources more thinly across larger families and increasingly channel those resources into obtaining more wives.

(e) While polygyny increases the value of women in the marriage market, women do not realize the added value since men manipulate social institutions in ways that facilitate their control of women. These institutions include early and arranged marriages, the payment of brideprice, easy divorce and the devaluing of romantic love. Among the costs are depressed mental health for women and poorer outcomes for their children.

(f) Women in polygynous relationships are at an elevated risk of physical and psychological harm. They face higher rates of domestic violence and abuse, including sexual abuse. Competition for material and emotional access to a shared husband can lead to fractious co-wife relationships. These factors contribute to the higher rates of depressive disorders and other mental health issues that women in polygynous relationships face. They have more children, are more likely to die in childbirth and live shorter lives than their monogamous counterparts. They lack reproductive autonomy, and report high rates of marital dissatisfaction and low levels of self-esteem. They also fare worse economically, as resources may be inequitably divided or simply insufficient.

(g) Children in polygynous families face higher infant mortality, even controlling for economic status and other relevant variables. They tend to suffer more emotional, behavioural and physical problems, as well as lower educational achievement. These outcomes are likely the result of higher levels of conflict, emotional stress and tension in polygynous families. In particular, rivalry and jealousy among co-wives can cause significant emotional problems for their children. The inability of fathers to give sufficient affection and disciplinary attention to all of their children can further reduce children's emotional security. Children are also at enhanced risk of psychological and physical abuse and neglect.

(h) Early marriage for girls is common, frequently to significantly older men. The resultant early sexual activity, pregnancies and childbirth have negative health implications for girls and also significantly limit their socio-economic development. Shortened inter-birth intervals pose a heightened risk of problems for both mother and child.

(i) The sex ratio imbalance inherent in polygyny means that young men are forced out of polygamous communities to sustain the ability of senior men to accumulate more wives. These young men and boys often receive limited education as a result, and must navigate their way outside their communities with few life skills and little social support.

The judgment, handed down on November 23, 2011, was hailed by women's groups across Canada and around the world. The archaic demands of fundamentalists had been challenged and stopped. It's a sign of the times. As the woman in Bountiful said when I slipped past the gate so many years ago, "When the silence is broken, the secrets will lose their power."

Still, as this book went to press, the provincial government of British Columbia had taken no action against the polygamists of Bountiful.

3

Cultural Contradictions

If your culture oppresses women, change it. — FARIDA
SHAHEED, UNITED NATIONS INDEPENDENT EXPERT
IN THE FIELD OF CULTURAL RIGHTS

Justifying violence in the name of culture is an old story. I've been its unhappy witness while reporting on the status of women in a dozen different places. I remember a UN official in Kandahar speaking to me with the patronizing air of a functionary in January 2001 about the Taliban rules that didn't allow women to work outside their homes and forbade girls to go to school. He asked me, "When are you going to get it through your head that what's happening to the women of Afghanistan is cultural?" I remember a diplomat in New York telling me, with exaggerated patience, "What you need to try to understand is that practices such as female genital mutilation and child marriage are cultural, and it's not our business to interfere."

In fact, in most of the countries where I work as a journalist, the thugs in power are quick to tell me, "You're not from here. You're not part of our culture, so you have no right to write about our women." Speaking up about someone else's culture is indeed a delicate task. Exposing the truth about cultural contradictions—about the price women pay for the so-called belonging that being part of a culture implies—has been a hazardous voyage for the courageous women who dare to risk the wrath of those who see themselves as the keepers of the cultural key. Culture flies like a banner of pride. But it also covers a host of misogynist acts that have oppressed women for centuries.

Farida Shaheed was appointed as the United Nations Independent Expert in the Field of Cultural Rights in 2009. It was surely a sign of the times, as the UN had assiduously avoided tangling with "cultural" issues such as child marriage in the past, lest they inflame one country or another with comments seen as interfering. Shaheed's appointment was tantamount to an announcement that "culture" is no longer acceptable as an excuse for the ill treatment of women and girls. She has worked for women's rights in Pakistan for three decades, first starting an NGO called Shirkat Gah in Lahore so that women could be educated about the laws that govern them and then as one of the founders of an organization called Women Living Under Muslim Laws (WLUML).

"Violence against women is always justified in the name of culture," she says. "Whether the culture is translated into laws [such as the personal status laws in Egypt] or is part of the system [the presumed and approved behavior of a tribe], this is always the excuse. And it is not acceptable." She's taken a daring new stand that is bound to contribute to the revolution going on in the lives of women today. In her new position, she asks women to shift the paradigm from culture as an obstacle to rights to demanding the cultural rights that are prescribed in the UN's International Covenant on Economic, Social and Cultural Rights. She refers to the precise wording of the covenant that says, "All peoples have the right of self-determination. By virtue of that right they freely determine their political status and freely pursue their economic, social and cultural development." Her goal is to flip the thinking from "I can't (go to school, work, decide when to marry) because of my culture" to "I can decide for myself because of my cultural rights."

Rather than backing down in the face of fundamentalists who claim that culture is no one else's business, she asserts that one can freely determine cultural development. It's a bold position. Cultural rights presume the right to freedom of association and conscience and action. Shaheed doesn't mince words. "Too many states say, 'This is our culture and we can't change it, can't make progress.' The whole world backs down when someone says, 'It's our culture, not yours, so mind your own business.' We need to say no matter where oppression exists or to whom it is happening, it's not acceptable. These are minimum standards we have all agreed to as an international community and we're not accepting deviations regardless of what the excuse is. I don't care if it's traditional or new, if [a practice is] discriminatory, it's just not acceptable."

Women in more than seventy countries who work with WLUML have been laying the foundation for this kind of discussion of culture since they started in 1984. Their goal was to provide information, support, and a collective space for women whose lives are shaped, conditioned, or governed by laws and customs said to derive from Islam. Almost immediately they started asking the tough questions: How does your [religious leader's] interpretation of my culture affect me? Who is deciding my fate? What right do you have to do that? How did the jurisprudence of this country arrive at the laws it uses? The answers to these questions, or more precisely the courage the women displayed in even asking them, have contributed to the tipping point that women are reaching today.

WLUML's work has spread to more than seventy countries, from South Africa to Uzbekistan, Senegal to Indonesia and Brazil to France. Since they are trying to reach women whose lives are controlled by Muslim law, they work in countries or states where Islam is the state religion, or in secular states that have Muslim majorities, and also in Muslim communities where political groups are demanding religious laws. In fact, wherever Muslim women live, this organization is available to strengthen their individual and collective struggles for equality and rights.

One of the first issues the organization tackled was the notion that the Muslim world was one big homogeneous family. It is not.

Islam is complicated when it comes to interpretation: laws said to be Islamic vary from one context to the next and originate from diverse sources (religious, customary, colonial and secular). WLUML needed to immediately uncover the different layers of laws that affected women from one country to another and to determine how they differed within cultural, social, and political contexts. For example, in one Muslim state women were required to cover their faces, and in another they didn't even have to wear headscarves.

The network achieves its goals by moving Muslim women out of isolation, creating links between them and equality-seeking women around the world. By demystifying the diverse sources of control over women's lives, the network shows women how to challenge the rules they live with.

Combating violence against women is a theme that cuts across all of WLUML's projects and activities. In 2010, the organization published a particularly astute book, *Control and Sexuality: The Revival of Zina Laws in Muslim Contexts* by Ziba Mir-Hosseini and Vanja Hamzić, a collection of essays that explain how culture and/or religion are invoked to justify laws that criminalize women's sexuality and subject them to cruel, inhuman, and degrading forms of punishment.

Shaheed feels that the publication is very timely, coming out just as issues of culture and human rights are being debated, often for the first time, in Muslim states, and subjecting the hated Zina laws (relating to "unlawful sexual intercourse," including extramarital and premarital sex) to a rare public examination. The authors explain that Zina laws were almost obsolete when the resurgence of Islam as a political and spiritual force late in the twentieth century saw them revived, codified, and made part of the criminal justice system in several countries. In Pakistan, they were reactivated in 1979 by the military ruler Muhammad Zia-ul-Haq when he announced the Islamization of Pakistan with what was called the Hudood Ordinance. While many, including Farida Shaheed, saw the move as an attempt on Zia's part to stay in power by appealing to extremists, the refreshed Zina laws were perilous to women. The legal punishment for adultery under the Zina code was death by stoning. The law required a raped woman to produce four male witnesses to prove she hadn't caused the rape. Shaheed and her colleagues in Pakistan worked tirelessly to overturn these draconian laws, and finally they did it. "Rape and sexual assault in Pakistan have gone back to the penal code; the Hudood Ordinance has been reformed," she says of their victory in the courts in 2007. "But it took twenty-seven years."

Challenging the sacred texts that fundamentalists insist underpin such laws is a tricky business since criticism of Islam is considered to be blasphemous, and blasphemy is punishable by death. But women's groups such as WLUML are using international human rights law to force a dialogue with political Islam.

They are well aware that improving women's legal and social positions is a nonstarter as long as patriarchal interpretations of the Quran remain unchallenged. The gender-based discussion that has started between traditionalism and modernism in the Muslim world is being hailed as progress for women. But it's also a flash point for politically motivated fundamentalists, who heap scorn (and sometimes worse) on women who speak out for equality rights. A few years ago when I was in Kabul, Afghanistan, I got into a discussion about women's rights with a mullah who was clearly appalled by the suggestion that women were equal to men. He said, "Get out of here with your Western human rights."

As far as I know, human rights aren't Western or Eastern, they're human.

After 9/11, the world was drawn to the human rights catastrophe taking place in Afghanistan. U.S. president George W. Bush claimed that he was invading Afghanistan to rescue the women, but a more honest explanation was that American soldiers happened to stumble over burqa-clad women on their way to avenge the attack on the World Trade towers. In fact, throughout history, no military or government has ever gone anywhere to rescue women, particularly to a place where the unequal treatment of women is ordained as the holy word of God. Women have learned that if they want to make change, they have to do it themselves.

The story of the women of Afghanistan is a blueprint for moving from centuries-old oppression to the tentative beginnings of emancipation. When I first visited that country in the spring of 1997, about six months after the Taliban had taken power, the women told me they had no voice—they had been silenced. They said, "Ask the women of Canada to be our voice. Let the world know what has happened to us."

They already had suffered from second-class citizenship, but when the Taliban swept into power and legislated misogyny for women with rules that threatened their health and safety, the status of women moved from oppressed to endangered. And Afghan women began to plot a way out of the dark ages for themselves. They opened clandestine schools for girls. They moved medical supplies from village to village as though they were transporting a cache of stolen diamonds. When radios and televisions were banned, they buried radios under the floors of their houses. As one woman told me, "News became as important as food."

When the Taliban were ousted, women started to work openly for change: researching traditions and practices such as polygamy and tribal laws that were harmful to women. They forced their way into discussions about the new constitution and made sure women were included. They ran for public office and sat in the parliament holding up their flags—green for "I agree" and red for "I disagree"—and demanded that women have the right to participate in every debate.

Much has changed for women in Afghanistan. But as in other places where oppression and second-class citizenship have defined the status of women, creating sustainable change requires time and tenacity.

One of the toughest objectives for women today is to eradicate the so-called cultural practices that physically harm them. Honor killing, for instance. Scholars of Islam say honor killing has nothing to do with the Quran and that the prophet Muhammad called for an end to it. But femicide has burgeoned recently and sent deadly tentacles into Pakistan, Afghanistan, and Iran, where women are stoned to death for presumed infidelity, and in the Middle East, where they are shot, choked to death, and bashed over the head with slabs of cement to rid the family of some perceived stain. Honor killing has cropped up in immigrant communities in Europe and North America, in Australia and New Zealand, too, when the female children of first-generation immigrants stray from the orbit of their fathers. The way men in some tribal cultures see it, a man is the sole protector of the girl or woman, so he must have total control of her. If his control slips, he loses honor because either he failed to protect her or he failed to bring her up correctly.

This obsession with the purity of women has survived the centuries to a greater or lesser extent throughout the Middle East and parts of Asia, as well as in Brazil; honor killing is practiced by Christians, Muslims, and Hindus. The good news is that today, a sisterhood of women in groups such as WLUML is defying the old order, rescuing women and keeping them in safe havens while they lobby for change. Accused of promoting promiscuity and destroying the traditional family, activists who have been challenging political, cultural, and religious forces for the past decade are poised to win the culture wars. And millions of women are cheering for their success.

On June 30, 2009, the bodies of three sisters and their father's first wife were found in a car at the bottom of the Rideau Canal in Kingston, Ontario. The coroner declared that drowning was the cause of death. But rumors that their deaths were actually honor killings swept across Canada. Three weeks later, on July 22, Mohammad

Shafia, fifty-nine; his second wife, Tooba Mohammad Yahya, forty-two; and their eldest son, Hamed, twenty-one, were arrested and charged with first-degree murder. The family, including four surviving children, had recently immigrated to Canada from Afghanistan. Over the eighteen months that followed their arrest, Canadians tracked an investigation that held honor killing up to the light. What the evidence suggested was that duplicity, ego-driven face-saving, and colossal entitlement were the forces behind the murders.

If pushing a car occupied by your three daughters and your first wife into a canal so they will drown is an act of honor, why pretend the death was an accident? If it's all about family honor, how come it's a secret?

The jury had to endure statements and explanations so convoluted and astounding that journalists covering the trial reported that individual jurors sometimes rolled their eyes. They heard that the Shafia daughters had been confined to the home, forbidden to wear Western-style dress, beaten for any whisper of defiance, and threatened with more serious harm: treatment revealed as abhorrent in the courtroom but that had been overlooked by outsiders who bowed to the familiar, specious argument that "it's not your culture, so it's none of your business."

During the trial, witnesses took the stand to try to explain a culture that is entrenched in blaming women and saving face, a culture that allows a father to give his underage daughter to a man three times her age, knowing she will be sexually assaulted. A culture that allows him to send his child back to a husband who has blackened her eyes and broken her arm. It is the same culture that prescribes that a woman wear black garments that absorb the blazing heat so she will avert the eyes of men who strut about in white robes that deflect the heat. It's a culture that creates men who can ask a daughter how she was dressed—was it modest enough?—when the rapist attacked her and then suggest that her loss of chastity is her own fault, that a man can't help himself.

In the case of the Shafia family, the eldest girl, Zainab, had the temerity to report the physical and verbal abuse being heaped on her at home. What's more, she dared to have a boyfriend. The second daughter, Sahar, also reported family abuse to the authorities. The youngest daughter, Geeti, paid the price simply for being with her sisters that night. The first wife, Rona Amir Mohammad, was also seen as expendable that June day in 2009 when the family set off on what was billed as a two-day holiday to Niagara Falls, Ontario. They'd taken two vehicles—a Nissan that the girls and their father's first wife were driving and a Lexus carrying Mohammad Shafia, Tooba, and Hamed. In what Mohammad Shafia at first called a terrible accident, the vehicle that the girls and Rona were in wound up at the bottom of the Rideau Canal in Kingston.

The police investigating the scene soon suspected that the Nissan had been bumped into the canal by the Lexus and got warrants for wiretaps on conversations between the three suspects. Those conversations were profoundly incriminating. For example, Mr. Shafia is heard telling Tooba and their son, "May the Devil shit on their graves." When asked in court to explain what he meant, he replied, "The Devil would check their graves and then God would decide their fate."

The court also heard his wiretapped comments to Tooba: "Were they to come back to life, I would do the same thing a hundred times." But when asked on the stand if he knew how the girls and Rona wound up in the water, he replied, "I didn't know anything [about the accident] until the eighteenth of July, when they showed us where the car went in." That was nineteen days after the girls and Rona had drowned.

During the trial, there was plenty of public discussion, particularly in online commentaries, about the use of the words *honor killing* versus *murder*. Many wondered how honor killing could be seen as a cultural phenomenon rather than an act of derangement. Invariably, those who defend honor killing and other assaults on women and girls are quick to challenge a critic with "This is our culture, our religion; it's none of your business." But when misogyny is passed off as "our way," when women and girls are denied an education, denied access to health care, exposed to daily rations of violence, even killed, then surely it is the obligation of everyone to speak out, to insist that what is happening here is not cultural but criminal.

The philosopher Hannah Arendt wrote, "Evil thrives on apathy and cannot exist without it; hence, apathy is evil." She argued, further, that when injustice encounters inertia it uses that passivity exactly as though it were approval; in the absence of protest, evil is nourished and can flourish. People who are next-door neighbors or United Nations observers are beginning to shed the "not my business" mantra and are bringing the truth to light. In country after country, women are speaking up; their neighbors, colleagues, and international partners are echoing their call for justice and change. The days of malignant presumptions about cultural practices being no one else's business are being challenged, and the human rights argument is beginning to trump the influence of the tribal past.

On January 29, 2012, the jury in the Shafia trial returned a guilty verdict. Looking straight at the three convicted murderers, Judge Robert Maranger of the Ontario Superior Court told the courtroom, "It is difficult to conceive of a more despicable, more heinous, more honorless crime. The apparent reason behind these cold-blooded, shameful murders was that the four completely innocent victims offended your completely twisted concept of honor, a notion of honor that is founded upon the domination and control of women."

He sentenced the Shafias to life in prison with no chance of parole for twenty-five years. If there is a legacy for the four innocents—Rona, Zainab, Sahar, and Geeti—let it be the public airing and censure of shameful traditions.

Honor killing is usually tied to public "knowing"—the family's need to take action to save face. If the "crime" (which can be anything connected to a girl's or woman's sexuality, even talking to a man she's not related to) is not disclosed, there's less pressure to take action. But if everyone in the village knows that a girl was walking with a boy who was not her brother, taking that girl's life becomes the tool to silence the gossips and rescue the family's honor. If a man wants to get rid of his wife because she's sick or he's tired of her, all he has to do is claim that he saw her with another man. He doesn't require witnesses. With preserving his honor as his shield, he can crush an inconvenient wife's skull, shoot her, drop her down a well, or slit her throat. She'll be dead. He'll have saved his honor.

Curiously, although honor killing is claimed as a cultural right, those who practice it invariably attempt to cover it up with a tapestry of lies and protestations of innocence. I once interviewed the chief coroner for the Palestinian Authority in East Jerusalem, Dr. Jalal Aljabri, who said he sees plenty of corpses that have all the marks of honor killing, but he hardly ever sees a case in which honor killing is the official cause of death. "In our culture, everybody knows but nobody says. I get cases that say the cause of death is a firearm injury. I know inside what really happened, but what can I do? I sign the certificate and say, 'Bye-bye; that's it.'"

And this is indeed the point—a cowardly response to a vile act. Dr. Aljabri exemplifies the "enlightened" Palestinian man. Ask him about the price that women sometimes pay for safeguarding the family's name, and he says he's strongly against honor killing. Ask him about his own family, and the tone changes. He's the father of eight, five boys and three girls. What would he do if one of his daughters became pregnant and wasn't married? He's aghast even at the question. "A girl knows she cannot be pregnant. She cannot have sexual relations. She must understand what would happen." So, I asked him again, what would he do? "I don't know," he replies.

I also remember an astonishing discussion with an educated man in Afghanistan about the case of a girl who'd been "given in Bad" to settle a dispute. Bad is a tribal law—illegal but still practiced—that basically says if your tribe has a fight with my tribe and my tribe wins, you are obliged to give me a girl child, preferably about the age of four, or maybe two or three little girls depending on the size of the harm done. The child in question was eight. She had just escaped after four years of being housed with the livestock, of being tethered to a harness and being used as a plow horse, of being sexually assaulted by the men of the house at night. I said to the man, "How can anyone treat a child like that?" His reply? "I know it is wrong, but it is our way."

So how is it that children's rights, women's rights, human rights are hailed as the way forward in some places while the concept can hardly get traction in others? The recorded human rights debate started long ago, in the thirteenth century BCE. The concept developed slowly over the centuries, and the idea that women have rights is a relatively recent invention. Women tried to change their status and even scored victories here and there century after century but were either thwarted or sold out before their elusive equality rights could become recognized.

"Universal brotherhood" and the "common good" are themes in the earliest writings about the idea of human rights. There is evidence of such laws, though paternalistic in nature, having been enacted to secure the common good in the earliest religious doctrines. For example, despite the derisive language about women in his Letters to the Corinthians, Paul the Apostle in Acts 17–19 says that God created all humankind and individuals of all races equal under his tutelage.

Although passages restrict women's rights and even allow a man to beat his wife, the Quran's Sura 12, 168–242 reads, "The rights of women apt to be trampled underfoot, now clearly affirmed." The Ten Commandments is a moral code that applies to men and women. So, too, do the early Buddhist writings. The duties, rights, and responsibilities of citizens were also written in the Hindu Vedas, the Babylonian Code of Hammurabi, and the Analects of Confucius.

In 300 BCE, Athenian women had no rights whatsoever, but Spartan women did. Plato's *The Republic* contains a defense of human rights for women at a time when women were entirely excluded from political life. His student Aristotle used the idea of the common good as the baseline for his *Politics,* which had a profound effect on the development of human rights, as did Cicero's ideas expressed in *The Laws.* But women's rights were not a priority even for these intellectuals. Just as in today's version of the debate, religious leaders relied on the Holy Scriptures for their arguments while scholars claimed that the concept of human rights was secular. In either case, women's voices were generally excluded.

By 69 BCE, Egyptian women had taken on a political role. In her new biography of Cleopatra, Stacy Schiff offers fascinating details of the lives of Egyptian women: the right to choose her own husband, to inherit equally, to hold property, to divorce. Women lent money and operated barges, served as priests, initiated lawsuits, hired flute players, and owned vineyards. Schiff writes, "As much as one third of Ptolemaic Egypt may have been in female hands."

At that time, their Roman sisters were expected to be silent and invisible in intellectual and political life. A Roman woman remained without political and legal rights, even though the Roman Empire devoted considerable energy to developing natural law and the rights of citizens for the next four hundred years.

The Quran began its life as a holy text by promoting women's rights in marriage, divorce, and inheritance. It also prohibited female infanticide and recognized women as full persons. How the interpretations of the Quran went from being the most progressive in the thirteenth century to the least in the twenty-first is a holy paradox.

It wasn't until 1405, when a novel called *Le Livre de la cité des dames* by the French poet Christine de Pizan was published, that women's rights got the attention needed to try to alter the status quo. Pizan has been hailed as the first female author to make her living by writing and by Simone de Beauvoir as one of the earliest feminists. In her novel, she constructs three allegorical foremothers—Reason, Justice, and Rectitude. Together they create a dialogue that addresses issues of consequence to all women: a woman's right to education and to live and work independently, participate in public life, and take responsibility for herself.

The Enlightenment period that followed in the mid-seventeenth century saw the discussion of human rights moving onto center stage. Scholars such as Thomas Hobbes sought to protect the individual's natural right to life and security, but "individuals" were men, not women. Political thinkers from Locke to Rousseau, Kant to Robespierre were claiming individual human rights and freedom from religious authority but didn't take up the cause of women. Then as now, it was women who had to demand that human rights be applied equally to females. The French playwright and political activist Olympe de Gouges presented her *Déclaration des droits de la femme et de la citoyenne* to Queen Marie Antoinette in 1791. In it she included the right to bodily integrity; the rights to vote, to hold public office, to work for fair or equal pay, to education, to own property, to serve in the military, and to enter into legal contracts; and marital, religious, and parental rights.

A year later, Mary Wollstonecraft wrote *A Vindication of the Rights of Woman* and addressed the consequences of violence against women. Her husband, William Godwin, was a campaigner for women's rights, as was the poet Percy Bysshe Shelley, who would marry their daughter.

The notion of human rights flourished along with the concept of socialism during the Industrial Age in the 1800s, probably due to the miseries associated with industrialization, says Micheline Ishay, author of *The Human Rights Reader*. She lists the emancipation of women, along with the prohibition of child labor, the establishment of factory health and safety measures, and universal voting rights, including a woman's right to vote, as major advances promoted in the writings of Pierre-Joseph Proudhon, Karl Marx, Friedrich Engels, and John Stuart Mill. In his 1869 essay, "The Subjection of Women," Mill wrote, "We are continually told that civilization and

Christianity have restored to women her just rights. Meanwhile the wife is the actual bondservant of her husband; no less so, as far as the legal obligation goes, than slaves." Mill, a member of parliament, called for women to have the right to vote and in 1867 proposed that the term *man* in relevant legislation in the House of Commons be replaced with *person*.

If the Industrial Revolution set the stage for human rights as a worldwide phenomenon, it was the dawn of the twentieth century that saw the first recording of those theories in international documents. In 1902, prompted by the women's suffrage movement, international law delegates meeting in The Hague adopted a series of conventions aimed at setting international standards for marriage, divorce, and the custody of minor children. It was the start of a century of change for women.

Following the Paris Peace Conference after the First World War, the Covenant of the League of Nations was drawn up in 1919 and included legislation supporting "fair and human conditions of labor for men, women, and children." After the international catastrophe of the Second World War, the Allies and other nations set out to invent an institution that could prevent global conflict, negotiating the ground rules and charter of the United Nations. The language of that charter when it came to gender was controversial. Eleanor Roosevelt, for example, balked at changing the wording "all men" to "all people" or "all human beings" because to her the term *all men* referred to all people. The Status of Women committee that worked on the drafting of the charter went to bat for rights-based language but was rebuffed. After much deliberation, the committee agreed on "all people, men and women," but due to an error in a previous draft, the phrase "all human beings" was approved and adopted in the final report. Still, despite their best efforts, the use of "mankind" and "he" persisted in parts of the document.

The next milestone came in 1948, when the Universal Declaration of Human Rights was written and adopted by the United Nations General Assembly. The declaration asserted that all people are equal "without distinction of any kind such as race, colour, sex, language . . . or other status." It was the first international agreement to proclaim sex equality as a fundamental human right. In doing so, it created a historic catalyst that sparked internationally agreed-upon strategies, standards, programs, and goals to advance the status of women worldwide.

However useful the UN charter and declaration and the covenants and conventions that have followed are in the fight for human rights, they don't have enforcement power. The UN wields no iron fist of accountability. Even the authors of these documents knew that human rights for everyone—women as well as men, disabled as well as able-bodied, poor as well as rich—would be a tough sell. And to try to find a mechanism to make states accountable for failing to fulfill the intent of the documents and covenants that they signed was a step too far. Accordingly, the documents, while useful in the politics of embarrassment, remain dependent on the will of signatory governments to enforce them.

It's been sixty-six years since the Declaration of Human Rights was written, almost six and a half decades of trying to make it work for "all human beings." Despite the fact that men and women were presumed to be equal by the United Nations in 1948, equality in the home and the workplace did not follow. In most Western countries a man was not usually prosecuted for beating his wife, and a married woman could not open a bank account without her husband's signature. Nor could she go to a hospital for treatment without her husband's consent nor take her child to the hospital for treatment without her husband's permission. A widow discovered that her husband's assets did not automatically belong to her. There were quotas at universities that kept the number of female students to a minimum. Women were not allowed to play team sports at the Olympics until 1964, and then they could only play volleyball, as it was considered a non-contact sport. They weren't allowed to compete in the marathon until 1984 because the men who ran the Olympic Games claimed that women would find it too strenuous to cover the twenty-six-mile distance. There was clearly a lot of work to do on the freedoms and rights declared by the United Nations.

Since most laws have been written by men, are applied by male jurists, and have only very recently been analyzed in the context of the lives of women, the rights of women continue to be marginalized. Domestic life has traditionally been viewed as private and not the law's business. Yet that is the world that women in Asia, Africa, Europe, and America live in today. They share their stories over laundry at the riverside and while tending the cornfields, at the office watercooler and in quiet cafés. They whisper about abuse, neglect, and oppression. Their suffering is part of a private world.

The women's rights activists and scholars Charlotte Bunch and Samantha Frost describe the public-versus-private conundrum in their essay "Women's Human Rights: An Introduction": "A major effect of the gender nature of the public/private split is that human rights violations of women that occur between 'private' individuals have been made invisible and deemed to be beyond the purview of the state. . . . Thus, abuses done to women in the name of family, religion, and culture have been hidden by the sanctity of the so-called private sphere, and perpetrators of such human rights violations have enjoyed immunity from accountability for their actions."

As the second wave of the women's movement (with its strong focus on eradicating the distinction between the personal and the political) gained momentum during the 1970s, the General Assembly of the UN declared 1975 International Women's Year and organized the first World Conference on Women in Mexico City. The UN subsequently declared the years 1976 to 1985 the UN Decade for Women.

Although 126 UN documents were written to establish the status of women, the most definitive instrument on women's equal rights was the creation in 1979 of the Convention on the Elimination of All Forms of Discrimination against Women (CEDAW), which has been signed by nearly every country in the world, including places such as Saudi Arabia, Swaziland, and Afghanistan. CEDAW is often used to try to bring states that oppress women to account with what is called "shadow reporting." This is how it works: the CEDAW oversight committee meets three times a year to discuss issues that need highlighting, such as a country that agrees to provide health care for women but locates clinics so far away that it is impossible for women to access the help they were promised. In that case, the country in question files a "shadow report" written by the women affected by the issue in question rather than by the government in charge. Then the CEDAW committee in New York sends a team to investigate the complaint and hold the country to account.

Two more international conferences on women's issues were organized in the eighties—in Copenhagen in 1980 and in Nairobi in 1985. The conferences launched a new era in global efforts to promote the advancement of women by opening a worldwide dialogue on gender equality. In 1993, at the UN World Conference on Human Rights held in Vienna, women were ready to present a new vision of human rights. They questioned why women's rights and gender-based violence were left out of human rights considerations. They prepared the Vienna Declaration, which says, "The human rights of women and of the girl-child are an inalienable, integral and indivisible part of universal human rights."

The fourth World Conference on Women, held in Beijing in 1995, concentrated entirely on the human rights of women and girls. The resulting Platform for Action—asserting that women's rights are human rights—was mainstreamed into all policies and programs of the United Nations. The slogan "Women's Rights Are Human Rights" went viral and became a rallying cry for women the world over.

Centuries of change have seen women move from being absent in the human rights debate, to taking part in it, and finally to lobbying for laws that protect their rights. But even now one problem is confoundingly persistent: in many cultures, women are taught to believe that suffering is their lot. Farida Shaheed says her research shows that women who are oppressed need a space where they can gather to share their experiences in the public sphere: "They can't do this at home because for many women it isn't a safe place to discuss power and empowerment. When they hear others' stories, they realize, 'It's not my bad fate or bad luck that my husband beats me.' They realize that other women have the same issues and that they can make changes in their lives. Families are the best supporter, but they are also the worst oppressor. Women need to build social capital beyond their families."

Talking to other women was key for Western women in the 1960s and '70s. And it's the best step toward change for women seeking change today. Women in places like Afghanistan now know that other women elsewhere in the world don't live with inexplicable laws and suffer indefensible treatment at the hands of their fathers and husbands. The questions they are posing about the legality of tribal law and polygamy, about transparency in government and the judiciary, are starting a public conversation. Despite the protestations of the fundamentalists, such conversations are giving rise to the change the women seek.

Women in countries that practice female genital mutilation are asking questions about where traditions like this came from and what the medical consequences are. These are brave steps of reform that sprung from the new definition of human rights as women's rights. Women murmured to one another about medical abnormalities and the cost of procedures to correct them, but to go public, to actually denounce ancient customs like FGM or early marriage or forced marriage, was an invitation to ostracization. International diplomats, Western feminists, and health leaders have tried for decades—for the entire twentieth century, in fact—to stop the two-thousand-year-old custom of circumcising women in Asia and Africa. But none of the outsiders have succeeded.

In 1997, I visited the women of Malicounda Bambara in Senegal because I heard they had eradicated FGM, a custom that their people had been practicing for centuries. Within a year of those women taking a stand, thirty more villages followed their lead, abandoning excision, as it's known in French-speaking Senegal. I followed the work of these women, and their leader, Molly Melching, for the next seven years as their cry of "Never again, not my daughter" spread to villages throughout Senegal.

I went back in 2004 to update the story because the women had extended their campaign to reform harmful cultural practices such as child marriage. Could they do it again—turn the tide on a practice that was grossly damaging but fully accepted, even expected? I was in for a lesson in the power of youngsters.

The day that changed everything started out like any other school day in the remote village of Polel Diawbé in northern Senegal. Khadia, ten, was sitting in her third-grade classroom when suddenly there was a ruckus at the door. Khadia's uncle pushed his way past the teacher, yanked Khadia from her desk, and announced that her school days were over. Then he hauled her off to the mosque to prepare her for a marriage to her twenty-two-year-old cousin. The uncle was acting on orders from her father, an immigrant worker in Ivory Coast. Her mother had had no say.

Khadia's future was no secret. Although she was only ten years old, she'd be forced to consummate the marriage, and once she started to menstruate she'd soon be pregnant, as was the custom for many young girls. But what happened next surprised everyone in Polel Diawbé, a village of 2,666.

After the little girl had been taken away, Khadia's friends stormed out of the school to confront the village chief at the community administrator's office. Her teacher followed. The news traveled from one thatch-roofed hut to another, and within minutes, centuries of silent obedience gave way to a call for change.

The girls begged the village chief to intervene. They left his office to go to the community hall to make posters: PARENTS HAVE PITY! NO MORE EXCISION! NO MORE EARLY MARRIAGE! NO MORE FORCED MARRIAGE! Then they brought those posters back and began to march in front of the administrator's office. Boys, more girls, teachers, and parents soon joined them. Even the director of the school walked with them. Someone ran several miles to the highway to find a phone to alert the media. National radio and local and national newspapers rushed correspondents to the scene. This was unheard-of—a collection of ten-year-olds demanding change.

In the middle of the protesters was little Khadia, shielded by her friends and marching with the others. She'd run away from her uncle's house, picked up a poster, and joined the historic scene that was unfolding in Polel Diawbé.

At first, Khadia wouldn't talk to anyone. The village leaders invited her to come inside the administrator's office; once there, she could only cry. One of the men said, "We've come to help you. You're young, you want to learn, you have a future. We're going to do everything we can to have this marriage stopped." Finally Khadia spoke: "I don't want marriage. It's wrong. I want to go to school." In just a dozen words, she had spoken for every girl in the village.

The protest was all over Senegal's radio programs the next morning, and phone-in lines were flooded with callers who wanted to show their support for the little girl. The president of Senegal sent gendarmes to the village with a stern reminder that despite tribal customs, girls under the age of sixteen were forbidden by law to get married. The prefect (district chief) arrived on the scene. Two days later, Khadia was back in her classroom, the marriage plan canceled.

Where diplomats, international health experts, and NGOs had failed, a group of preteens took a brave step into the future, bringing their village after them.

The year before the incident with Khadia, one young girl in a neighboring village who'd been married off at eleven and become pregnant at twelve had died in childbirth. Everyone knew it was because she was too young to be having a baby. Everyone also knew she'd been subjected to female genital cutting, which hadn't been banned in her village and made her first delivery more dangerous.

More than 130 million women who are alive today in twenty-eight countries have been sexually mutilated in the name of tradition. Every day, an average of six thousand little girls are taken to old women known as "the cutters," who excise their clitoris and labia with a razor and then sew them up. There's no anesthetic, no sterilization. There's just agony, a future of pain and sometimes death. And there's a powerful taboo against speaking of the procedure to anyone.

Polel Diawbé is situated in the heart of the most conservative district of Senegal, where taking action against a practice seen as a religious and cultural duty risked insulting the elders, enraging the religious leaders, and isolating families who broke with tradition. Still, the village broke the taboo and stopped performing the procedure.

So what was behind the villagers' rebellion? There'd been a lot of discussion about child marriage in Polel Diawbé, where children are supposed to go to school until grade six and marry at the age of twelve or thirteen. Their actions grew out of classes held by an organization called Tostan, which means "breakthrough" in the Wolof language. It was started by Molly Melching, a force of nature who came to Senegal as a twenty-four-year-old student from the University of Illinois on a six-month exchange program at the University of Dakar in 1974 and never left. She learned the language, adopted the styles of the people, moved into a village, and experienced an epiphany: change isn't an external event, it's internal. If someone tells you to stop doing something that you think is right, you'll reject the advice. "But given the opportunity to gather the information needed for change, you'll make the best decision yourself," says Melching, a charismatic woman who is six feet tall and fills a room with her presence. "If it's your idea, it'll work." That realization inspired Melching and her Senegalese team to create a program that would help women to make their own decisions.

Tostan has been teaching courses in health and human rights in Senegal's villages since 1991. In 1997, the first victory was posted by the women of Malicounda Bambara, who had taken the courses and then banded together and declared an end to FGM. Within the next year, other villages made the same public declarations. Since then, Melching estimates that girls in more than fifty-five hundred communities have been spared the procedure. In 2001, the Senegalese villagers added early and forced marriages to their reform of harmful cultural practices, and one by one the villages are banning it. Today, Senegal is on the verge of becoming the first country to entirely abandon both FGM and child marriage.

The rainy season began the day I traveled to Khadia's village in 2004. Along the highway in this northern district, which is known as the Fouta, black plastic bags litter the ground and cling to tree branches like hooded vultures. Eighteen-wheeler trucks belch brown fumes onto the acacia trees that stand silhouetted across the landscape. The Sahara desert is encroaching on this area, pushing its sand dunes onto the arable land that the villages depend on for food, and shepherds herd bleating goats to the scarce patches of green. Here old Africa is bumping into the modern world, rocking the rhythms of life uncomfortably. For Molly Melching, this village has been a watershed.

She'd been in this region before in 2002 to try to start the Tostan program and found herself held hostage in a hotel in nearby Ourossogui. Men from the town surrounded the building, burning tires and threatening her. They feared that if they let her out of the hotel, she'd change their women, erase their past, alter their culture. To these men, Melching posed too big a threat to what they saw as their way of life. "It's so frustrating with fundamentalists," she says. "It's like, 'My mind is made up, so don't confuse me with the facts.'" Even the district prefect, who said he agreed with ending female genital cutting, told her not to come back because he couldn't protect her. The women sent another message: "Come back. We will protect you ourselves."

Senegal's former minister of communications, Aïssata Tall Sall, a woman known for her tough stand on women's issues, says, "I come from this region. It is so conservative that I would have been beheaded for mentioning FGC [female genital cutting]. But Molly did it. She's a very courageous woman."

Social anthropologists have usually assumed it would take hundreds of years to end female circumcision, but Gerry Mackie, then a researcher at Notre Dame University in Indiana who has written extensively about foot binding in China, disputes this conclusion. He says, "Melching's approach indicates that FGM will end suddenly and universally."

Like FGM, foot binding had gone on for more than a thousand years. No one understood how it started. Many tried to stop it, worried about the painful medical consequences to women. Then, at the end of the 1890s, a small group of women in China formed the Healthy Foot Society. They held public meetings to talk about the value of having feet that grew naturally so women could walk easily. Then they created marriage societies where parents made a public pledge that they would never bind their daughters' feet and would never allow their sons to marry a girl whose feet were bound. In twelve years, the practice had stopped almost completely in the eastern coastal cities. The success, says Mackie, came from the public pledge.

He told me during an interview I did with him after I first met the women of Malicounda Bambara, who had also taken a public pledge to stop female genital cutting, that going it on your own, against custom, leads to being ostracized: if you break with tradition, you or your daughter can't wash with the others, cook with the others, eat meals with the others. Vowing to stop together avoids singling out one woman or her family. Mackie said, "The women of Malicounda copied the techniques of the anti-foot-binding reformers when they took part in the Tostan program." The other key, he explained, is the fact that Tostan provides the education but never tells people what to do.

Part of that education is starting a dialogue that includes the whole village. Incredibly, Senegalese men claimed that they had no idea what was actually being done to girls and women who were circumcised. Since no one talked about it, most of the women didn't know precisely what had been done to them either.

The World Health Organization describes three types of FGM: type one, which is partial or total removal of the clitoris and/or the prepuce; type two, which is the partial or total removal of the clitoris as well as the labia minora; and type three, which is the narrowing of the vaginal orifice by cutting and/or removing the labia minora and labia majora and stitching the opening shut with thorns.

While types one and two are most common in Senegal, type three is practiced in some regions. And although any type of circumcision has been described as a violation of the human rights of girls and women by the WHO, for a girl who has type three, the price she pays is a lifetime of pain. If the girl doesn't bleed to death, if she doesn't die from shock or pelvic infection or tetanus, she will be left with an opening the size of her baby fingertip. Urinating, which can take as long as fifteen minutes for a girl whose entire vulva area has been damaged, hurts so much that she'll try to avoid it, which causes urinary tract infections, leading to kidney problems and sometimes blood poisoning. When she marries, she'll be recut with a razor to make intercourse possible. Then comes the agony of childbirth with a birth canal opening that has been mutilated. Labor is prolonged—three to five days is not unusual—so the baby is often starved of oxygen. Like so many women before her, she'll say, "The first one always dies. It is making a passage for the other children."

The roots of this brutal rite are as confounding as the business of stopping it. The practice started twenty-two hundred years ago in Egypt and spread westward. Some say it is a religious requirement, but though it is practiced by Muslims, Christians, and a Jewish sect in Ethiopia, it is not mentioned in either the Quran, the Bible or the Torah. Some say it improves the health and childbearing capabilities of women, despite irrefutable medical evidence to the contrary. Other bizarre claims are that it makes a woman more attractive and a better wife. In fact, it badly scars her, hobbling her with pain and sexual trauma.

Mackie told me that people trying to stop FGM had been asking villagers the wrong question. "The question is not, 'Why do you practice FGM?' The question to ask is, 'What would happen if you didn't practice FGM?'" Marriageability turned out to be the key. If a girl wasn't cut, she was considered unclean and unmarriageable. The consequences for a single family to give up the ritual would be devastating. There would be no marriage for their daughter, no grandchildren, no respect.

The tradition of early marriage also has murky origins. In many places such as Pakistan and Afghanistan, it is thought that a girl should not ovulate in her parents' home. In other words, if she is not married by the time she can produce a child, she might bring shame to her family. "Girls under the age of sixteen are simply not physically mature enough to be having babies, especially if they have been circumcised," says Melching. Moreover, married girls cannot attend school, so their education is halted. Enduring both early marriage and FGM, girls reach adulthood with disadvantages that last a lifetime.

Melching's program has a unique method of teaching with drama instead of written material, which could make the illiterate villagers feel inadequate. And Tostan's message is a combination of rights and responsibilities. "To have the right, you have to have responsibility," says Melching. Tostan literally acts this concept out in plays, stories, and poetry. When I visited one of the villages near Polel Diawbé, I watched a Tostan drama featuring a pregnant woman; I was taken both by the power of the story that the players acted out and by the reaction of the crowd watching the play. The central character was obviously sick and in danger of losing her baby as well as her own life. She had the right to pre- and postnatal care, but she didn't come to the health center until it was too late. The lesson was well taken by the villagers who gathered around the makeshift stage: you have the right to medical care, but it's your responsibility to get it.

In another village, the drama revolved around a girl who had to leave school to be married. When the cutter was called to reopen the vagina that was closed when she was circumcised, the girl began to hemorrhage. The silence among the twelve hundred villagers was poignant. The girl in the play died, and the onlookers burst into shouts of "Pak pak pak," which loosely translated means "Death to the harmful tradition." The play was so moving that the village cutters formed a circle around the players and tossed their tools for circumcision into a pot for burial.

There are fourteen thousand villages in Senegal, and not all of them have a history of FGM. Of the eight thousand that do, approximately fifty-five hundred have stopped the practice since 1997. The newspapers once chastised the women of Malicounda Bambara for rebelling against tradition. Now they hail them as heroes. The religious leaders once thought the women were going against the Quran. Now they say the women showed the truth. Koumba Tokola, a community manager in the Fouta, says, "We didn't know before that the practice led to these problems. Now we know, so we have to speak out. We're the women, the ones who were cut, the ones who endure the consequences, so we're the ones who have to stop it." Propaganda and prohibition failed to end FGM and early marriage. But Melching's program of human rights and health education and public declarations is succeeding.

Tostan's lessons about rights and responsibilities are far-reaching. In Senegal, more than 40 percent of the children don't have birth certificates and are therefore not registered as citizens. Birth registration is part of the Tostan program, as is vaccination. Lessons about the right to a clean environment have resulted in garbage cleanup, tree planting, and villagers adopting a more efficient stove that uses two-thirds less wood for cooking.

The cost of the Tostan program is about $100 per woman, or $20,000 per village. Melching figures she needs $20 million to finish the job she started in 1992. The program has spread beyond the borders of Senegal into Mali, Sudan and Guinea, Guinea-Bissau, The Gambia, and Mauritanian, and in East Africa to Djibouti and Somalia, so she believes that if Tostan finds the funds, FGM and early marriage will soon be history everywhere.

I watched her for a morning sending faxes and calling donors. I'm stunned that the woman who has found the formula for success in stopping cultural traditions that are damaging to women and girls can't get the budget to finish the job. When I talked to UNICEF in New York, I discovered that the power players hadn't held the meeting to establish costs and timelines; they simply hadn't made it a priority. Maria Gabriella De Vita, director of Child Protection at UNICEF, says the Tostan program works. "We know what to do, the strategy is there, but the international community has not created an agenda or set dates to reach the objectives." Bureaucracy was winning as the girls were waiting.

That's what was on Melching's mind when we turned off the single highway that forms a ribbon around the Fouta and negotiated the muddy flats on the way into Polel Diawbé, where I hoped to meet Khadia. Across the riverbed, the villagers gathered to greet their hero, Melching, with enormous applause. They wanted to show her the drama they had prepared for the upcoming ceremony to formally end FGM and early marriage. Before the play, we sat on the sandy ground, ten of us sharing a bowl of food, eating the spiced rice, glazed onions, and chicken portions with our hands. There was a delicious taste of victory in Polel Diawbé, but Khadia, the child I'd traveled such a long way to see, wasn't there. Her friends told me she was visiting relatives in Dakar and wouldn't be back until school began again. Dando, a classmate who had marched that fateful day in the village, said with all the solemnity a little girl can muster, "A tradition that harms is not one we should keep." Then she dashed off to join the other girls from Khadia's class, who were laughing, teasing, playing—acting their age.

The introductory speeches were loud, full of weighty proclamations about the future. The pageantry of the evening performance began in the fiery red glow of sunset and concluded in the soft mauve of dusk. The dancing, singing, drama, and storytelling spoke of a deep-rooted culture in Senegal that is still thriving despite the eradication of harmful customs once seen as crucial.

When I checked in with Melching again in the spring of 2013, she had a message for me from Maimouna Traoré, one of the leaders in Malicounda Bambara. Traoré wanted me to know this: "In the beginning, I was often called a traitor to my culture. However, I now consider myself more Bambara than ever before. Our deepest values are those of well-being, peace, and good health. That is why we abandoned this social practice that brought only pain and suffering into our community. We are proud to change those practices, which we learned are a violation of our deepest values."

Melching added, "When the history of the abandonment of FGC in Senegal is written, it will highlight the villagers themselves who traveled from community to community to promote human rights and better health for the girls and women of their family."

The change is not complete, but it is still an immense turning point for women and girls. In other countries where women suffer from so-called cultural practices, systemic change is well under way. "It's time for people, especially women, but men as well in Muslim society, to break the taboos about discussing the issue of sexuality," says Farida Shaheed. "In many ways sexuality is at the root of women's oppression. There have been huge attempts by men to control women's sexuality both in terms of how they dress and how they behave and in terms of their reproductive power. In our parts of the world, there's been a silence about that—it needs to be broken."

That silence *is* being broken. In Iran, for example, by women like the human rights activist and Nobel laureate Shirin Ebadi, who says, "Men who come from a patriarchal cultural background do not agree with full and complete equality for women and men, and the reason for it is that equality weakens their power. Those men exist in the government of Iran." And in Afghanistan, where Sima Samar, chair of the Afghanistan Independent Human Rights Commission, is also breaking the taboo against speaking up: "If a woman wears a short skirt, the men cannot control themselves. And that's not our mistake. If they don't have enough confidence to not be disturbed by the tap-tap of a woman's footstep [the Taliban forbade high-heeled shoes, as they didn't want to hear the sound of a woman approaching] or her hair showing or short clothes, it's their problem, not ours. They are the ones who are always shouting and using culture and religion to oppress us. The men who have confidence don't have problems with women's equality rights."

I can't resist adding a story about the temerity of some men who simply don't get the issue of human rights. In Newfoundland, in 2007, an Iranian student doing a PhD in engineering at Memorial University in St. John's was arrested for kissing a woman on her breast while the two—strangers to each other—were sharing an elevator in a building on the campus. The student, twenty-five-year-old Farhood Azarsina, told the court that he didn't realize the seriousness of the offense in Canada. "You can't expect all males to control themselves when the breasts are out," he said in his defense. The young man, obviously intelligent enough to be doing a PhD in engineering, felt that blaming the victim was appropriate and accepted, and he expressed no remorse. The judge sentenced him to two months in jail.

Figuring out how people arrive at such bizarre notions is one aspect of the story of change. But another aspect is exploring why men are so afraid of women. Many have speculated about the answer, including Louise Arbour, the former High Commissioner for Human Rights at the United Nations and now the president and CEO of the International Crisis Group. Arbour once said, "The natural response is that women give birth. They can control the future." Farida Shaheed touches on a similar theme: "In 1939, when Mulana Muduicky, a conservative scholar, was addressing men as to why women should not be educated, should not be allowed to do X, Y, and Z, he said, 'If women really try and strive against their nature, they can do anything. Men can never reproduce, cannot have a child, cannot do what women do.'" Shaheed says it's all about controlling women.

In 2000, a thirteen-year-old Nigerian girl named Bariya Magazu who was raped and became pregnant was sentenced in a Zina trial first to a hundred lashes with a cane on her bare back for fornication and then to eighty more lashes for slander: she was unable to prove which of the three men who raped her had fathered her child. The story quickly spread around the world, and the reaction of women was swift and direct. For all the so-called cultural respect that has in the recent past muted criticism of such barbarism, the outcry over Bariya's sentence quashed the presumption that the world would remain silent. Women lawyers gathered to prepare a defense. The child's future was debated far and wide. Zina laws were exposed as duplicitous, deceitful, and probably illegal. The world was talking. The fundamentalists were furious.

The reaction didn't prevent her punishment—Bariya was indeed whipped a hundred times with a cane (claiming a court error rather than an international outcry reduced the flogging from 180 lashes to one hundred)—but her case received so much publicity that the government was shamed into saying that a trial like hers would not happen again in Nigeria. So far it hasn't.

4

Herstory

It enriches a whole country to have the shackles of inequality removed from half its people. — MARY EBERTS, HUMAN RIGHTS LAWYER

There's no shortage of stories about women with the moral courage and intellectual heft to alter previously unjust, unfair, and often life-threatening customs. I have been lucky enough to meet them in villages and cities all over the world. Some of them, like Sima Samar from Afghanistan and Shirin Ebadi from Iran, are already international icons of change. Others, like Naomi Chazan from Israel and Mama Darlene from South Africa, are heroes in their own countries. But most women game-changers are best known in their own villages or to the women and girls they serve. They're valiant and determined; they bide their time, watching for opportunities that will improve the status of women. They're protective and brave, tenacious and daring. They're also argumentative and occasionally vengeful. They aren't beyond gossip, dishing about local big shots—sometimes deliciously. They have been known to overreact. In other words, they are not saints but warriors, and, like women we all know, they are people we can emulate. Their collective effort is what has brought women to the tipping point that we're heading toward today.

In this chapter, I want to tell three stories: of the Israeli and Palestinian women who are trying to untangle the fractious file that is the Middle East; of Siphiwe Hlophe of Swaziland and her allies, who insisted that if the women in Africa didn't speak up, they'd all be dead from HIV/AIDS; and the story of Hangama Anwari, a human rights commissioner in Afghanistan, and her supporters, who started the Women and Children Legal Research Foundation so that Afghan women will know what the laws actually say and which ones are the bogus imaginings of fundamentalists.

The Middle East

When peace negotiations stall and, worse, collapse, when delaying tactics are employed as a means of staying in power, new actions are required, and it's women who claim to have them: fresh ideas and the temerity to speak up and demand a seat at the decision-making table. The women I've met on the West Bank and the Gaza Strip, and in Israel, have been struggling with a plan to end the conflict in the Middle East for decades.

Their story begins with two organizations: Women in Black, a worldwide antiwar movement led by women in Israel who want an end to the occupation of the Palestinian Territories, and the Jerusalem Center for Women, which is the Palestinian counterpart. These women don't have blood on their own hands, yet they pay a very high price for war. They are fed up with waiting for the men on both sides to do something about the conflict.

It was in 1988, during the First Intifada, that Women in Black decided to stand weekly vigil in public places, such as busy intersections, to demonstrate their abhorrence of the Israeli occupation of the Palestinian Territories. Inspired by women who demonstrated in the streets of South Africa to end apartheid and in Argentina in search of the disappeared, the vigils became a constant in the lives of Israelis: every Friday, women dressed in black held up placards—a black hand with white lettering that read END THE OCCUPATION—and banners that said the same in Arabic and Hebrew. Some passersby heckled and abused them, yelling "whore" and "traitor," but many others honked their car horns to show support.

While the Women in Black never shouted back since it was their policy to maintain silence and dignity, people who opposed them at regular Friday rallies that soon sprang up were not so restrained. On one trip I talked to Lizaz, sixteen, who belonged to the Kahane Party, which wanted to transfer all Arabs out of Israel to create a pure Jewish state. "Israel belongs to the Jews," she told me. "We can't live with the Arabs. This is our land. The Bible says that." To underline her point, she added, "Most people in Israel agree with me, but they can't admit it because they think it's too violent." The man standing beside her, who refused to give me his name, said, "Destroy these Arabs. They're human garbage."

The Women in Black weren't the first to speak on behalf of women for peace—the Women's International League for Peace and Freedom, formed in 1915, holds that distinction. Women in Black became part of an extraordinary international call for action when they held a vigil attended by three thousand women at the United Nations World Conference on Women in Beijing in 1995 and called for "a world safer for women." In November 2000, the Coalition of Women for a Just Peace brought the Women in Black, the Jerusalem Center for Women, and nine other Israeli and Palestinian women's peace organizations together to push ahead with the only peace agenda they thought would work: two states, an end to the occupation, a shared city of Jerusalem, and a cessation of violence.

The idea of "fighting for peace" is contradictory to these women, who approach peace negotiations from a different angle. They use compromise and embrace persuasion. And over the years, they've made some progress. In 1997, only 20 percent of Israelis felt that a Palestinian state was viable, and only 3 percent believed that Jerusalem must be shared. In 2002, partly due to the work the women had done, 80 percent of Israelis said that a Palestinian state was inevitable, and almost 30 percent agreed that Jerusalem had to be shared.

The women's groups on both sides of the conflict soon attracted more than a hundred peace and anti-occupation initiatives from around the world that had mobilized in response to the insufferable situation in the region. One was Machsom Watch, a women's human rights organization that monitors checkpoints to try to prevent Israeli soldiers from abusing Palestinians who needed or wanted to cross into Israel. I traveled with Ronnee Jaeger, one of the founders of Machsom Watch, to see conditions for myself. She said that when she was on duty she had witnessed more than twenty women forced to give birth while stopped at the checkpoints. At least four of the babies and two of the women had died because they were not permitted to get to a hospital. "Just by acting as observers, we stop a lot of harassment," she said. "But still we see people being lined up face to the wall and waiting as long as three hours for no apparent reason before going through the checkpoint."

The women's groups saw their work as critical: some observers said Hamas (the Palestinian Islamist organization that has formed the elected government in Gaza since 2006 and whose military wing claimed responsibility for most of the suicide bombings in Israel) was attracting a hundred new members a day who wanted revenge for the harassment and humiliation they faced at the checkpoints. (The Israelis claimed such humiliation was a small price to pay if it stopped even a single suicide bomber.)

The polarization of right-wing and left-wing attitudes defied reconciliation on my trip a decade ago, just as it does today. The right says that Israel would be a sitting duck if the occupation ended. The left says that the violence won't stop until Palestine is a sovereign state. The right says, "Our army is in the occupied territory, so we have to support it." The left regards the Israeli settlements in the occupied territories as bones in the throats of the Palestinians. Many blame the deeply held belief among Israelis that God wants Jews to have this land as the underlying barrier to peace. Samia Khoury, a Palestinian who was born in Jaffa in 1933 and has lived all her life here in this ancient land, says, "There is too much injustice based on biblical interpretation."

Khoury comes from a long line of community leaders that includes the founders of Birzeit University, the Palestinian school chartered in 1953. She remembers being chased out of her home in Jerusalem, where she was a student in 1948. "There's not a single family who hasn't been hurt by this," she says. Her brother, who was president of Birzeit University, was expelled from the Palestinian Territories for almost twenty years and only permitted to return as a goodwill gesture by the Israeli government. "In every family, someone has been killed, deported, or humiliated," she says, but she says the real danger lies in the fact that the new generation of Palestinian kids has never known Israelis as anything but occupiers, whereas she knew them as friends and neighbors.

Speaking to me at her home in East Jerusalem, Khoury said she was living in "sorrowful painful times." Like almost everyone in Israel and the Palestinian Territories, she thought the situation had never been as bad as it was during the Second Intifada. She feared the future, especially for her five grandchildren. "When the children go to school, they have to cross checkpoints. Families can't even visit each other. Our lives are consumed with fear. We are constantly asking, did they cross, did they reach, did they arrive?"

The women on the front lines of the peace process think women on both sides understand each other. Gila Svirsky, who has been a Woman in Black since the organization began, accuses the politicians of being the obstacle to peace. "The leaders are driven by power needs and conflict," she said. "Militarism is pervasive in both societies: glorification of the fighter, giving one's life for the homeland, a hero's halo around the martyr or fighter pilot—this has to stop."

If it were up to the women, Palestine and Israel would have signed a peace accord in the late 1980s, Svirsky says. Women from both sides met in Belgium in 1988 to find a path to peace. They had to meet offshore because there was a law that said Israeli citizens could not meet members of the Palestinian Liberation Organization (PLO) on Israeli territory. At the time, Svirsky says, "Every Palestinian with self-respect belonged to the PLO." In her opinion, the ongoing meetings by women's groups at that time built up a pro-peace attitude on both sides.

But despite the much-heralded U.S.–sponsored peace talks in subsequent years, the women have not been invited to the table. Even after the United Nations adopted Resolution 1325 in 2000, which called for "equal participation and full involvement of women in all efforts for the maintenance and promotion of peace and security, and the need to increase their role in decision-making with regard to conflict prevention and resolution," the negotiations were left to the male warriors, the seekers of power, turf, and control: precisely the people that women peace activists see as part of the problem.

On May 7, 2002, Israeli and Palestinian women took their plea to the UN Security Council, where Terry Greenblatt of Bat Shalom (part of the Jerusalem Center for Women) spoke on behalf of the women's peace movement: "We envision a settlement based on international law, which would endorse sharing the whole city of Jerusalem, the dismantling of the settlements, and a just solution to the question of refugees according to relevant UN resolutions," she said.

Approximately two thousand people had been killed and countless more wounded since the Second Intifada began on September 29, 2000. An Israeli military action, presumably to rout the terrorists in the Palestinians' midst, had precipitated both that intifada and the rash of suicide bombings that followed. Suicide bombers started vaporizing themselves and innocent Israeli citizens in the name of God, and although the Quran does not sanction suicide, many clerics in the Middle East supported the violence and declared the bombers martyrs.

I met the Israeli and Palestinian women in 2002, when my editor sent me to Israel and the West Bank to find out what women were doing about the peace process. The Second Intifada was raging. Suicide bombings had increased in frequency. Israeli army incursions into the West Bank and Gaza Strip had become more brutal. Everyone was in harm's way.

Remarkably, these Israeli and Palestinian women were working together to try to turn the intifada into peace talks. Even an Israeli mother who had lost a child to a suicide bomber spoke of the need to stop the occupation. Her name—Nurit Peled-Elhanan—had become synonymous with the double-edged sword in the Middle East. Her heartbreaking story was made even more so by her sense of justice and fairness.

As I climbed the stairs to her house in West Jerusalem, the scent of flowers spilling out of pots on every step leading to the family's apartment caught my attention. At the top of the stairs, the entrance to the house was under a canopy of vines and blossoms that suggested a paradise off the beaten path. But a bold sign on the door—FREE PALESTINE—and the intertwined Israeli and Palestinian flags stuck underneath it suggested that there was more to this Israeli home than the aromatic stairway.

Inside, I came face-to-face with an almost life-size photo of Smadar Elhanan. Her big brown eyes were happy, trusting, twinkling back at me, the essence of innocent childhood. Smadar was just two weeks shy of her fourteenth birthday when a Palestinian suicide bomber blew himself and this beautiful girl to bits on September 4, 1997. Four others died in the same attack, as well as the three suicide bombers. Two hundred were wounded, mostly young people who had flocked to Ben Yehuda, a popular pedestrian street, to meet their friends.

A few hours after the tragedy, Smadar's mother, Nurit Peled-Elhanan, received a phone call from Benjamin Netanyahu, then the prime minister of Israel; she'd known him since high school, when they were classmates. But his condolences were of little consolation to a woman who believed the government was complicit in the violence. She told him his government was responsible for her daughter's death and hung up the phone.

Elhanan and her family had paid an unspeakable price for the fifty-year struggle between two peoples. By 2002, suicide bombing had created an air of near panic in Israel, and the attacks by the Israeli army on the West Bank only fueled the fires of revenge. Palestinians and Israelis alike claimed the tension and terror had never been as bad. Together, they were perched like birds on the branch of a burning bush.

Nurit Elhanan, a lecturer in language education at Hebrew University, was part of the groundswell of Israeli and Palestinian women who were furious with the politically intractable positions on both sides of the conflict. Although Elhanan didn't belong to any one group, she spoke at their rallies and told me, "The women's peace movement is the only one that's active, serious, doing something about this."

She believed it was her insistence that her children needed to make up their own minds that led her daughter into harm's way. Elhanan knew the dangers of the streets, and on the day Smadar was killed, Elhanan had told her that she couldn't go downtown alone. Smadar replied, "This is my city. I must be able to walk in it. If you say no, then I will have to go without your permission."

Five years later, her mother was still consumed by every detail of the day her daughter went downtown to sign up for jazz-dancing lessons and instead met death. We sat in the garden below the flower-filled staircase while Elhanan told me about Smadar's growing independence. "My husband and I had taken the kids on a vacation to the Sea of Galilee some weeks before, and my older sons had asked if they could bring along a couple of friends. One of them made quite an impression on Smadar. Although he was several years older than she was, she had sort of a crush on him."

He was the one who called Elhanan to say there'd been an explosion and that he'd seen her daughter in the area. Smadar had approached the young man on Ben Yehuda Street, but he'd waved her off because he was talking to a friend. Elhanan told me he's now consumed with guilt, wishing he'd talked with Smadar, even for a moment, so she might have lingered where he was and not walked into the path of the suicide bomber. "I raced to the street and looked and looked for my little girl," Elhanan said. But she did not find her.

Grapefruit trees were laden with fruit, and songbirds were feeding from the nut-bearing bushes as the sun was starting to set. A woman who had suffered too much and too long, Elhanan didn't seem to realize that her right eye twitched when she talked about her child. The twitching stopped only when the conversation turned to the politicians she was enraged with.

She described the bomber who killed her daughter as one of the consequences of mistreating innocent civilians. "Look at these Palestinian kids. They suffer hunger, humiliation, oppression, torture, and they see their parents suffering that, too. It doesn't take much to convince them to kill those happy kids in downtown Jerusalem. It's the Samson story. Only we are the Philistines." She knows that those kids, as she calls them, are used by a larger organization: "Someone is in charge of training the suicide bombers. The organizer brainwashes the kids who do it. The parents of suicide bombers invariably say they haven't seen the kids for a couple of years."

After every suicide bombing since, Elhanan said, she got a phone call from investigators saying, "That was your guy." She believed the calls were made to taunt her for speaking out on behalf of peace—to imply that the same person who masterminded Smadar's death had struck again.

A lot of people said the politicians were stalled because neither side wanted to make the first move. Elhanan believed the crisis was not as complicated as the politicians suggested. For instance, she said, a casino had been closed in Jerusalem when Palestinian and Israeli business tycoons couldn't agree on who had jurisdiction. But because their own livelihoods depended on it, politicians from both sides of the conflict soon reached a deal and reopened the casino. That didn't take an American intervention, she said. "This shows that when an issue affects them directly—unlike the deaths of children—they are quick to find a solution. All of us, Israelis and Palestinians, are victims of politicians who gamble the lives of our children on games of honor and prestige. To them, children are worth less than roulette chips."

Elhanan picked at flower pods that were strewn on the garden table. Her voice dropped as she flicked the floral debris off the table. "You have to put off your truth, your opinion, your belief, and study the others to communicate. Men can't do that. Women are all the time in a 'polylogue,' having several conversations at once, bridging differences, adjusting to each child that is born." It's women, she insisted, who understand the price of violence.

After one of the suicide bombings, she wrote an essay using the Dylan Thomas poem "And Death Shall Have No Dominion" to reflect the crisis in Israel. "Here death governs: the government of Israel rules over a dominion of death," she wrote. "Each attack is a link in a chain of horrific bloody evens that extend back thirty-four years and have but one cause: a brutal occupation."

Later, we left the solace of the garden to walk down the street to a protest rally with nine-year-old Yigal, Elhanan's youngest son. Her older sons had moved to Paris. She didn't even want them to visit, as she couldn't bear the fear she felt when they went downtown to meet their friends.

It was dusk when I left Elhanan. Her story, her courage, and her profound sadness stayed with me while I walked the streets of Jerusalem. But it was her soul-searing words about the legacy of these terrible times that haunt me still: "In the kingdom of death, Israeli children lie beside Palestinian children, soldiers of the occupying army beside suicide bombers, and no one remembers who was David and who was Goliath."

The intifada didn't end until 2005. The women who saw themselves as the best bet for peace had at last persuaded the United

Nations to take action on Resolution 1325, which was five years old, and to organize a way to bring women into the work of negotiating a peace. Later that year, under the auspices of UNIFEM, the International Women's Commission for a Just and Sustainable Israeli-Palestinian Peace (IWC) was launched. The commissioners were twenty Israeli women, twenty Palestinian women, and twelve internationals who came together to try to bridge the conflicting narratives between Israelis and Palestinians by providing an opportunity to tell the story of the conflict in a way that acknowledged the suffering on both sides. It promoted a women's rights perspective, which the women felt had been absent from efforts to build peace. Over the course of five years (2006–2011), IWC members engaged in high-level political advocacy at home and abroad, drawing on the words and insights of women experiencing the impact of the conflict in their daily lives. Like others who had worked on a peace plan for the region, the women on the IWC agreed on the two-state solution based on the 1967 borders. But they added a new goal: they would mobilize a million women and thirty-two heads of state to carry the plan to the UN. Committees were formed to move the plan forward.

During the 2009 election in Israel, the majority of the political parties moved to the right. The left-leaning parties as good as collapsed. The support for the peace plan that the women had worked on since 1988 went from 70 percent in favor to 70 percent claiming that a two-state solution would never happen.

Then tensions flared among the commissioners over whether Israel should be held accountable for the damage done by their treatment of the Palestinians over the decades. The Palestinian women said they wouldn't continue without accountability on the part of the Israelis. The Israeli women said it was too soon to accommodate that issue. They couldn't come to an agreement. Tempers flared. The women at the table committed the sins of the fathers: "my way or the highway." The negotiations collapsed not just because the two sides could not agree but also because the arguments became so heated that the space for compromise evaporated. Finally, in May 2011, the IWC members decided to formally disband. The great sadness of this failed commission was that everyone at the table—Israelis, Palestinians, and international members—knew that the women on both sides could carry the negotiations to a peaceful conclusion, and yet here they were, walking away from the table, as others had done before them. The commission members had no sooner decided to begin disbanding than the women were in touch with one another in cyberspace, hoping a new committee would rise from the ashes of the old one and find a way to restart the conversation. Most people agree that Palestinians and Israelis are very much alike as people, and somewhere in that similarity, surely they could find common ground. Nurit Elhanan had explained that to me: "We have the same deep values, such as the way we treat our children, how we receive people in our houses. We feel good with each other. But the education system here in Israel promotes how much Jews are hated elsewhere, how fearful they need to be." And the system on the other side promotes the same distrust and fear of Israelis.

In the meantime, every Friday, the Women in Black still hold their weekly vigil at Paris Square in West Jerusalem. The women drift into the square from the five avenues that converge there. They pick up their placards and take up positions facing the traffic on three sides of the square.

But it's the men across from them on the fourth side of the square, waving Israeli flags, who now get the lion's share of the honking and cheering. Gila Svirsky tells me that she's disappointed that the number of women who stand with her has decreased, but she still feels a political solution is out there. Ultimately, she believes, the point of view the women have promoted since 1988 will win the day.

Swaziland

If ever there was a country that needed a game-changer, it's Swaziland. For all its trouble—the highest HIV/AIDS infection rate in the world, the most deaths per capita from HIV/AIDS, and a life expectancy of thirty-three years—the women of Swaziland are coming to the rescue of the country. They're being led by a dynamo called Siphiwe Hlophe. She is heralded as the woman who is turning the pandemic around in sub-Saharan Africa. One of the aces she holds is the powerful support of Stephen Lewis, the codirector of AIDS-Free World. When Lewis was the UN secretary general's special envoy for HIV/AIDS in Africa from 2001 to 2006, he soon identified Hlophe as a beacon of light in the darkness of the pandemic.

When I caught up with her in the summer of 2012, she said, "It's the women who bear the brunt of the HIV/AIDS epidemic in Swaziland: 31 percent are positive, compared with 20 percent of the men. There are 130,000 children orphaned by the pandemic, and here in Swaziland, 70 percent live in abject poverty." Grim statistics.

The Kingdom of Swaziland is a tiny landlocked territory of a million souls, home to Africa's only absolute monarch, King Mswati III, forty-five. He keeps a harem of thirteen wives (although three have recently left, claiming abuse and causing a monumental scandal in the royal household) and spends a king's ransom on cars, palaces, and parties. Crime, especially in Manzini, the business center, is bold and rampant. A thief will steal your cell phone while you're making a call, or snatch your purse from a restaurant table while you're sipping lemonade.

During the apartheid era, Swaziland was a haven for mixed-race couples from South Africa, which borders it on three sides (Mozambique is to the west). It was a British protectorate until 1968. It was selected as the site of one of the first United World Colleges, Waterford Kamhlaba. Nelson Mandela's children attended this school. So did Bishop Tutu's.

Unlike other African countries, there's just one tribe, Swazis, subdivided into dozens of different clans, living in fifty-five constituencies under half a dozen hereditary chiefs and one elected in-gula (head man) per region. The king is the leader of them all.

The power of superstition is strong in Swaziland. Most people seek medical help from witch doctors, who provide concoctions for every conceivable illness. They have even been enlisted by the ministry of health to cure people with HIV/AIDS, which has led to a shocking rate of death as well as a disturbing rise in ritualistic killings. Body parts, preferably cut from a living person, are said to lend potency to the witch doctors' treatments. More than half a dozen mutilated bodies, mostly those of children or elderly people, are found every year, flesh from armpits and bits of internal organs removed, the gory details splashed in the newspapers.

Twins are seen as bad luck. It used to be acceptable that one newborn twin would be killed so the other would be a whole per-son. Even well-educated Swazis speak in whispers when asked about these practices. Women cover their heads and avoid standing in the same line (for food, services, banking) as the men, fearing the con-sequences of a dozen different curses.

But for all Swaziland's black magic, the biggest wrong that needs to be righted, according to Siphiwe Hlophe, is the situation of the country's women. They are considered minors with no legal status. The combination of tribal law and government law works against women's interests in cases of domestic violence, forced marriage, and sexual demands.

Hlophe, fifty-three, is the executive director of Swaziland for Positive Living (SWAPOL). She started the program in 2001, when she discovered she was HIV positive and felt that if someone didn't do something to stop the spread of AIDS in her country, they'd all soon be dead. And so she created a network of women whose chal-lenge was no less than to take on the myths, superstitions, and an-cient male-dominated laws of the entire country—and even the king.

Swazi women have no rights when it comes to sex; polygamy, a practice that denigrates women and spreads the HIV/AIDS virus, is the norm. A woman can't say no. She can't demand that a man wear a condom. She can't make decisions on her own, cannot practice safe sex. She can't even go to the hospital without her husband's permission.

The constitution says that women and men have equal rights, but Doo Aphane, a women's rights lawyer, says, "Nobody observes that—not even the royal family, where women have privileges but not equality with men." She says all the rules are stacked against women. "When I started talking about women's rights, I was treated like someone who should be put in detention without bail."

But then Aphane took the attorney general to court to prove that women had "immoveable property, bonds, and other real rights" registered in their own names. On February 23, 2010, she made history for women in Swaziland when a judgment was handed down by Justice Qinisile Mabuza that effectively redressed forty-two years of injustice and subordination of "women married in community of property." The ruling also set the stage for examining all laws that still treat women as minors.

Although Aphane had been to court to fight for change before, this particular case came about when she and her husband tried to buy land and register it in both their names. They were told that having a woman's name on the registry contravened the Deeds Registry Act and were refused. Like the girls in Kenya who sued their government for failing to protect them from being raped, Aphane relied on constitutional arguments to make her case. Swaziland's constitution (like those of Kenya, Canada, and even Afghanistan) claims to secure equal rights for all citizens. But Aphane's was the first case to test the effectiveness of that claim.

I met Aphane and Siphiwe Hlophe for the first time when I went to Swaziland to cover an HIV/AIDS rally on World AIDS Day in December 2007. Hlophe is one of those women who command a lot of attention simply by entering a room. Ask for her at the airport, and the customs officers will tell you how to find her—they'll even telephone her for you. In fact, ask anyone anywhere in the kingdom and they all know the former trade union leader who declared war on oppression, a battle that puts her in direct confrontation with the powerful king.

I found her that December in the overcrowded SWAPOL office in Manzini. Boxes and plastic garbage bags stuffed with materials to be delivered to the rally she was holding the next day took up every inch of space. Staff and volunteers stepped over them to negotiate a path to her desk, bringing her papers to sign, waiting for her okay on a course of action. She handled it all while taking two phone calls at once—one on her cell, the other on a landline. Her trademark is hearty laughter—as the rolling belly laugh fills the room, her head falls back and a grin wreathes her face.

She told me that when she was diagnosed with HIV/AIDS, she knew the infection had come from her husband, but she felt the sting of blame that women in Swaziland live with. "The culture here is that men don't bring sickness to the house. Sickness is caused by women. And if a woman is sick it's because she's been sleeping around. It's never, ever presumed that she might have got it from her husband."

The government even supports that sort of thinking. On that trip I heard a radio ad that featured a woman on the telephone asking a man, "Can you come and see me?" The man replies, "I'm sick of you women bringing disease." Hlophe explained that the campaign had been run by the National Emergency Response Council on HIV and AIDS (NERCHA). "That ad hurled the fault for the pandemic at women. We had to stop the campaign," she said. "It was promoting the stigma and discrimination against women. The very organization that should eradicate such thinking was promoting it."

Popular radio programs were contributing to the colossal misinformation campaign. I heard one commentator scoff, "Condoms have worms. Fill one with water and you can see them moving around." He went on to say, "The drugs [antiretrovirals] are being brought in to kill us." The myth of the virgin cure was widely held, as it is in many sub-Saharan countries. Not surprisingly, it had contributed to a startling increase in the rape of girls.

Since the men in Swaziland see polygamy as their right, wives have no say in whom their husbands have sex with. "If he's cross with one wife, he can go to another. If she talks too much, he goes to the third," said Hlophe. The country has signed CEDAW, the Convention on the Elimination of All Forms of Discrimination against Women, but the principles are simply not observed. "We want to empower women on issues of rights such as no condom, no sex," Hlophe said. "To do that, we need to join hands and change a lot. The government is denying the statistics, promoting our culture, but every day people are dying left and right."

If a girl suffers an assault and goes to the police, she told me, "They'll demand to know where she was, what she was wearing, how she was behaving. You go in there in hysterics, and they humiliate you and make you feel responsible." And although the parliament had a bill before it to stop forced marriage, it didn't pass, and the practice still goes on all over the country.

When I was there in 2007, before Doo Aphane's day in court, a married woman needed permission from her husband for every significant act. She couldn't apply for a passport or own land. Customary patterns of inheritance dictated that land ownership was through a male relative, even in cases such as that of Aphane, who bought the land herself. A widow was expected—in fact, forced—to marry her husband's brother. There were no shelters for abused women, and women thought they didn't have the right to go to court. They'd been taught to take their complaints to the district chief, who invariably threw them out and told the woman to go home and listen to her husband.

SWAPOL's project coordinator, Cebile Dlamini, twenty-seven, told me, "When I get married, if my husband wants more wives, there's nothing I can do. If he doesn't want to use a condom or get tested for HIV/AIDS, he doesn't have to. If I refuse sex with him, he will send me back home and say, 'I'll take another wife who will respect me and do as I say.' "

She and the other Swazi women I met were working to change those presumptions; they wanted an end to polygamy. But they believed that level of change would have to start with the king. Although grassroots change has been proven to be more effective in most parts of the world, in Swaziland, the king and his family have an almost mystical hold on the people. Reformers agree that if he stopped having multiple wives, the district chiefs would think it was the right thing to do.

In fact, many of Swaziland's woes can be laid at the doorstep of King Mswati, who was educated in England and is seen as the country's father figure despite behavior that has attracted international condemnation. As Stephen Lewis wrote in his book *Race Against Time*, "His subjects are dying in numbers that would have made Malthus weep. And all of us are quiet; nary an audible peep from the UN family."

Unabashed by the criticism leveled at him, Mswati still owns a fleet of expensive cars (in 2012, ten BMW SUVs and a German luxury car called a Maybach 62 that sells for $500,000). He spends his time in a string of luxurious palaces and bought a personal jet for about $90 million. Lewis called it "monumental extravagance in the face of pernicious illness and misery."

Finding a member of the royal family to defend him is nearly impossible. You are told that the prince, or whoever is representing the royal household, is away today and coming home tomorrow or tired from yesterday's journey and available tomorrow. The day I called, the king was in seclusion, preparing for Incwala, which is the Thanksgiving holiday (although very few Swazis had much to give thanks for that harvest season). During Incwala, old men and young boys do traditional Swazi dances in the presence of the king, and pubescent girls perform the reed dance, bare-breasted in grass skirts, as part of a ceremony called Umhlanga, acting the part of young virgins who weed the king's fields. The ceremony is rather less benign, since the king often chooses a new wife from these girls. Hlophe's youngest daughter, Lxolile (pronounced Holilay), sixteen, danced for the king in 2004; her friend wanted to go and persuaded Lxolile to come with her, convincing the teenager that it would be an interesting experience. When I asked her how it was, she said flatly, "I hated it." When I asked if she would like to be married to the king, she replied emphatically, "No. He's too old and he's got too many wives. When I get married, there will be no other wives. If the man took another wife, I'd break up with him."

King Mswati made international headlines in 2002 when he sent minions to pluck eighteen-year-old Zena Mahlangu off the street to make her the tenth wife in his harem, after he'd seen her in the reed dance. He hadn't counted on the reaction of Zena's mother, Lindiwe, who filed a lawsuit that accused the king of kidnapping. Lindiwe Mahlangu was manager of postal and telecommunications in the ministry of communications in Swaziland, and said her daughter had been invited to the reed dance by a friend who was Miss Swaziland at the time. A few days later, Zena left for school as usual and vanished. Her mother found out that she'd been taken to a royal guesthouse and was being prepared for marriage to the king.

If the king chooses a new wife from among the girls at the reed dance (or later while he examines videotape of the dance), he is bound to ask the girl's father or grandfather for her hand. In this case, he hadn't asked, so Lindiwe pressed ahead with her suit, even though a letter from the palace instructed the three judges to throw the case out or face dismissal.

A widow who has known her share of trouble (her youngest son was killed in a car crash in 2006), Lindiwe eventually came to an agreement with the royal family before her daughter married the king. She told me, "My daughter is married now and has a son. I am a grandmother. I went to court before she was married. So I don't talk about that anymore." When I asked her if she was happy with the result, she picked her words carefully. "Happiness is an event. Something happens to make you happy. You can't characterize your life around happiness. I have joy—from God—which is permanent. That's what helps me to carry on."

I drove with Doo Aphane from Manzini to the rally that Hlophe had planned in the far-flung district of Mahlangtja on a hot mid-December day that revealed the stunning extremes of the Swaziland terrain. The valleys that rolled out of granite-topped mountains in a kaleidoscope of muted colors made the countryside look as if it had been art directed. Puffs of mist appeared and disappeared as if by magic, revealing and concealing forests of zebras, rivers of hippos, cheeky vervet monkeys, blue-headed iguanas and geckos. Guinea fowl pecked at grain in the morning dew and hid their chicks from the crowned eagles soaring overhead. Hibiscus in flower and the massive albizia shade trees were stunning; the nonindigenous gum and jacaranda trees also looked wonderful but suck up sixty gallons of water a day apiece in this water-challenged country. Near the capital city of Mbabane is Sibebe Rock, the second biggest freestanding rock in the world (after Ayers Rock in Australia). There's much that is remarkable about the Kingdom of Swaziland, the smallest country in Africa with the biggest problems.

Gossip about the king, although regarded as treasonous, was rife at the Mahlangtja rally to mark World AIDS Day. There were rumors that he was having sex with women other than his own wives and that his wives were having sex with their bodyguards. His first wife, Inkhosikati LaMbikiza, said polygamy, which the king sees as a royal birthright, should end because of HIV/AIDS. But the spotlight at the rally was on Hlophe, who could gather people in the thousands, attract the media, get the attention of the government, and press her demands for change. While her mantra was women's rights, SWAPOL's program was about income generation (sewing, gardening, crop production) and drug treatment for HIV/AIDS. At the time, her organization was supporting fifteen child-headed households and paying the school fees of 500 orphans (by 2012, the numbers had increased to thirty-five households and 577 orphans). She received funding from several sources, but the largest portion came from the Stephen Lewis Foundation, which was providing $100,000 annually.

Amid music, song, and conga lines, the irrepressible Hlophe negotiated the jagged line of dignitaries and politicians with her belly laughter and her wide-open embracing arms. Watching her in action as she moved into the crowd—all HIV positive and wearing white T-shirts with "Stop AIDS—Keep the Promise" written on the back—it was easy to see how her enthusiasm caught the imagination of everyone there.

As she delivered her speech about the importance of making change on that hot windy afternoon, the crowd fell silent when she described a better tomorrow. Hlophe was treading a fine line— the minister of public service, S'gayoya Magongo, was actually in the audience—when she told them, "Even the minister agrees with me— it's in the constitution—women should have the right to choose." The minister had no choice but to nod, knowing Hlophe had co-opted him for her battle. She ended her oration by reminding the HIV/AIDS victims in the audience of the responsibility born by the members of government, who were all sitting behind her. A courageous woman.

One of the ministers at the rally referred to the national pride they should all have in the decline of the HIV/AIDS rate of infection from 42.6 percent of the population to 39.2 percent. "It's nothing to be proud of," Hlophe told me later. An administrator from Manzini, Catbird Khumalo, put it more bluntly, "We will all die if we continue to adhere to the culture of polygamy and continue to sleep with our relatives' wives under the custom of Kungena [the right of the dead man's brothers to have sex with his widow]."

Evening began to fall. The puffs of mist that had seemed so magical early in the day were rolling together into thunderclouds. The tourists in the safari camps an hour's drive away were likely sipping their gin and tonic, watching wildlife drink at the river's edge.

At Mahlangtja, the rally was over and a thousand disposable plates littered the field. The members of the crowd, grateful for the meal they'd been served, were drifting back to their mud huts in villages that were as far away as a two-hour walk. Hlophe declared the day a success. "We raised five thousand dollars," she said, while helping to clean up the field. "Tomorrow we'll start again."

If she had to do it one rally at a time, she was determined to alter the status of women in Swaziland.

Afghanistan

In early December 2011, just before the critical meeting in Bonn, Germany, that brought all the players on the Afghanistan file together to decide what the next best steps would be, President Hamid Karzai dropped another gender bomb onto the international scene. He announced that he was pardoning a woman who was in jail—who had, in fact, been in jail for two years—for the crime of being raped. The outrage about a woman actually serving jail time for being raped spread around the world. Initially news media reported that he'd given a pardon to the woman because she'd agreed she would marry the man who had raped her and who was the father of the child she had delivered while in prison. The woman's lawyer insisted that this was not the case, that there were no conditions to the pardon. Most of the world felt that if any conditions needed to be placed, it was on Karzai and all his male cronies in government. That a woman who was raped should have to be pardoned? That she should be in jail in the first place? That the rapist had gone free? That being raped was her fault, so she must be punished? These are the cockeyed notions that women and girls in many places live with until other women speak up, challenge seemingly intractable attitudes and traditions and turn the tide on inequality.

The thing about making change is that you have to do the research, prepare the data, present the facts, and take them back to the power brokers again and again and again. As Marilou McPhedran says, when it comes to seeking change, "The single best tool to use is the law and the words in the law that say there are promises of equality and justice."

That's what convinced Afghanistan's Hangama Anwari and her colleagues to form the Women and Children Legal Research Foundation. Anwari was a commissioner with the Afghanistan Independent Human Rights Commission when she realized that Afghan women didn't even know what was written in the existing law or that their newly adopted constitution guaranteed equal rights for women. Worse, most politicians didn't know what was legal and what wasn't. Anwari and her associates decided to try to make the justice system work for women and girls. "Women who have access to information have a stronger voice in the family," she says. "They can have an opinion about a daughter's marriage, for example. The goal is to improve the situation of women and children in Afghanistan by providing the knowledge the women need in dealing with laws that affect them."

Afghanistan relies on a patchwork of criminal and civil law, as well as sharia (Islamic religious law). Add to this picture the large sections of the country that still operate under tribal law, and it's little wonder that people don't know what their rights are.

The foundation started with examining practices that harmed women and children. For example, the tribal law I mentioned earlier, called Bad: the exchange of little girls between feuding families to settle disputes. "When a girl is given by the perpetrator's family to the victim's family, both sides think the problem will be solved by creating a relationship between the two families," says Anwari. "But it rarely happens. The families continue to fight with each other, and the girl child pays the awful price of being owned by people who see her as the enemy."

Another harmful practice is child marriage. "Most of the girls are underage—seven, eight years old, even three years old," says Anwari. If a girl who has been married off to a man (often old enough to be her grandfather) runs away and is caught and goes to the village jirga, or council, to plead her case to the elders, those elders may order her to be stoned to death or executed by another form of honor killing, even though it is illegal under the government's laws. "I realized we didn't have study cases or proper documentation to show that these actions are illegal. There was no local organization to do this work, so we started the research foundation."

They began with a survey that asked five thousand Afghans how they felt about the religiously sanctified practice of polygamy. They asked those with more than one wife why they had chosen that path. The results showed that a stunning 86.5 percent of Afghans were against it. But the Quran allows polygamy under four particular circumstances: if a woman cannot bear children; if she is sick; if a man wants more wives and can provide for them; or if the first wife is in agreement with taking a second wife. Since Afghanistan is an Islamic state, criticizing anything in the Quran is considered blasphemous. And blasphemy is punishable by death. These change-makers needed to proceed with great caution.

"We started with what verses in the Quran said about polygamy. The four conditions allowed in the Quran were the basis of our research. But our research showed there are twelve reasons given for polygamous marriages in Afghanistan. Since only four of them are legal according to the Quran, by way of elimination, we began to whittle away the numbers. We concluded that Islam is against the way polygamy is practiced in Afghanistan."

She said it felt like a major achievement when the results of the study were presented to the government as well as to the public. But she admitted, "Changing behavior and attitudes is a sensitive and time-consuming task. We need to use different strategies. Advocacy at the national level is not enough. So we decided to take our research findings to the village." In the course of talking about their findings with the villagers, they empowered the people to make changes such as building schools for girls, hiring teachers, and buying materials such as books and science kits. Like so many game-changers, they saw the opportunity to talk about polygamy as an opening to discuss the value of girls' education and the dangers involved in child marriage.

The foundation began in 2003. The last time I caught up with Anwari, in the spring of 2011, she had an impressive list of research papers that had been prepared on topics such as the situation of the girl child in Afghan families, violence against women, women's access to justice and equal access of women to marriage rights. With the data her team collected, they examined a woman's marriage rights, using passages from the Quran to prove that the prophet said there must be mutual consent between the man and the woman before marriage. Then they tied those verses to the articles of the United Nation's Universal Declaration of Human Rights. The goal was to make the facts available not just to women but to governments, judiciaries, elders, and villagers. Without that, said Anwari, "You cannot make change in a society."

One of the aims of their work is to decrease the horrifying rate of self-immolation among Afghan daughters and wives. In 2011, there were twenty-two thousand known cases of attempted self-burning; two thousand cases required hospitalization and 234 women died. The Afghanistan Independent Human Rights Commission released a report called *Reasons of Women's Suicide in South-Western Afghanistan* that year. It states that "most of the respondents have mentioned the issue of forced marriage as one of the important factors for self-immolation. Twenty-two percent of the victims interviewed said they had been married without their consent and because of force. Others talked about marriage in exchange for money or Badal [another tribal law that exchanges daughters for marriage]." Accurate statistics on self-immolation are not available, but the report concluded that stopping forced marriages was one of the solutions for decreasing the incidence of women's self-immolation.

A measure of the foundation's growing success is the welcome the villagers extend to the women who run the workshops that teach about access to justice in the villages. Anwari explained: "We teach people what the law says, to help them to understand their own rights. Showing them how to make changes takes a lot of time, so I decided that conducting workshops was the best way forward." She and her colleagues have noticed increased optimism among the women they work with. What's more, local elders who have enormous social influence are increasingly onside with the women. The workshops are the topic of conversation all over the village, and attendance has steadily increased.

When Anwari began, the government thought that tribal law had a legitimate role to play. Her organization proved that it does not. Most people thought polygamy was not only religiously sanctified but also culturally blessed even by women. Immense problems remain. Forced marriages and child marriages still take place, and violence against women is still very much a part of many Afghan marriages. But now there's a sense at least that change is possible. As in other countries where women have been oppressed, the women of Afghanistan are now in a dialogue with their mullahs and with their village elders, but most important, with one another. It's a discussion that they have never had before.

Dr. Sima Samar, who still fights like a lioness for women's rights in Afghanistan, is the woman who defied the Taliban decrees to close her medical practice and shut down her girls' schools. In spite of death threats, she kept both the schools and her health clinics open. She became the first minister of women's affairs when President Karzai took office in 2001 and subsequently became the first chair of the Afghanistan Independent Human Rights Commission. Today she says, "The status of women is much better than it was during the Taliban time and even before that, during the mujahedeen government and the previous regime as well. The women in the cities gained a lot of rights and have access to work, to information through the media, and to job opportunities and health care. But in the rural areas it is still the same, particularly in areas controlled by the Taliban. Women are not allowed to get educated or to go to work; they might be allowed health care if the clinics have female staff, but they can't raise their voices or exercise basic rights like freedom of movement, choice, and speech."

She says the question everyone needs to ask is, why should a man look at a woman as a sexual object rather than as an equal personality? She described a conference she attended in Uruzgan province: "There were all these mullahs complaining that their people didn't have access to education, to female teachers or doctors. I listened to each one complaining. I spoke last and said change needs to come from your own society. Who is going to be the lady doctor to deal with your wife and daughters if you refuse to send your daughters to school? Who will be the teacher to teach your girls? Your daughter's mind is not smaller than mine. You respect me. I come from the same society as you. I am able to do the work. Your daughters can too."

Afghanistan has been known as a country where being a woman is to be a target for religious extremists, an object of so-called cultural practices. It's to be the child who is fed last and least, the one who is denied education. It's to be sold as chattel, given away in a forced marriage as a child bride and used in any manner that benefits a father or brother.

The world has grown weary of a place that has taken so much in the way of troops and treasure, and the international community is making plans to leave. Rumors of a Taliban return to power are rife. But the Taliban have never been a large fighting force. They could never go toe-to-toe with any military, which is why they resorted to suicide bombing and improvised explosive devices. Many Afghans see the Taliban as a menace and a throwback to the dark ages. Its support comes mostly from thugs and malcontents and the Pakistan secret service. The biggest obstacle to a Taliban return is the women, particularly the young women active in Afghanistan today.

As I described in this book's introduction, Young Women for Change (YWC) is challenging old customs and is growing dramatically. Recently, fifty young men and women marched from Kabul University to the offices of the Afghanistan Independent Human Rights Commission carrying placards that called for women's rights in the streets of Afghanistan and handing out pamphlets that explained their position about street harassment. Some bystanders were shocked by the brazen behavior of the young Afghans, but the majority of onlookers accepted the pamphlets and joined the marchers.

In an initiative that suggests they are trying to inspire another Banksy, the iconoclastic British graffiti artist whose work is brilliantly displayed on the wall that separates Israel and the West Bank, YWC launched an art competition in January 2012 that invited artists to create posters to promote the organization's causes. The rules stipulated that the work must embrace gender equality, women's power, the peaceful campaign for women's rights, and the participation of women in society, with a focus on the elimination of violence and street harassment. Such a contest would have been absolutely unheard-of even a few years ago.

The resulting works were hung all over Kabul City, featuring such slogans as STOP THE VIOLENCE AGAINST WOMEN; DON'T BEAT ME; LET US GO TO SCHOOL; I WANT TO GO OUTSIDE WITHOUT FEAR OF HARASSMENT; and MORE THAN 75 PERCENT OF KIDS IN AFGHANISTAN FACE FORCED AND EARLY MARRIAGE. One of the male recruits of YWC, Zafar Salhei, said, "We printed fifteen hundred posters and put them up in crowded places where people would see them. Our aim is to change the mind of people." Some of the posters were damaged by critics who saw women's rights as the work of the Devil; some were totally destroyed; but most stayed on the walls of Kabul's buildings, sending out a message of change. Women and girls are seen in a different light in the Afghanistan of today. Not everyone is in favor, of course, but women like Dr. Samar and Commissioner Anwari continue to promote change, and the young generation is leaping at the opportunity.

. . .

Measuring the changes by wins isn't always the best strategy. These women I've described fighting for change in the Middle East, in Swaziland, and in Afghanistan know that it takes time to reform laws and attitudes, and patience too. But they also know that, at last, their voices are being heard, that the status quo is not sustainable and that victory is out there.

5

Breaking the Cycle of Poverty

Equality for women and girls is ... a social and economic imperative. Where women are educated and empowered, economies are more productive and strong. Where women are fully represented, societies are more peaceful and stable. — UN SECRETARY GENERAL BAN KI-MOON

The economist Jeffrey Sachs has a view of poverty and the economy that tips a lot of dismal thinking upside down. Director of the Earth Institute at Columbia University and adviser to the UN on Millennium Development Goals, whose aim is to reduce poverty, hunger, and disease by 2015, he says, "If you treat the symptoms, your patient will die. If you treat the causes, you will save the patient." Simple words. Profound truth.

One of the most remarkable examples of Sachs's idea of treating the causes, not the symptoms, of poverty can be found with Muhammad Yunus, the Bangladeshi banker, economist, and founder of the Grameen Bank, an institution that has been providing microcredit—small loans to poor people possessing no collateral—since the mid-1970s. Yunus was among the first to see women as the way forward, the way out of the intractable cycle of poverty. And the success of his strategy of extending microcredit to women has become a legend. I was fortunate enough to hear the story firsthand at the State of the World Forum held in New York City in September 2000, where Yunus was a luncheon speaker, along with former chief of the U.S. defense staff Colin Powell. Powell went first.

A tall man, broad-shouldered and seemingly comfortable with the mantle of power he wore, Powell addressed a room of approximately fifteen hundred delegates. His remarks about the state of the world's security almost exactly a year before 9/11 were well received with a round of polite applause. Then Yunus came to the stage. A short man wearing a Bangladeshi shalwar kameez, he required a step at the podium to be able to see his audience, and even then he was barely visible. Speaking conversationally in his characteristically soft voice, he quickly created a hush: people held their breath so as not to miss a single word. He told us he'd been working at a bank in Dhaka when he got the idea that ultimately launched the Grameen Bank. Each day on his way to work he walked by a group of women using bamboo to make stools and tables and trays. He and the women wished each other good morning, sometimes commented on the weather, and the encounter soon became part of his daily routine. One day curiosity made him stop to speak to the women, which is how he discovered that they were paying a lender usurious fees for cash to buy their bamboo. At work that day, he suggested to his colleagues that the bank lend money to these women at an honest rate. They were dumbfounded. "Lend money to poor people? Unheard-of. You'll never get it back."

Yunus pondered their reaction for a long time, and then he decided to lend the women the money himself. "I made a list of people who needed just a little bit of money. When the list was complete, there were forty-two names. The total amount of money they needed was $27. I was shocked." He had figured out that the women were not only paying too much interest on the loans but, worse, the arrangement they'd made included selling the finished product to the lender, who was grossly underpaying them. "I wanted to give money to people like these women so that they would be free from the moneylenders to sell their product at the price which the markets gave them, which was much higher than what the trader was giving them."

That was in 1976—it was the beginning. Soon he was lending money to poor men as well as poor women, but he discovered it was the women who paid back his loans in total and on time. His Grameen Bank stopped lending to men and became the lender to poor women—and known around the world. His philosophy: lend money to women and they will break the cycle of poverty; lend it to men and they will spend the money on themselves. "My greatest challenge has been to change the mind-set of people. Mind-sets play strange tricks on us. We see things the way our minds have instructed our eyes to see." Then he said, with characteristic understatement, "Poverty is unnecessary."

He was speaking his truth: "We have created a society that does not allow opportunities for those people to take care of themselves because we have denied them those opportunities." The prolonged applause he received spoke for the agreement that the delegates to the State of the World Forum had for the Yunus method of breaking the cycle of poverty.

In 2006, Yunus and his Grameen Bank were awarded the Nobel Peace Prize for developing microcredit into an ever more important instrument in the struggle against poverty. His methods were praised the world over, but some in Bangladesh resented a native son they believed was rising disproportionately in the ranks of the famous. In a highly controversial move, the government of Bangladesh fired him from his post as managing director of Grameen Bank in 2011, claiming he had started it without proper permission and also asserting that Yunus, then seventy, had failed to retire on time. Yunus and his bank are appealing the decision.

In the meantime, his lesson lives on. Increasingly, economists see women as the solution to poverty. For example, the World Economic Forum *Global Gender Gap Report* shows that where the gender gap is nearest to being closed in a range of areas—including access to education and health care, economic participation, and political participation—countries and economies are more competitive and prosperous.

The first-ever economic summit on women, sponsored by the Asia-Pacific Economic Cooperation (APEC), was held in September 2011 in San Francisco. Hillary Clinton, U.S. secretary of state, was the keynote speaker at the gathering, which drew the largest number of foreign diplomats to the city since 1945, when representatives of fifty nations had gathered there to sign the United Nations charter.

The room was filled with the who's who of the business of the economy, which many saw as a portent of the future of women. Hillary Clinton certainly did. She opened her address with this: "To achieve the economic expansion we all seek, we need to unlock a vital source of growth that can power our economies in the decades to come. And that vital source of growth is women. With economic models straining in every corner of the world, none of us can afford to perpetuate the barriers facing women in the workforce. By increasing women's participation in the economy and enhancing their efficiency and productivity, we can bring about a dramatic impact on the competitiveness and growth of our economies. Because when everyone has a chance to participate in the economic life of a nation, we can all be richer."

Backroom strategists have long warned elected officials about the perils of being too honest, of daring to talk about issues that are controversial. But Clinton was fearless. She has always said the unsayable, whether talking about China's high abortion rate of female fetuses during her trip to that country or, in Congo, claiming that conflict is better settled by women. She has also regularly employed a tactic unusual in a politician: citing concrete statistics to back up her claims. At the economic summit, she called for "a fundamental transformation, a paradigm shift in how governments make and enforce laws and policies, how businesses invest and operate, how people make choices in the marketplace." She was taking a page from Muhammad Yunus's book, writ large. "As information transcends borders and creates opportunities for farmers to bank on mobile phones and children in distant villages to learn remotely, I believe that here, at the beginning of the twenty-first century, we are entering the participation age, where every individual, regardless of gender or other characteristics, is poised to be a contributing and valued member of the global marketplace." In essence, she said, "A rising tide of women in an economy raises the fortunes of families and nations." There are plenty of statistics to back up her claims. For example, *The Economist* reports that the increase in employment of women in developed countries during the past decade has added more to global GDP than China has. In the United States, a McKinsey study found that from 1972 to 2012, women went from holding 37 percent of all jobs to nearly 48 percent; in terms of their contribution to the bottom line, they were punching well above their weight.

But Clinton also highlighted the realities that women face. "A web of legal and social restrictions limit their potential," she said. She was referring to women who are confronted with a glass ceiling that keeps them from the most senior positions; women who don't have the same inheritance or property rights as men, so they can't inherit property or businesses owned by their fathers; women who are unable to have citizenship conferred on their children, which leaves the rights of the children in limbo. Some countries charge women higher taxes than men, deny women loans, prohibit them from opening bank accounts, signing contracts, purchasing property, owning businesses, or filing lawsuits without the permission of a male guardian.

These strictures have to change, Clinton argued, for reasons of survival: "When we liberate the economic potential of women, we elevate the economic performance of communities, nations, and the world."

She cited a Goldman Sachs report that shows how reducing the barriers to female labor force participation would increase America's GDP by 9 percent, the eurozone's by 13 percent, and Japan's by 16 percent. The same report claims that unlocking the potential of women by eliminating the gender barrier in the workplace would improve economies, including those of China, Russia, Indonesia, the Philippines, Vietnam, and South Korea.

It seems to be working in the United States. In her book *The Richer Sex,* Liza Mundy, an award-winning *Washington Post* reporter, refers to "breadwomen" as the new normal and says that today, 40 percent of American women earn more than their male partners. She estimates that within a generation this percentage will grow, until for the first time in human history women will earn more than men. She charts not only why this is inevitable, but also why it is a state much to be desired by both women and men because, to quote from her subtitle, "the new majority of female breadwinners is transforming sex, love, and family."

Research on women and the economy shows that women save more money than men, that they use their money to feed and educate their children, and as a result their families are healthier and better educated. But in many countries such statistics fall on deaf ears. Despite Jeffrey Sachs's analysis that the status of women and the economy are directly linked, there are countries, such as India, where the economy is red hot and the status of women deeply unacceptable. India can boast that some of its most prominent people are women political leaders and bankers and investment company chief executive officers. But as Isobel Coleman cautions, "Look at the local village level, where women are bought and sold like chattel, honor crimes are promulgated by local unelected leaders, female fetuses are aborted at high rates. There's little value on the girl child or on women." Indeed, a country that's now described as an economic powerhouse can be medieval in its social practices.

Hardest hit among India's women are the Dalits, formerly called untouchables. In 2004, I went to India to research an article about how those women were managing in the midst of the fastest-growing economy in the world. What I found was the intractable face of poverty. I started my quest in a village near the bustling city of Bangalore. There in southern India, I met a woman named Gowramma and saw firsthand how the cycle of poverty is reinforced.

It's the water pumps that I remember most powerfully. Soon after I arrived, Gowramma walked me to a roadway that was maybe a hundred yards from her home and explained how that dusty dirt road, which she did not dare to cross, separated her from the water she so badly needed for her six-month-old baby daughter, Dikshitra. On the other side of the road, in the village of Etangur, there was a tap in every house with fresh cool water twenty-four hours a day. On Gowramma's side, there were three water pumps for two hundred families. The water was turned on every three days. That was not enough for her needs, so when the pumps weren't running, she had to risk the one-and-a-half-mile walk to another village that would allow her to have water, a walk that took her past jeering men who threatened her with rape and worse.

The word *dalit* is Sanskrit and means "broken people." Like 200 million Dalits in India, Gowramma lived outside the mainstream Hindu society, according to the abusive unwritten rules that have governed her people for centuries. The caste system in India is the largest hierarchical system in the world today, with roots that trace back to between 1500 BCE and 1000 BCE. The idea and practice of ranking people according to their caste still exists in many countries in Southeast Asia, including Japan, Bangladesh, Pakistan, and Nepal, but the vast majority of untouchables live in India, a country where birth status condemns almost 20 percent of the population to poverty and abuse.

In Indian society, Hindus are stratified into four varna, or caste categories: the Brahmin, the priestly caste; the Kshatriya, warriors; the Vaisya, the trading and artisan caste; and the Sudra, manual laborers. The rest of the population is outcaste—literally untouchable to the four castes. Just twenty-five miles from Bangalore, the center of India's high-tech industry and often referred to as Silicon

Valley East, Gowramma and her daughter were living in appalling conditions. She was forbidden to walk on the street of the Hindu village across that road, enter the temple, drink from the same well as the upper caste, or even eat the same food. She and her kind could not hold marriage processions or carry their dead on the streets as part of a funeral. Village flour mills would not provide service to them. Like many other Dalits in India, Gowramma's family was kept by the upper caste as bonded laborers. They were forced to do jobs such as cleaning latrines and removing dead animals, sometimes with their bare hands, as they rarely owned gloves. In some villages in this state of Karnataka, Dalit girls as young as seven and eight were designated as the village concubine. To defy this ancient system was to invite brutal revenge from the higher castes.

Police files are full of atrocities. In 1995, Bhanwari Devi, a worker in the Women's Development Program in Rajasthan, reported the child marriage of a one-year-old girl to the authorities and was gang-raped by friends of the man she accused. When she reported the rape, the police said she was too old and unattractive to merit the attentions of young men and ignored her case. When she finally managed to get charges brought, the judge acquitted her rapists, reasoning, "Since the offenders were upper-caste men, including a Brahmin, the rape could not have taken place because an upper-caste man could not have defiled himself by raping a lower-caste woman."

When I was there in October 2004, a thirty-eight-year-old woman from Keela Urappanur village in Madurai District spurned the advances of an upper-caste man and was forced by a mob to drink excrement mixed with water. Then the crowd threw a bucket of excrement on her children, who were watching. In another incident that October, a sessions judge in Uttar Pradesh murdered a Dalit and wasn't even suspended from his duties, never mind charged. He continues to function as a judge.

In India, you're born into your caste; it's predetermined and immutable. Although the minority populations of Christians, Muslims, and Buddhists are considered outside the system, everyone else's caste is stamped on their school ID card, which is then used for identification, education, and job applications. If you're born a Dalit, you die a Dalit.

In 1950, the newly independent India attempted to deal with the malevolence of the caste system, not by annulling it but by giving the untouchables a new name: "the Scheduled Castes." At the same time, the government allocated 17 percent of civil service jobs and 17 percent of parliament seats to the Dalits. The practices of untouchability were forbidden by law and made punishable under the Indian constitution. Moreover, the new laws said the state had to protect the Scheduled Castes from social injustice. The government also created scholarships for Dalit children so they could get an education. Although some Dalits prospered—K. R. Narayanan became president of India in 1997 and Bhimrao Ambedkar wrote the new constitution—the government's experiment in emancipation failed. Ninety-nine percent of Dalits are still living the lives of untouchables.

Even though the Dalits who live in India's teeming cities are relegated to slum living, low-paying jobs, and discrimination, they do have more access to the laws designed to protect them. But 70 percent of India's 1 billion people live in villages, far from the magistrates and urban courts, and it is there, out of the sight of the lawmakers and among traditionalists, that the ancient indignities heaped on the outcastes, particularly the women, flourish.

Back in Etangur, Gowramma's baby was fussing because she was thirsty. A twenty-five-year-old mother of three, who'd been married at the age of thirteen, Gowramma couldn't leave on her trek for water until Dikshitra fell asleep: she couldn't carry the baby along with the heavy water jugs. She pointed to a pathetic collection of vessels hooked over the dry spout of the water pump in her village. Everyone was waiting for water.

Eventually, a neighbor came by to watch over Dikshitra, and Gowramma began her dreaded walk for water in the heat of the noonday sun.

Gowramma's husband works as a bonded laborer because they once needed to borrow money from the landlord for food. He earns about 25 cents a day, barely enough to repay the debt and provide a low-calorie cereal that his family eats three times a day. As she walked, Gowramma shared a dream with me: "We have two cows. I want to start a dairy. I could provide milk to the people, earn enough money to get us out of bondage. But the upper castes won't allow me to do that." Gowramma's plan to sell milk would not only get their family on its feet, it would also contribute to solving the problem with food shortages in the region. But she couldn't make it happen.

When women such as Gowramma are confronted with barriers limiting their right to start a business, it has the same negative effect as when women elsewhere are denied access to markets, social networks, and credit: everyone loses. Even in high-income countries, social norms and market barriers still contribute to keeping women away from opportunities that can move them into better-paying jobs. When Hillary Clinton addressed the economic summit on women, she raised the issue of women farmers with a view to explaining how, if given a chance, the women can reduce food shortages and boost nutrition levels. "Take just one sector of our economy—agriculture—to illustrate what I mean. We know women play an important role in driving agriculture-led growth worldwide. . . . They sustain every link in the agricultural chain: They plant the seeds; they care for the livestock; they harvest the crops; they sell them at markets; they store the food; and then they prepare it for consumption."

Then Clinton drew the big picture: "Despite their presence in all of these kinds of jobs, they have less to show for all of their work. Women farmers are up to 30 percent less productive than male farmers, and that's not because they are working less or are less committed. It's because women farmers have access to fewer resources. They have less fertilizer, fewer tools, poorer-quality seeds, and less access to training or to land. And they have much less time to farm because they also have to do most of the household work. When that resource gap is closed and resources are allocated equally—and, better yet, efficiently—women and men are equally productive in agriculture. And that has positive benefits. In Nepal, for example, where mothers have greater ownership of land because of their inheritance rights, there are fewer severely underweight children."

Clinton outlined the consequences of ignoring women farmers. "Close the resource gap holding women back in developing economies, and we could feed 150 million more people worldwide every year, and that's according to the Food and Agriculture Organization, and that's in addition to the higher incomes for families and the more efficient markets and the more agricultural trade that would result."

One of the organizations working to alter Gowramma's situation is the National Federation of Dalit Women, which seeks to educate and organize women like her. They are pursuing legal action against caste-based atrocities. They seek political empowerment for Dalit women and plan to get it by building self-confidence in women, sharing knowledge of the law, and developing leadership. "The government of India has failed in its responsibility to almost 20 percent of the population," said its leader, Ruth Manorama. "This level of human rights deprivation is worse than racism." Manorama was the sort of woman they needed to upset three-thousand-year-old traditions. Feisty and in-your-face, she had a lot to say. "Despite the benefits promised by the government, there's an unholy alliance between the state and the upper castes that perpetuates a shameful level of apartheid. Police actively collude with the upper castes to perpetrate violence against Dalits." The superiority of the upper castes is so entrenched that the abuse is sometimes no more than sport but always a reminder that in India, status overrules human rights. Manorama also started another organization, Women's Voice, to reach out to women in the slums and the villages. One of the women in her program was Gowramma.

But nasty habits die hard. A stunning report first written by Smita Narula for Human Rights Watch in 1999, and updated in 2011, exposed the Dalits' situation to a worldwide audience. Narula found that sexual abuse and other forms of violence were used to crush dissent within the community. Women such as Gowramma, who dream of change, and other Dalits, who contest political office in village councils and municipalities, vying for seats constitutionally reserved for them, are threatened with physical abuse if they persist.

It's not as if the state is unaware of the ongoing problems. Consider the wording of the Prevention of Atrocities Act, passed in 1989, which lays out punishments for offenses such as forcing a member of the Scheduled Caste "to drink or eat any inedible or obnoxious substance"; parading a person "naked or with painted face"; assaults on women "with intent to dishonor or outrage her modesty."

As for the international community, even in the recent past, many development programs were designed without consulting women or considering the crucial role they played, whether it was funding agricultural training initiatives that targeted men, even though women often represented the majority of small farmers, or building wells in areas where women could not go, never mind that women were the ones responsible for fetching water.

Gross inequality is a reality in the lives of Dalits. Clearly, the caste system has to go. But unless the upper castes face real consequences under the law, they are not about to give up their power and privilege. They live in a country that has not only one of the fastest-growing economies in the world but also the second-biggest population after China. Wealth is increasing in India, even as Dalits suffer in poverty. In July 2003, India even asked twenty-two countries to stop sending foreign aid, in an attempt to better its chances of joining the G7 group of countries with major economies.

Gowramma credited public pressure for slight revisions to the rules she and her neighbors lived with. They used to have to remove their sandals and the men also had to remove their shirts in the presence of the landlord. They couldn't ride bicycles on the same street as Hindus. At one time, they could be whipped if they happened to step into the shadow of a member of the upper caste. After the rules changed, she said, an upper-caste person would give a Dalit food as long as it was on a separate plate, one that the Hindu family didn't have to touch.

But Dalit women still suffer sexual exploitation cloaked as "religious" ritual. Outlawed practices, such as Bettale Seve, nude worship, which allows upper castes to strip Dalit women and men and parade them naked through the streets, still happen. So does devadasi, the Hindu practice that in part sacrifices a young girl's virginity to the gods to satisfy the wants of village chiefs and ward off evil spirits and bad omens.

While she was getting her sons ready to go to the Dalit-only school they attend in the village, I asked Gowramma how she untangled this injustice for her children. "I tell them, 'You are a human being. God has not created people to be upper or lower caste. It's people who have divided society. So, don't you feel inferior. Go to school; study well so you can get a good job.'"

After the boys left for school, she sounded less optimistic. "It's so hard," she said quietly while breast-feeding Dikshitra. "We work so hard, get such low income, have no money for good food. We need to change this."

As the baby drifted off to sleep in her arms, I was reminded of *A Fine Balance,* Rohinton Mistry's novel about India's untouchables, whose theme is how narrow is the distance between hope and despair. For Dalit women such as Gowramma, hope and a growing demand for justice may be the only way out of despair. It's easy to dismiss a poor woman and her two cows as a minor problem, one that won't solve the food shortages or human rights atrocities that the Dalits suffer. Spending time with Gowramma made it abundantly clear that it is crucial to change the rules so that a woman can milk her cows and sell the milk to people who need it and can afford to pay for it. Allowing a woman such as Gowramma to sell her milk is the way to turn poverty into production.

The Food and Agriculture Organization of the United Nations (FAO) estimates that if women had the same access to productive resources as men, they could increase yields on their farms by 20 to 30 percent. This increase could raise total agricultural output in developing countries by 2.5 to 4 percent and reduce the number of hungry people in the world by 12 to 17 percent, or up to 150 million people.

Isobel Coleman sees a core economic argument here. "When you invest in women and girls, it's the best way to break cycles of poverty. Poor states aren't necessarily failed states. But it's difficult to emerge as a peaceful, functioning, stable country when living in dire straits of poverty." Her advice: "Invest in women and girls—break negative cycles and create positive cycles that would benefit the women and girls and country as a whole at a macro-economic level."

While it's an economic issue, Coleman says, it's also a human rights issue. "When women are sold, bartered, neglected, aborted as baby girls, all sorts of bad things are happening in those countries— it's a real marker for the health of the civil society, the political life, the core of the nation. Countries that stone young women or have high levels of honor crimes, or don't allow women to take part in the social fabric, or vote, or participate as equals, have a whole range of problems, the role of women being the most obvious. Women are half the population. These aren't women's issues, they are core economic issues, security issues, human rights issues."

The surest path to the eradication of poverty is the economic empowerment of women, who make up the majority of the world's poor. Studies done by the International Center for Research on Women in Washington, D.C., claim that discriminating against women is economically inefficient; that national economies lose out when a substantial part of the population cannot compete equitably or realize their full potential. Gowramma's story is ever more meaningful in the face of data that says women who are economically empowered contribute more to their families, societies, and economies. They invest income in their children, which is the definition of sustainable development.

Koraro is a village in Ethiopia that was selected as a Millennium Village by Jeffrey Sachs and his Millennium Goals team to demonstrate how a little outside help could lift a village out of poverty. The Earth Institute and the UN Development Programme kicked in the funds to jump-start Koraro from hardscrabble poverty—rampant malaria, no schools, no health clinics, food shortages—to development, complete with a local school, a clinic, and much-improved agriculture. Although they have a distance to travel before becoming self-sustaining, Sachs credits the girls in the village with showing how the empowerment of women can lead to success for the entire village. Each year, a dozen girls were given scholarships to attend secondary school in another town. The classes included instruction in skills that led to jobs as plumbers and electricians and to improved farming techniques. Education changed their lives. Exactly as Sachs had predicted, the girls married later and had fewer children, and those children are healthier. When he visited the village in 2010, he sat in the classroom while the first wave of graduates talked to primary schoolchildren about the value of getting an education. Sachs believes that these young women will improve Koraro's education level and create new jobs along the way.

That was the sort of successful experiment that caught the attention of Margot Franssen, a businesswoman who brought the Body Shop franchise to Canada. "When women aren't included in the conversation, in equal rights, when they don't have the whole menu of opportunity, it affects the entire world. We need to invest money in women and girls so they can sit at the table and bring their voices to the table. We need the men too."

She believes that too many people, from government representatives to corporate bosses, still simply don't get it; they don't understand the big picture—how important it is to invest in women and girls. "People believe if you buy someone a cow, you settle poverty. If you have a shelter built, that's the end of violence. That's like saying, 'We have an emergency ward so we don't need the hospital.' People like simplistic solutions, but we need to look at this in a more holistic manner."

Franssen became the co-chair of Women Moving Millions (WMM) for precisely that reason. "In my life of dealing with business and commerce and funding women and girls," she says, "I discovered that just because it's legal doesn't mean it's moral, and just because it's moral doesn't mean it'll be put into law. No amount of laws will make women strong. We need to step in and give them a voice." WMM funds women in impressive numbers and at significant levels: millions of dollars. Women of means in Canada and the United States pledge $1 million each to fund organizations that are moving women into a world of self-sufficiency. Franssen gave her pledge money to the Canadian Women's Foundation (CWF), an organization whose motto is "The power of women and the dreams of girls," so it can research, fund, and share the best approaches to ending violence against women, moving low-income women out of poverty, and building strong, resilient girls.

WMM started in 2007 with a goal to raise $150 million for the advancement of women and girls. Franssen remembers, "Everyone said, 'You're crazy. You'll never make it.' By 2009, when the rest of the world was falling to pieces, we had raised $185 million. Now we're realizing we should be thinking billions. It's not about us deciding where the money will go, it's us saying if you really want to invest well, give your money to an organization that promotes women and girls."

She supports CWF because she's seen that it makes a significant difference in the lives of women and girls. When, for instance, it funded Aboriginal women in Winnipeg, Manitoba, who wanted to become carpenters, it was unheard-of that women would join the union of carpenters in the province. Even while they were apprenticing, the women feared they'd never get jobs. With CWF funds over a five-year period, they put together a co-op carpentry company and hired themselves out. In short order, all thirteen newly qualified female carpenters were fully booked. They eventually disbanded the co-op but only to go on to work for developers and renovators, having built careers for themselves. The cost of helping these women was a fraction of what it would have cost the state to subsidize them with social assistance.

"Through CWF, we fund the most marginalized people in our society," says Franssen. "One woman in Niagara Falls, Ontario, who had been abused by her husband was out on her own without work and wondering how to make ends meet when she came to us with a plan. She knew how to preserve food and was making jellies and jams. We funded her. She's now the CEO of Niagara Presents, a hugely successful company that hires women who come from the same situation she was in."

There's another CWF initiative that draws particular attention among businesswomen in Toronto. The foundation released the plan as an IPO (initial public offering) and invited women to join. Here's how it works. The organization's research established that it takes $2,500 to launch a woman out of poverty, much less than the cost of paying welfare over her lifetime. So CWF set a goal to raise $2,500 from each participant to launch twenty-five hundred women out of poverty. It became a wildly successful program, pitched each year by Franssen, who stood up in front of about a thousand women at one of those ghastly early-morning breakfast fund-raisers and begged: "Come on—it's $41 a month on your Visa. That's less than a pedicure." CWF met its goal in three and a half years, raising more than $6 million. Franssen says, "Women are looked at as a problem. We need to look at them as an asset—their inner strength, intuition, their smarts, and their ability to nurture and see into the future. I believe that things are changing for women and girls. The last decade has shown us that. We're becoming a bigger voice and are using that voice."

Speaking of the corporate women who come to those CWF breakfasts, research shows a correlation between the number of women on boards and higher corporate profits. One analysis found that companies with more women board directors outperform those with the least by 66 percent return on invested capital, by 53 percent return on equity, and 42 percent return on sales. Another study indicates that one-third of executives reported increased profits as a result of investments in employing women in emerging markets.

In the United States, the productivity gains attributable to the modest 11 percent increase in women's overall share of the labor market over the past forty years, as documented in the McKinsey report mentioned earlier, accounts for approximately one-quarter of the country's current GDP. The dollar amount is more than $3.5 trillion—more than the GDP of Germany, and more than half the GDPs of China and Japan.

There's no shortage of sobering statistics that present a strong moral case that funding women is smart economics. For example, women produce nearly 80 percent of the world's food but receive less than 10 percent of agricultural assistance. Even *The Economist* is on board: an editorial written in April 2006 was titled, "Forget China, India and the Internet: Economic Growth Is Driven by Women."

Some of the most heart-wrenching and seemingly impossible cases in the poverty file are being handled by innovative women—some of them octogenarians who bring new meaning to necessity being the mother of invention. These are the grandmothers in sub-Saharan Africa who were called on to care for their sons and daughters who had HIV/AIDS; when their children succumbed to the disease, they became the guardians to the next generation—their grandchildren and great-grandchildren. Stephen Lewis, once the UN Special Envoy for HIV/AIDS in Africa, says, "This is the redefinition of the family. An entire generation is missing—the one that keeps the economy going. We don't know what impact that will have."

I went back to the Kingdom of Swaziland in May 2010 to meet some of these women who are trying to turn the economy in their own lives around, and to witness an extraordinary event called the Gathering.

The streets of Manzini swayed with their presence; curb to curb for block after block they marched—more than two thousand women hoisting placards demanding pensions, voices ululating and chanting "Viva Go Gos" (the Swazi word for "grandmothers"). They came from thirteen African countries and Canada (where Lewis had alerted First World grannies to the needs of African grannies) for the Gathering, which started as a passionate and persuasive call for change and became the birth of a movement to empower older women.

Much of a generation—the sons and daughters of the women marching—had been wiped out by the HIV/AIDS pandemic. The African grandmothers are tasked with raising their orphaned grandchildren—getting up for two A.M. feedings and pleading with teenagers to keep their curfews at a time when they thought the anxiety of child rearing was behind them. They were joined by Canadian grandmothers there to bear witness, express solidarity, and gather evidence that would describe the needs of these African grannies back home in Canada so they could raise money to lighten their burden.

Most of the Canadian women cut their teeth on protests that demanded social change. As they marched down the streets of Manzini, they reminded me of marchers who followed Pete Seeger, Doris Anderson, Martin Luther King Jr., and Harvey Milk.

This is what it takes to launch a movement; these kinds of marches for peace, for women's rights, for civil rights, and for gay rights invariably lead to change. "We aren't simply a collection of retired teachers and nurses and social workers," said Leslie Starkman, sixty, a delegate from Toronto, "we're boomers and hippies and activists." Working for change is in their DNA.

Bringing the African and Canadian grandmothers together was the brainchild of Ilana Landsberg-Lewis, the director of the Stephen Lewis Foundation. "We were funding hundreds of projects in Africa that provide food, school fees, medicines, and microcredit earning initiatives, and it occurred to me that most of the people receiving the funds were grandmothers." For Landsberg-Lewis, the penny dropped. She held a press conference in Canada with a trio of famous grannies—the country's former governor general Adrienne Clarkson; Shirley Douglas, the actress and activist daughter of the Canadian political icon Tommy Douglas and the mother of Kiefer Sutherland; and Landsberg-Lewis's own mom, the journalist Michele Landsberg.

The launch of the program was in August 2006 when the Stephen Lewis Foundation brought one hundred grannies from Africa and two hundred from Canada together in Toronto to address the life-and-death problems the African grandmothers were facing. Many were themselves HIV positive. All of them were financially stretched and physically exhausted. Grief suffused the heartbreaking stories they shared. The promise that their sons and daughters would take care of them in their old age had disintegrated with the ashes of their dead children.

At the close of that first meeting, the Canadian grandmothers made a pledge: "We are acutely conscious of the enormous debt owed to a generation of women who spent their youth freeing Africa, their middle age reviving it, and their older lives sustaining it. We will not rest until they can rest."

Then the African grannies serenaded their Canadian sisters with "We Shall Overcome." The Canadian grannies sang right back to them, with "Amazing Grace." Laughter and tears bonded the women into a powerful international network of activists. About twelve thousand Canadian grandmothers have since raised more than $10 million for the cause.

Some of the African grannies came from the township of Khayelitsha, about forty minutes south of Cape Town, South Africa. I visited them before the event in Swaziland and found a tiny room full of committed if slightly overwhelmed grandmothers.

A single note in a clear contralto resonated through the room as I walked into the little building that houses Grandmothers Against Poverty and AIDS (GAPA), where a dozen women bent over beadwork, sewing machines, and knitting needles. Like a choir director's baton, the note raised the other women's voices in powerful, soulful harmony—the kind that vibrates against the ribs, swells the chest, seeps into the soul, and makes the hips sway. The music, like the rhythm of life, was the sound of solidarity in this place, which when the grannies first began to gather was the center of unspeakable sadness and despair.

One of the women, Constance Sohena, sixty-three, told me that after her daughter died of AIDS, she locked herself in the house and wouldn't come out for six months. But once she met the other grannies, she began to recover, could devote herself to raising her grandson and leading a granny support group, in the process turning into a formidable human rights activist—a transformation that made Sohena laugh when she thought about the despair she started with. Alicia Mdaka, sixty-nine, lost two daughters and a granddaughter to AIDS. She was raising four orphaned grandchildren and said, "I wished at first that I would die too. When I heard about the GAPA grannies, I realized I'm not alone." In fact, the strength she gained from the group propelled her to accept an invitation to fly to Malta in 2005 to address the Commonwealth Heads of Government Meeting, in order to tell the world of the plight of the GAPA grannies.

While her great-granddaughter, thirteen-month-old Salome, played happily under the sewing table where Mdaka was working, she recounted how she felt at the start of that journey. "I'd never been on a plane, never left South Africa. But I'm not scared of anything now." She credited GAPA for pulling her back from the brink of suicide. She scooped up Salome, who snuggled into her arms for her morning bottle, and said, "A granny can never be useless. You get thread, you sew, you sell what you make, buy bread for the children and electricity so your house will be light." Her daughter Olive died in 1999 and left her with three children to raise, and then three-month-old Zizipho, her eldest daughter's child, was born HIV positive and died in 2000. A year later, two of her sons were murdered in the violence-racked township. Then Zizipho's mother succumbed to AIDS and left her son in Mdaka's care. "My shack burned down that year. So I had no house, no place to have a funeral for my daughter, no money to bury her." Today, she looks after two more sons who are mentally ill and cannot work. A third daughter is living with full-blown AIDS because the antiretroviral drug that can control the illness arrived in time to save her.

Mdaka seemed like a miracle of survival in the mean lottery of HIV/AIDS. She was determined that her troubles were behind her. "I live in a block-brick house now—no more shack. There's no water inside yet, but next year I'll put my sinks and bath inside. I sew pinafores, drape covers, dresses, and pillowcases. I sell them at the pay points [where pensions are handed out] and at the train station and taxi ranks—wherever there are plenty of people."

Inside the little gray brick house, surrounded by a patchy lawn and a six-foot wall topped with barbed wire—the headquarters of the project for 410 grandmothers in Khayelitsha since 2004—newspaper accounts of the first grannies' gathering in Canada covered the bulletin board. One of them described the visit: "It was marvelous in Canada. It's quiet, clean, no shacks, big buildings. The people in Toronto are helpful. They don't have racism. Whites are with blacks—even married to blacks."

Of that event, Mdaka told me, "We met other African grannies who are in chaos and could tell them how to start a group, find others, unite, get some beads, make some dresses. Then you have money for bread." They also received newfound support from Canadian grandmothers who vowed to be there with dollars and deeds until the wretched pandemic is tamed.

The statistics are mind-boggling. Of the 40 million people with HIV/AIDS worldwide, 25 million live in sub-Saharan Africa and 57 percent of them are women. Thirteen million children are orphans, a number that's expected to rise to 18 million by 2013. There are seven thousand new cases of HIV/AIDS a day, nine hundred of them in South Africa. In 2008, only 20 percent were getting the antiretroviral drugs they needed to survive. The rollout is better now but still not enough.

Statistics on grandmothers are scant because they haven't been included in the studies done on HIV/AIDS. The tragic myth in these afflicted countries is that the grannies are HIV negative and therefore AIDS-free, which means rape is rising among this already vulnerable group.

The first study on grandmother-led households and HIV/AIDS was done in 1999 by the Institute of Ageing in Africa at the University of Cape Town. At the time, the researchers established that grandmothers were the sole supporters of hundreds of thousands of newly orphaned children and that they didn't have the financial means to cope. The stigma surrounding HIV/AIDS meant that their houses were being attacked and burned. They were ostracized. They had no one to talk to. Those who had jobs had to give them up to care for their dying children at home. Traditional funerals—a weeklong mourning period during which visitors have to be fed, a marquee raised in front of the house, a bus hired to get everyone to the burial, a cow or several sheep slaughtered for the reception—cost a fortune, and many of the grandmothers couldn't afford them.

The findings of the report were made public at an international conference on aging in Madrid in 2002, and the plight of the grannies was on the map. Kathleen Brodrick, an occupational therapist from Cape Town who was already familiar with the developing catastrophe in Khayelitsha, had been hired by the researchers to interpret the data. "We needed to start support groups, which meant finding people who would discuss a topic that was taboo," she said. At first seventeen grandmothers turned up to meetings she arranged, then thirty, then huge numbers of desperate women in crisis joined. They started with patchwork—sewing together bits of donated cloth to make pinafores, blankets, anything they could stitch and sell to bring in money. While they sewed, they talked. "They were sickly-looking, with a gray pallor, miserable and quiet when we started," says Brodrick. "By the time the four-week trial period was over, their self-confidence was growing, they looked better, and they said, 'What now? We can't stop this meeting.' "

That was the beginning of GAPA. Brodrick stayed on as a volunteer; today she does the fund-raising and planning, and the group has a full-time manager and their own meeting house—the one I visited. "It is not a handout organization," says Brodrick firmly. "It's a hand up. If people need money or food, we send them to the agencies that can help. GAPA is about figuring out how to help yourself." At the workshops, every one of them run by a grandmother, the grannies learn about human rights, parenting skills, how to access government grants and draw up a will. There is counseling for grief, coping with child raising, and finding health care. And in Canada and elsewhere, the groups funding the initiatives are also run by grannies.

It would be easy to dismiss the well-heeled southwestern Ontario grandmothers' group called Oomama (which means "our mother") as guilt-ridden do-gooders, but that would underestimate a powerful force of women whose aim is nothing short of international solidarity. Carole Holmes, for example, was running a bed-and-breakfast in upscale Niagara-on-the-Lake when I met her. Ask her about her own granddaughter, Calliope, and she chokes up, describing the relationship she has with the thirteen-month-old child who calls her Mamm (she hasn't quite mastered the *gr* in Gram). Her hopes for this child are palpable. "The thought of other grandmothers wanting to feed their grandchildren, get them educated, with no support, no means, is heartbreaking to me. This is not about knitting booties and making quilts, it's about making change." Holmes and her extended family kicked in $6,000 for the Stephen Lewis Foundation one Christmas, donating the money they would have spent on Christmas gifts.

Or listen to Sherry Ardell, who recalls reading a story about Stephen Lewis's work in *The Globe and Mail* on January 4, 2003. "I didn't know what I could do. I only knew I had to do something. I was born at the end of the Second World War. When I asked my parents, they didn't seem to know what was going on in the camps [in Germany] but now we know [what's going on in Africa]." She raised $22,000 at a garage sale that summer and put on a speaking event featuring Stephen Lewis in her hometown of Oakville, at which she tripled the garage sale total.

Then there's Bev LeFrancois, a woman who's been in the trenches for change for thirty years and counts the struggle to include women's rights in the Canadian constitution as one of the battles she helped fight and win. "This grandmothers' issue in Africa is just one more terrible example of the way women are treated. How is it we can afford to make war but can't help these women to care for the orphaned children? I hope we can get resources to do for those grandchildren the way we are privileged to do for ours."

Back in Khayelitsha, the cemetery was full. Some families had had to bury one member on top of another. Hand-painted signs reading COFFINS FOR SALE dotted the street corners. When I asked the grannies where all the men were, they said, "They're either dead or have gone off with a younger woman."

"It's difficult to raise up a grandchild," said Constance Sohena, who suffers from elephantiasis and lives in a two-bedroom house with five of her grandchildren, her surviving daughter, two sons, and her husband. "They are demanding and not satisfied whatever you are doing. You never know if teenagers are angry with you or with something else." She was referring to an incident that happened when she came home with new shoes for thirteen-year-old Sonwabo. He threw them to the floor in disgust, saying, "I won't wear them," and stomped out of the house. The running shoes were not "Toughies," the black oxford-style shoes that the other boys were wearing. Like most style-conscious teenagers, Sonwabo didn't want to be uncool.

Sohena's daughter Amanda died in her arms in 1999. She was devastated. "I lost my passion, was angry all the time. One day a woman came and told me about the workshop. She talked me into going with her. I wanted to know more about this disease that took my child away. I began to accept that I'm not alone. I came to terms with HIV. I talked about it for the first time. We learned from each other."

She learned plenty, discovering she had rights, such as a pension, that were being denied by the government. "I know about my rights now. No one can come and tell me what to think. I think for myself." Five years after her daughter died, one of her sons was stabbed to death. No one was charged with the killing. Sohena went to the police and demanded an investigation, but they said the docket with the information about the incident had been lost. She said they'd better find it. They did. Her son's murderer was arrested and is now in jail. Everyone in the area knew not to mess with Sohena when it comes to women's rights, violence, and abuse, or the treatment of HIV/AIDS patients.

The task these women have inherited is immense. They worry about living long enough to raise the children to adulthood and wonder who will be left to bury them and whether the old traditions will be lost because no one can afford to keep them.

Thenjiwe Madzinga, sixty-nine, had been raising four grandchildren since her daughter Christina died in 2003. "I had another daughter, Nyameka, and a son, Jorda—they were both working, bringing me money to take care of the children. But both died last year—they followed each other within one month. All I can think about is if God will keep me here until these children are grown and can do things for themselves."

A dozen blocks away from the GAPA house, in the two-room, four-by-four-yard shack she's painted bright blue, Madzinga had greeted me with a warm smile, but her equanimity collapsed when she told the story of nursing her daughters and son, how they suffered, that she had nothing for them, no drugs. "I wish I'd had enough food in the house for the children. I wish there was someone to take care of me. I'm not happy," she admitted.

As for her grandchildren, they adore her. Said eighteen-year-old Zekhaya, "She's the best grandma; she's always there for us. We have everything we need because we have her." Zekhaya scoffed at the rampant crime in their neighborhood, where doors are kicked in during the night, people are stabbed and robbed. "Not us," she said. Zekhaya planned to start studies at the University of Western Cape the next year if she could find the funds to pay the fees. "I'll be the first in my family to go to university."

Finances are an ongoing struggle. Although grandmothers in South Africa receive a pension of 700 rand a month (about $112) and a stipend of 500 rand (about $80) per child under eighteen, in other African countries there's no subsidy at all. And even in South Africa, that money often feeds and clothes up to twenty family members. Also, half the grandmothers in the GAPA program are between fifty and sixty, and the pension doesn't kick in until they turn sixty.

The enormity of the crisis is paralyzing. At the macro level, universal treatment with antiretroviral drugs is required, and a vaccine or a cure needs to be found. New drugs, such as the microbicides that can be used vaginally before sex to prevent HIV but allow conception, need to be made available. But all of that requires an international commitment of funding. And so far, apart from superstars such as Bono and philanthropists such as Bill Gates, no one is stepping up. Passing out condoms simply isn't solving the problem.

At the Stephen Lewis Foundation office in Toronto, the messages attached to the project reports coming in from Africa reflect the ongoing terrible consequences of the pandemic. One hastily scribbled note reads, "Sorry to be late. We couldn't get the report to you on time because the leader passed away." Another says, "The house was burned down; we had to write the report again." Still another reads, "The lawyer helping us died." It's hard to measure the progress that will ameliorate the effects of the pandemic when the virus hasn't yet been tamed.

At the Gathering, there were five hundred official delegates from thirteen African countries and forty-four Canadians who represented 240 grandmother groups from across Canada. The goal was to amplify the voices of the grandmothers in sub-Saharan Africa, to validate their needs and establish the economic link between getting their orphaned grandchildren raised and educated and the future of the thirteen countries they represented. The visiting Canadian grannies vowed to press their government to maintain its commitment to the Global Fund to Fight AIDS and to make the less expensive generic drugs available to Africans.

On the day of the march, grandmothers from all over Swaziland joined in, swelling the numbers. Organized by SWAPOL, the three-day conference and workshops let the world know that in the face of great darkness, women from two sides of the world quilted together a patchwork of survival.

One of those women was Sabina Muale from Zambia, who'd made contact with the grandmothers' group in her area, the Busy Bees, just weeks before coming to the conference. She wasn't sure of her age but assumed she was more than seventy. She'd had twelve children—strong sons and daughters who worked hard, raised their families, and looked in on their mama every day. Then the pandemic struck. Every one of her children died. Every single one. She wound up taking care of the orphaned grandchildren—eight of them between the ages of three and sixteen. The four-year-old was HIV positive. The kids weren't in school because Muale could hardly earn enough to feed them, never mind pay school fees. She was doing what she calls "yard work"—weeding and hoeing—to earn money for food. She was worn out, her dulcet way of talking muted by her own exhaustion. With her gnarled fingers clenched in her lap, she said, "I never, ever thought I'd be in this position. My children would have taken care of me." Then she shrugged, turned her arms inward as if to cover her heart, and said in a barely audible voice, "I'm just me now," and she began to cry. This was the picture of despair.

The conference, however, became a turning point for Muale. She'd made small rag dolls to sell. The Canadian grandmothers snatched them up as though at a fire sale. Muale also got to know other grannies, both Canadian and African. She felt the solidarity, attended the sessions. She came away with a new sense of hope. "It lessens my burden," she said. "I see others in the same situation. My heart is heavy at home. It's gentle here. And I know after this gathering that if I go, other grannies will take care of my babies. I have the courage to carry on now."

Although Swaziland's royal household had displayed a shocking disregard for the catastrophe that had brought the country to its knees, just days before the event, the spin doctors at the palace realized that there was a public relations coup at their doorstep and suddenly announced that the royal household would host the opening night of the conference.

There was hoopla and pomp; there were ceremonial swords and dancers. The much-loved Queen Mother presided at the head table, along with the crown prince and four of the king's wives (who spent much of the night talking on cell phones). It looked as though the royal family had hijacked the event.

But when the Queen Mother instructed her musicians to strike up, a bit of serendipity entered the proceedings. With little warning and no planning, the African and Canadian grandmothers leaped from their seats and boogied arm in arm to the dance floor, taking the event back into their own hands. It was a remarkable sight. These women, who had traveled great distances because the welfare of grandchildren was at stake, briefly laid down their burdens and danced the night away.

The workshops that began the next day dealt with the harsh realities of their lives: the grinding poverty and a particularly heinous form of violence—the beating, rape, and robbery of vulnerable grannies. They sought means to stop the violence, and they examined the law to find a way around the customary tradition of a surviving brother taking all his brother's assets, including the widow, as his rightful property and leaving the children penniless.

And they talked about the means of raising money: the grannies from Canada relied on the tried-and-true methods of bake sales and quilting bees and silent auctions and stuffed dolls with no-skid slippers. The African grannies, on the other hand, do their part tilling the soil and weeding the gardens of those who have money to pay. They grow vegetables, make soap, knit blankets with wool from old sweaters, and sell everything they make at a market.

When the marchers reached their destination at the community center on the final day of the conference, the grannies read the Manzini Statement: "We are the backbones of our communities. Africa cannot survive without us." They called on their governments to help their HIV-positive grandchildren; they demanded food security and microcredit financing, social security, a stop to violence, and a change in the jurisprudence that results in the disinheritance of their grandchildren. The closing line of the statement was "We are strong. We are visionary, we have faith, and we are not alone. Together we will turn the tide of AIDS. Viva!"

Siphiwe Hlophe, the director of SWAPOL and the host of the event, was exhausted the morning after the march as she waved off busload after busload of grannies heading back to their own hearths in Zambia and Zimbabwe, in Ontario and British Columbia, in

South Africa and Rwanda, in Quebec and New Brunswick. The Gathering had been all she hoped for and more. "A lot has changed since last we met in Canada," she said. "In 2006, the African grandmothers were grieving. They were needy, disconnected, and exhausted. Now many more can put food on the table, clothe the grandchildren, and send them to school, but, more than that, a movement started here."

Gloria Steinem has seen women come together to alter their status in North America as well as Africa. When we sat down to talk in New York, she said, "It's all about having faith in women." She shared a story about being in Zambia for a meeting about sex-trafficking and discussing strategies to stop it. "After the meeting I ended up on the Zambezi River with a huge group of women. There were too many different languages being spoken. I wondered how we were going to communicate, but experience told me that circles of women always work; someone speaks the truth, and then it works."

Gradually out of the babble of discussion came the fact that what the local women needed was to grow maize so they would have food security for a year in order to pay their kids' school fees. "They explained that the maize they grew was being eaten by the elephants. They needed a fence to keep the elephants out and didn't have the funds to buy one. To earn money so they could buy food for the children and send them to school, the women were going to Lusaka and joining the sex trade."

Steinem ended up helping to raise money for an electrified fence so the elephants didn't come and eat the maize. "When I went back the next year," she said, "they had a bumper crop of maize; they were singing songs to the maize, dancing under the trees to the maize. What it meant was they could stay at home and not go to Lusaka, where they'd be sex-trafficked. If someone had told me an electrified fence would be the answer to sex-trafficking, I couldn't have believed it. You've got to listen to women, to the wisdom of women in each situation."

. . .

Putting morality and social justice to one side for a moment, we can see that investing in women simply makes good economic sense. Hillary Clinton predicts a change in the economic climate for women, and there's research data to support her view. Economists estimate that women-owned businesses will create nearly a third of the new jobs anticipated over the next seven years. Globally, women will control $15 trillion in spending by the year 2014. Narrowing the gender gap could lead to a 14 percent rise in per capita incomes by the year 2020, and a reduction in barriers to female labor-force participation would increase the size of America's GDP by 9 percent, the eurozone's by 13 percent, and Japan's by 16 percent. By 2028, women will be responsible for about two-thirds of consumer spending worldwide.

The World Bank's 2012 World Development Report on gender equality and development argues that gender equality is a core development objective in its own right. Greater gender equality can enhance productivity, improve development outcomes for the next generation, and make institutions more representative.

Women used to be viewed as victims of poverty and illiteracy, of violence and seemingly unbreakable cultural traditions. Melanne Verveer, the U.S. ambassador-at-large for global women's issues, says, "Promoting the status of women is not just a moral imperative but a strategic one; it's essential to economic prosperity and to global peace and security. It is, in other words, a strategy for a smarter foreign policy." There are millions of women around the world— some of them grandmothers, some of them teenagers—who would say Verveer is absolutely right.

6

The Ascent of Women

Until women around the world are accorded their rights . . .
global progress and prosperity will have its own
glass ceiling. — HILLARY CLINTON

Like Sisyphus, women have been rolling a rock uphill for millennia. Our victories, while significant, have invariably been tempered by backlash as well as hampered by cultural and religious dogma. Today, I believe that women are poised, at last, to reach the summit. Given the rapidly changing status of women, an optimist could even suggest that women are at a tipping point when age-old oppression is seen as damaging to the economy and the health of the community and its opposite—emancipation—is seen as the prescription for prosperity.

How these coming changes play out will differ from place to place. The women of Afghanistan have found their voices and are demanding change. The women of Liberia banded together and elected a female president for the first time in 2005 because their lives were in danger in the hands of the men who were running the country. In the Democratic Republic of the Congo, a place where it's more dangerous to be a woman than a soldier, women are organizing a Silence Is Violence campaign and breaking a taboo that has historically demanded that they keep the abuse in their lives a secret.

A vast collection of knowledge and learned ways of dealing with particular circumstances inevitably feed a tipping point. One of them is changes in language itself. Language matters. It creates a response, sets a scene, delivers legitimacy. Calling the widespread rape, murder, and displacement of a people "ethnic cleansing" lets its perpetrators off the hook. To call it what it is—genocide—makes them bear some responsibility. When the adage "boys will be boys" is applied to a carful of racist young men hurling insults at Aboriginal women walking on the roadside, it cultivates acceptance. Saying that you are acting in the name of God can be either a blessing or a curse: feeding the poor and caring for the sick in the name of God is one thing; being denied an education and health care in the name of God is another. Dismissing violence as cultural rather than criminal excuses the act. Until we call crimes against women (and humanity) by their true names, we'll not only fail to stop the violence against women that is endemic throughout the world, we will be endorsing it.

Circumstances also contribute to a tipping point. For example, women in Saudi Arabia had never attended the Olympic Games as athletes. They were not allowed to attend athletic events at home and were discouraged from playing competitive sports. During the buildup to the London Olympics in 2012, the absence of Saudi female athletes began to get a lot of attention. The pressure from probing media increased almost daily. The Olympic Games are a place to showcase national accomplishment; denying women the chance to participate became too big a stain for the Saudi kingdom to wear. It caved in, and with weeks to go before the opening ceremonies, two female athletes—one in judo, the other in the eight-hundred-meter track event—were added to the Saudi Olympic team. Other Gulf States, such as Qatar, followed suit. When those women walked into the Olympic Stadium in London, they made history. They became part of a growing collection of circumstances that are contributing to the tipping point for women.

It's not just "firsts"—first governor general, first cabinet minister, first chair of the board, first firefighter—that clear the way for women, it's a sea change in attitudes about the treatment of women. Stories about underage girls being forced to marry or become prostitutes are no longer dismissed as "the way those people live." They make headlines, go viral, wind up on YouTube. When a fifteen-year-old child bride named Sahar Gul was rescued in 2011 by Afghan police from a home that was a torture chamber—the girl said her mother-in-law had pulled out her fingernails with pliers—the news made headlines in the foreign press. Gul had been married off to a man twice her age, and soon after the nuptials, she was told she had to become a prostitute to bring money home to her new husband's family. When she refused, they beat her, pulled out her hair, burned her with cigarettes, cut off pieces of her flesh, and locked her in a windowless toilet. The neighbors called the authorities after hearing her crying and moaning day after day.

Even a short time ago, Gul's story would likely have been ignored, first by the police, as it would have been seen as a domestic issue and nobody's business, and then by the media, who would not have been alerted by the police or the neighbors. During the Taliban regime, the atrocities committed against women and girls in Afghanistan were shockingly brutal. One eighteen-year-old girl was in labor for forty days while the Taliban forbade medical help because she was a woman. Her family tried to help her with hot compresses that burned her abdomen and endless concoctions that made her sick. When Dr. Sima Samar at last was able to travel to the girl's home, she did a Caesarean section to save the girl's life and remove the fetus, which had been dead for most of the forty days. Afterward, Samar said to me, "Losing the baby wasn't the worst thing that happened to that girl. I had to do a hysterectomy because all the reproductive organs were infected. Now she'll be relegated to being someone's slave because she cannot bear children."

There was almost no media attention on the fate of Afghan women at the time, most assigning editors concluding that what was
happening to them was "someone else's culture, none of our business." For most news agencies, the women became a story only after the Americans toppled the Taliban after 9/11.

Although Sahar Gul's husband fled before the police arrived,
her in-laws were arrested and charged. And in a sign of the times
in Afghanistan, Noorjahan Akbar, of Young Women for Change,
named the Internet café that the organization opened on International Women's Day in 2012 after the girl, to honor her and keep
her story alive. Reporting the story is one thing. Naming a café
after her so that her story will never be forgotten is an example of
how women's issues have taken on a new status in places where it
seemed as if such change would never happen.

The international community has historically been cowed by
accusations that by protesting injustice and abuse they are interfering in someone else's culture. By suggesting that rape was an inevitable consequence of war, they normalized it. In the guise of a
message from God, oppression of women seemed acceptable. Diplomats and activists were silenced by thugs who'd hijacked their
culture and their own religion for political opportunism, and bowed
to the finger-wagging of self-appointed guardians of cultural and
religious codes. While endemic mistreatment still goes on in many
places—which country would tell a Saudi Arabian prince that his
oil was not wanted as long as his country lashed women for driving—at least women are winning the public relations war on oppression and subjugation.

Case in point: on March 31, 2009, the international community
did a major about-face that altered the course for women in Afghanistan, as well as for the men who oppress them. At a NATO
summit meeting on the war in Afghanistan in Strasbourg, France,
Hamid Karzai announced that he had signed the Shiite Personal
Status Law, which rolled back the gains women had made in Afghanistan since the Taliban were ousted. Among other draconian

measures, the law blesses marital rape, accepts child marriage, and forbids wives to leave their homes unless the right to go to work has been written into their marriage contract. It stripped women of custody of their children after divorce and of the ability to inherit property. Article 132 (3) stated, "The couple should not commit acts that create hatred and bitterness in their relationship. The wife is bound to preen for her husband, as and when he desires."

Shiite Muslims make up about 20 percent of the Afghan population; they are mostly Hazara, the most persecuted tribe in Afghanistan. But Shiite women have been vocal about the need for change. They are often first to register for literacy classes and take every opportunity to upgrade their skills. So the passing of such a law was a blow to their new emancipation. They, like most Afghans, had presumed that Karzai would let the issue float: he'd claim in public that the retrograde measures were being discussed, even taken seriously, but would never table such a law. In fact, behind the scenes Karzai was being pressured by the fundamentalists to sign the Shiite law. But here he was meeting in Strasbourg with the very people who had committed troops and funds to get his country back on its feet and announcing a return to the dark ages. The reaction was swift and excoriating. The *Guardian* newspaper reported that it was Canada's prime minister, Stephen Harper, who spoke first. "If you support that," he told Karzai, "we can't support you." Leaders from the international community lined up to condemn the Afghan president and to stand together on the line that Harper had drawn in the sand.

Why did Karzai choose such an inopportune moment to make his announcement? Given the history of the international community's response to women's issues, you'd be hard-pressed to accuse him of misjudging his audience. In the past, the United Nations in particular had turned a blind eye to equally ridiculous pronouncements and edicts. There was little other than lip service about improving the lives of women and girls to suggest that the men and women Karzai consulted, accepted bailouts from, and paraded around as his pals would stand in his way. But they did. And Karzai backed down, first saying that the version of the law released to the media was different from the one he had signed, then that he had signed the law without ever reading it.

Most people wondered how the president could have made such a blockhead decision in the first place. Afghans said it was all about the upcoming presidential election. Karzai's numbers were dropping, and there were two or three credible candidates who could maybe have beaten him. He'd crunched the numbers and then had done what power-hungry people do (or are forced to do when extremists and warlords are holding the key to power): he attempted to sell out women to win over the fundamentalist vote that would secure an electoral win. But for once, the tactic backfired.

The international community had, for the first time since the insurgency in Afghanistan began, refused to be bullied by the argument that says "this is our culture and is none of your business." Referring to the various international treaties, mostly under the auspices of the United Nations, that Afghanistan has signed— covenants and conventions that protect the rights of women and girls—progressives demanded that the Afghan government honor them. Pressure from inside the country to heed the Afghan constitution, which also protects the rights of women and girls, increased as well.

Karzai was caught off guard; when he'd given a sweeping amnesty to the war criminals in his country, for example, the international community and his own citizens had mostly succumbed to the old dodge "there's nothing I can do." Not this time. Women in Kabul marched in the street. Media reports showed men throwing rocks at them, but a ring of policewomen moved in to surround the marchers and keep the men back. The protesters demanded a meeting with Karzai when he got back from Europe. They got it. At the meeting, they demanded changes to the Shiite Personal Status Law. They didn't get all they asked for—the law is still a thorn in the side of anyone who seeks fairness and justice—but Karzai did amend it. For example, under the law, a girl was deemed mature and marriageable at her first menstrual period, which could be as young as nine or ten years old. The age of maturity for boys was set at fifteen. Amendments changed the girls' legal "marrying" age to sixteen. Karzai also agreed to change the law forbidding women to leave the home. They can now leave for work or school or medical treatment without having previously signed a marriage contract allowing such trips.

It wasn't the end of the rights debate, of course, but it did herald the fact that by banding together (as the women in Senegal did to end female genital mutilation and the women in sub-Saharan Africa did to turn the tide of HIV/AIDS), Afghan women could alter their own destiny.

Indicators of grassroots change in attitudes toward women's rights had been cropping up in unusual places throughout the first decade of the new century. Since 1999, the second brutal civil war had raged in the West African nation of Liberia. One corrupt dictator, the infamous Dr. Doe, had been replaced by another—the psychopath Charles Taylor. The usual complement of horrors had overtaken the country: mass raping of women; abducting children and turning them into child soldiers; a campaign of torture, dismemberment, and killing that paralyzed the people with fear.

In 2002, when it seemed as if the civil war would never end—and Liberian women figured they'd sacrificed their entire lives to the carnage and bloodletting of conflict, to the fear of being raped in the ongoing violence—a young woman named Leymah Gbowee, who had become involved with two nascent regional peace movements, had a dream in which she saw women of both the country's major religions, Christianity and Islam, coming together as an unstoppable force with a plan for peace. Soon after, she gathered

Christian women together to start a conversation about how they might contribute to moving the peace talks forward. Then a Muslim woman arrived at the meeting, asking how she could become involved. The two religious groups had known plenty of discord, so the first step was to settle their own differences. They talked through each issue and discovered that misinformation and suspicion were largely responsible for keeping them apart. Solidarity followed.

Calling themselves the Women of Liberia Mass Action for Peace, and armed with nothing more than the courage of their convictions, the women, under Gbowee's leadership, made signs, donned white T-shirts, and went to the fish market every day for months in 2003 because they knew that Charles Taylor, the president, drove by every morning in his motorcade. Their signs told him that he had to negotiate a peace and stop the violence. The protests were ignored.

What happened next astounded everyone, including the women. They decided to take their placards to the presidential mansion, where they chanted their demands for peace; their bold stand became the talk of the country. And it worked. Taylor was persuaded to attend the peace talks with the rebel leaders being held in Ghana, and the women followed him there just in case he changed his mind.

When the peace talks in Ghana broke down, the women staged an unforgettable scene. Linking arms, they circled the building where the negotiators were deadlocked and announced that they were taking them hostage on behalf of the women of Liberia. They vowed that they would not budge until a peace accord was signed. When commissionaires were sent to physically remove them, the women stood their ground and threatened to shed their clothes if the guards tried to send them away. It was a curse of nakedness on all those men, and the consequences of such a curse are formidable in Africa: men who are exposed to that curse are considered to be dead. No one will cook for such a man, or marry him, or do any kind of business with him. The security men left the women alone.

The next day, with the peace accord still elusive, the protesters announced a sex strike. No woman would allow her husband to have sex with her until the peace agreement was signed. They encouraged all the women of Liberia to join the protest, and a massive number did—sending messages via cell phones and runners to let their sisters in Ghana know that the sex strike was taking immediate effect.

A mediator came out at that point to negotiate with the demonstrators, who agreed to give the men two weeks to get the talks to the finish line. At the top of their list of demands was that the men at the table stop talking about the political appointments and rewards and access to the country's resources that they anticipated in the aftermath of the agreement and start talking about how to implement a lasting peace. To the astonishment of many, exactly two weeks later the peace treaty was signed, and Charles Taylor went into exile. UN troops were deployed to maintain the peace, and the women went home.

An army of women had confronted Liberia's ruthless president and rebel warlords and won. But the women didn't stop there. They went to work on the election campaign that brought Ellen Johnson Sirleaf to power as the first woman to head the Liberian state. Leymah Gbowee helped lead an army of women that ended the war in her nation and in the process emerged as an international leader who changed history. In a classic case of nonviolent action, she and the women of Liberia reversed the power equation. Gbowee would eventually win the Nobel Peace Prize in 2011 for her efforts, but the event that led to that international honor might have been missed except that the American filmmaker Abigail Disney heard about the commotion and turned it into a widely released and praised documentary called *Pray the Devil Back to Hell*. When I asked Disney where she got the title for the film, she explained: "Leymah said at one point in our discussions that Charles Taylor was such a fake religious guy he could pray the Devil out of hell. My director said these women were praying him back."

The film has been seen in thirty-two countries on all seven continents (including Antarctica, on a docked cruise ship). The story it tells has inspired the women's movements in Bosnia, Georgia, and Cambodia. It's influenced how the UN understands women who are trying to be heard at peace negotiating tables. And it's having an impact on the vital importance of women's voices being taken seriously in ending conflict.

Disney says, "Women mobilizing to stop war is our last best hope." Referring to the ever-increasing number of civil wars going on in the world today, she stresses, "We have been moving closer to perpetual war every day. One thing we've never tried, never given a chance to, is women's leadership. Women don't have magic in their chromosomes. But women do the work of peace. We do the living and carry out the dead and care for the sick and educate the children. Women are much more reluctant to go to war." The lesson of the film, she feels, is that it lets people know that you really can make a difference. "If you choose to lean into the answers, instead of backing away from the fray, you can do anything."

Liberia is certainly not trouble-free. Ellen Johnson Sirleaf won a second term as president, by a hair. The country wobbles on the stability scale. Rape, although much reduced, is still a problem. But the women know they made a difference, and, says Disney, "They are living proof that moral courage and nonviolent resistance can succeed, even where the best efforts of traditional diplomacy have failed."

One victory doesn't secure emancipation. Vigilance is the lot of women if they want to maintain equality with men. Look at Israel, for example. Ultra Orthodox (or Haredi, those who "tremble before God") men are actually making women sit in the back of the bus and chastising women who aren't dressed modestly in public. This kind of behavior started in 2010 on buses that run through Haredi neighborhoods, but three years later it has escalated to neighborhoods all over Jerusalem, and every woman is fair game, not just women in the Haredi community. The Haredim have been accused by non-Orthodox Jews of blacking out women's faces on billboards, barring women from speaking at the podium at conferences, even spitting on an eight-year-old girl because they deemed her to be immodestly dressed.

In a case that became the talk of Israel, a woman pediatrician, Channa Maayan, was being awarded a prize from the ministry of health for a book she wrote about hereditary diseases common to Jews. She attended the event with her husband, and they were told that they would have to sit apart, as women and men could not sit together. Then the official in charge said she was to stay seated and send a man to the stage to collect her prize. This in a country that boasts women pilots in the air force, women in parliament and even as chief of the Supreme Court, a country that once had the irrepressible Golda Meir as prime minister.

Another sign of the times for women: in May 2011, three women—Jody Williams from the United States, Shirin Ebadi from Iran, and Mairead Maguire from Ireland, all of them Nobel Peace laureates—came together to collectively tackle one of the most intransigent problems that women face: sexual violence in zones of conflict and post conflict. These laureates are part of a new force in the world called the Nobel Women's Initiative, which was established in 2006 by Williams, Ebadi, and Maguire, along with the late Wangari Maathai (Kenya), Rigoberta Menchú Tum (Guatemala), and Betty Williams (Ireland). In 2012, they were joined by the laureates Leymah Gbowee (Liberia) and Tawakkol Karman (Yeman) and honorary member Aung San Suu Kyi (Burma).

The three who initiated the May meeting were looking for strategies to end the scourge of rape and gender violence in conflict, which is one of the ugliest stories in the world today. Monsters are gang-raping women as a strategy of war in Congo, Darfur, and Zimbabwe, among other places, and getting away with it. This despite the attention of a high-powered collection of notables such as

Stephen Lewis, Hillary Clinton, Ellen Johnson Sirleaf, and the play-wright and activist Eve Ensler; despite the unprecedented step taken by the UN Security Council on June 19, 2008, when it declared rape a strategy of war and a security issue. Rape has horrendous personal consequences for women and their families, but it also undermines whole economies. For example, food production in Congo dropped by 70 percent starting in 2004 because traditionally the women are the planters of seed and the tenders and harvesters of produce, and they have been sexually assaulted so brutally and so often that they are too wounded to go to the fields—and when they've healed enough to work again, they often won't because they are too afraid of be-ing assaulted again. The World Food Programme has to supply food from an already strained international aid budget. What's more, the consequences of sexual depravity affect everyone: when the caregivers are unable to cope, the children are left to their own devices, and their health and nutrition suffer. The level of violence that the victims endure is almost unspeakable—they have been pa-raded naked in the town square, assaulted vaginally with a broken beer bottle, mutilated with a machete, gang-raped by soldiers eight and ten times a day. Some of the victims are newborns, others eighty years old.

The Nobel women invited 130 activists from all over the world to meet in Montebello, Quebec, to find a way to stop this increas-ingly horrific violence against women. They had a wealth of expe-rience in lobbying, protesting, and building public awareness: Jody Williams received the Nobel Prize for her work in banning land mines; Mairead Maguire was one of two women (the other was Betty Williams) honored for establishing peace in Ireland; and Shi-rin Ebadi is the Iranian woman who dares to continually speak out for the women of that country. The conference, held in an old log building surrounded by gently rolling hills, had a we-can-do-anything buzz from the moment the delegates arrived. Rose Mapendo had come from the Democratic Republic of the Congo, which had recently been named the second most dangerous place on earth for women (Afghanistan is in first place). A woman or girl is raped approximately every forty-eight seconds in Congo. Mapendo stood up to reply to a comment made from the podium and then, as though the floodgates had opened, she began to tell her terrible story. She'd been attacked by one of the roving militias in her country; she had witnessed the murder of her husband and the rape of her daughters and finally had been gang-raped herself. It was apparent that she had not planned to relate her experience, but the memories she'd been harboring had overpowered her reserve. She looked so alone and vulnerable when she began talking, wringing her hands, her voice rising and falling as she described some details that brought back the terror and others that reduced her to tears. Excruciating pauses punctuated her account.

"I'm a survivor of genocide. It's enough goodness for me to sit with women who make a commitment to make a difference." She stopped talking for a moment, trying to gain control of her voice as she choked on tears. Every one of us was on the edge of her seat, trying to send vibes of support to her. She began again. "It is hard to speak, but I choose to do this. Nobody can change my past. We learn from the past and from that we can change the present and future.

"Women can stand up for other women. I believe when women come together, something happens because we heard the testimony. Some people don't believe the rape or sexual violence, don't believe it is true—but it is true. I spent sixteen months in the death camps, under the gun twenty-four hours, seven days a week. At the beginning I was with my husband and children. They tortured the men, killed all of them, left the women. They said they couldn't waste bullets on women. We talk about rape—"

She paused again. One woman stood up and slipped an arm around her, and Rose continued. "We had no help. I thank the people who take action. The first step is raise awareness. Tell people this is true. Encourage the victim to speak out. Without our voice, nobody knows what is true exactly. That they raped women in front of their children. And take the life of husband. That they take their children and raped them in front of the mothers. How can you do that horrible thing to someone?

"My happy today is the women. Unite is power. To push the elephant together—nobody can do it herself. Empower those women; empower them to stand up. Culture makes women feel they are in shame. I am a victim. I believe I can help another victim. Because nobody knows what she's been through. Nobody can change outside, can change what's inside. It's not your fault to be raped. Not your choice. You can speak out, let it go—don't keep it inside.

"We are powerful. We can come together [and] make a difference today."

Her story, and the courage it took to tell it, brought the roomful of women to their feet in thunderous supportive applause. She stood for several minutes, perplexed by the outpouring of affection and sympathy and pride, not knowing what to say. Her call for women to come together to create a force of change, when she herself was so emotionally wounded, galvanized the participants to absolute solidarity.

Several more women shared their stories then—none of them seeking pity, all of them putting a face on an atrocity, a fact with an accusation. Binalakshmi Nepram from India was one. She leaned into the microphone and tried to make eye contact with every woman in the room as she described the little-known facts of wretched brutality in the northeastern Indian state of Manipur, where ethnic conflict is raging and women are being targeted by the Indian military. It's one of those places the government describes as "disturbed"—a code word, says Nepram, for merciless crackdown. But the military and the police sent to Manipur aren't into finding solutions, she said, but into punishing the people who live there.

She shared a story from July 2004. A young Manipuri woman was arrested in the middle of the night at gunpoint by Indian soldiers. The next morning her body was found with bullet holes in her genitals, the ultimate form of sexual violence. In an amazing act of defiance and nonviolent protest, a dozen women stripped in front of the headquarters of the Assam Rifles, challenging the armed forces to rape them as well.

Nepram told us, "Women in Manipur have joined together for community security and support. They patrol the streets with bamboo torches at night and physically tussle with the armed Indian soldiers to rescue women being held in their trucks."

Intervention is only possible when people such as Rose Mapendo and Binalakshmi Nepram decide to speak up. There were many moments of despair during the conference but also hard determination to work for change. When asked for plans, women eagerly came forward: provide cell phones so the women can get help quickly; use Twitter to spread the word and get real-time updates; issue a call to action; form an ad hoc committee; establish reachable goals.

The statistics reported and the stories told led the participants to form the International Campaign to Stop Rape & Gender Violence in Conflict, joining organizations and individuals already working on this issue to make a coordinated effort for change. On the final day, the three Nobel laureates issued a statement: "Together we will demand bold political leadership to prevent rape in conflict, to protect civilians and rape survivors, and call for justice for all—including effective prosecution of those responsible."

It's shocking to hear reports from states like Manipur, reeling in violence in a country that's said to be the fastest-growing democracy in the world. Congo is also a place of extraordinary violence but one that the international community tends to ignore. I'd traveled to North and South Kivu provinces in December 2009 to write about how Congolese women were managing. Aid workers had said they were hiding in the forest because the roving militias had burned their villages, chased off their men, raped them, and stolen their livestock.

Getting there was a story in itself. The east side of the country is so dangerous that all the humanitarian agencies except Médecins Sans Frontières (MSF) had left when I was there. But even MSF, known for its fearlessness, was taking exceptional precautions to keep its staff safe. For example, in getting from point A to point B, they used what's called a "kiss" maneuver. To get from Goma, the capital of North Kiro province, to Kitchanga, where I wanted to go, they sent a vehicle from both directions to meet at the middle and transfer the goods, the personnel, or, in this case, the journalist. Each truck also carried a person (known to the team as "the donkey") who stayed on a walkie-talkie, reporting their location every few minutes. As we drove on the rutted, spine-jarring road to Kitchanga, one of the MSF staff told me about the children who'd been sexually assaulted, most of them so traumatized that they were barely coherent.

The next day I met one of them, ten-year-old Siffy (not her real name). Her enormous round eyes were soul-piercing as she told me about the men who raped her and left her for dead in the forest. Her story came in fragments. Her mother, Pascasie, had searched frantically for two days after Siffy went missing, but it's hard to find a lone child in the African bush. At last Pascasie ran into a hunter who said he'd seen the girl's body and would lead her there. Siffy was lying on her back, as still as the air, her arms spread, her skin covered with mosquito bites. Then her mother saw her take an almost imperceptible breath. Siffy wasn't dead.

The merciless attack had left the girl perilously traumatized, but she lived to be an eyewitness to the worst atrocity known to women in a country convulsing with lawlessness. And by all accounts, it's the women themselves who are poised to yank this pitiless place out of its fifteen-year-old date with the Devil.

Siffy's conversation with me shifted between a deluge of facts and childlike requests to play. "The monsters are outside," she told me, her eyes still showing fear. "They want to kill us. They hurt me. I want to go home. But we can't go there now." She's not even a teenager yet, this child of Congo, a place where girls as young as she is know the difference between gang rape (one woman raped by many men), mass rape (all the women in the village raped), and re-rape (women raped again and again). "The monsters tortured my mother," Siffy said. "They took our food. I'm afraid of the monsters. They are still at my home in Kalembe." Then she switched the subject with such telling facility that I knew she could only recount pieces of it at a time lest her young mind take flight. A dazzling smile washed away the pain that had clouded her face while she spoke of the monsters, and she pulled me into play—she loved doing high-fives.

The war in Congo has claimed 5.4 million lives since it began in 1997. The Red Cross says forty-five thousand more die every month. The health system has collapsed. The economy is devastated. There isn't even an intact road to get from one side of the country to the other, and the DRC is bigger than Europe. June 30, 2010, marked its fiftieth anniversary of independence from Belgium, and for most of those years it's been convulsed by multiple wars, human rights abuses, and appalling suffering.

Congo is the country that Joseph Conrad described in *Heart of Darkness*. It's a place with lush but mountainous terrain and topsoil so fertile that you can kick a seed into the ground and have a plant by week's end. The rush of growth is the botanical equivalent of insanity: banana fronds big enough to shelter a grown man; floral excesses of orchids, lobelias, and lilies splashing the landscape in saucy orange; crimson and delicate pink while white datura lilies lifting off the lush green vegetation reaching for the sun. The earth is so mineral rich that the hillsides literally sparkle as though studded with broken glass. Endangered mountain gorillas live in Virunga National Park. Thatch-roofed huts are beginning to give way to corrugated steel roofs, but women and girls still carry goods on their heads and gather to wash their clothes in the streams that babble through the villages. The countryside is enchanting. But it is also where the pickaxe of the mining industry has unearthed a scenario so horrible that it suggests the loss of stability has led to madness.

Although the UN says the war is on the wane, there's nothing to celebrate yet. North and South Kivu have the richest mineral deposits in the world; seven different militias supposedly protect them, armed to the teeth, often drunk and guilty of atrocities against women and girls. The rapes and ongoing war are usually ascribed to ethnic revenge, the fault of the Interahamwe paramilitaries from Rwanda, who flooded into Congo seeking escape from justice after the genocide; or it's Ugandan and Rwandan militias intent on grabbing the country's mineral wealth while the West looks on with complicity; or it's the totally dysfunctional government of DRC's president, Joseph Kabila, and his equally guilty military. In every scenario, gold, diamonds, coltan (used in cell phones and electronic tablets), and cassiterite (tin ore) are presented as the raison d'être for the militias and, as a result, the cause of the carnage for women. Rape is said to be retribution, an initiation ritual, a torture, a morale booster for troops, a means to humiliate and terrorize the population, a strategy for ethnic cleansing, a weapon of biological warfare for the spreading of HIV.

But who would rape a newborn baby to death for any of these reasons? Who would gang-rape a woman while forcing her terrified children to watch? Why on earth would a pair of soldiers believe that holding a woman down and slicing off her breasts with a machete would help protect mineral deposits? The wretched truth is this: in the absence of civility during the past dozen years of war, the men with the guns have descended into savagery. They bury people alive; draw and quarter their living, breathing captives; burn the villages they come across and rape and mutilate the women and girls.

And yet for the most part, the world is silent. Indeed, mention 5 million dead and hundreds of thousands of gang-raped women and children, and most people will say they had no idea.

Congolese women realize that their path out of this abyss is empowerment. But first they need to heal. Médecins Sans Frontières is on the front line of this war on women and has brought in therapists to deal with a population traumatized and reeling. The psychiatric therapy they bring is as valuable as the battlefield surgery they're better known for. Ana Cristina Henriques is one of the MSF mental health officers in Congo. She stays in Kitchanga, a village that's deep in the bush about a four-hour drive from Goma, where she serves women who have escaped their burning villages and hidden in the nearby woods. Almost every one of them has been raped at least once.

Henriques met Siffy last June. "She was severely traumatized. The only piece of her own identity she could recall was her age—the number ten. If I asked how many pencils were on the table, or how many people were in the room, or how many candies she would like, the reply was always the same—*icumi*, the Kenyan Rwandan word for 'ten.' After three and a half weeks of sixty-minute sessions per day, she finally said her name."

Henriques had heard Siffy's story from her mother, Pascasie. It was much like every other story: the militia arrives in a village, they tell the men and boys to leave and shoot those who don't, then they set fire to the thatch-roofed huts, rape the women and girls, steal the livestock, and move on. But in this case, Pascasie had received warning that they were coming and ran to the hut she kept in the forest as a refuge, bringing Siffy and her three-year-old grandson with her. The militia discovered their hideout. They told Pascasie they knew she had a pig at home and instructed her to go with two of the soldiers to get it, and to take her grandson with her. They kept Siffy and promised they wouldn't harm her if her mother gave them her pig. Once they were back at the village, the soldiers whacked Pascasie across the back with a machete and told her to lie down. With her terrified grandson watching, first one then the other raped her. "When I got back to the hut in the woods, my daughter was gone. It was after I'd found her and carried her back to the shelter, washed her, and fed her, that I realized she was so traumatized she couldn't speak. Six days later, we were strong enough to walk to another village. She started to have seizures and panicked whenever she saw men. When I heard about the therapist at MSF, I brought her here to Kitchanga."

That's where I met her—at the MSF therapy hut. Henriques handed Siffy a doll. She kept washing it over and over again, telling the therapist that the doll was dirty, that the monsters had hurt the doll. She was sweetly vulnerable and quick to smile, but she suffered from panic attacks and often thought there was someone chasing her. She drooled almost continuously, but when her mother reminded her to hold her saliva, she was able to, for a while. She held her right arm tucked into her side like a bird's broken wing, but if you played high-five with her and suddenly switched from the left hand to the right, she poked that hand forward—not far, but the delighted look on her face made me think this blameless child might get her life back after all.

After the session, we walked to the hut where she lives with her mother in the woods outside Kitchanga and huddled on the soft earthen floor inside. Siffy had something she wanted to say, and she played with the buttons on her shirt while slowly getting to the point of a story that seemed to weigh like a stone on her shoulders. "There was shooting, a lot of shooting," she said. "They hurt me," she said again, as if to reassure herself that someone was listening. "The monsters have guns. They wear uniforms. They are soldiers. There was too much noise." She stopped talking then. We exchanged another round of high-fives, and she gave me a smile so sweet that it was contagious.

Then it disappeared and Siffy leaned forward and said, "I'm still afraid of the monsters. They're still in Kalembe. Someone needs to make them go away."

One woman who came to Henriques's clinic had witnessed her seven children and her husband being shot by the militia. After that, each of the men raped her in turn and she hoped she would die. When she didn't, she asked her neighbors to kill her so she could be buried with her family. Another woman was rounded up with the rest of her village while soldiers set fire to their huts. Terrified, the villagers watched flames soar into the smoky sky as the huts burned to the ground. Then the soldiers opened fire. She survived simply because she was at the back of the pack and fell to the ground with the blood of her children and extended family running over her. She lay still until the brutes swaggered out of the village.

On a cloudy morning outside a cabin on the edge of the woods where they live, thirty-five women gathered in a circle with Henriques. They talked about their dreams of escape and the ghastly nightmares in which they relive the atrocities. They described the life of a typical Congolese woman. She does all the heavy lifting: she plants the crop, straps a tumpline to her forehead to carry backbreaking loads of charcoal and wood to sell in the city, hauls the water, and fetches firewood for her family. Yet here in the circle, the women, who were between the ages of twenty-two and seventy-five, told me, "We're not equal to the men because we don't wear the pants." They spoke as one when they said, "We're seen as worthless."

But they also wanted to talk about how to change their condition. "No one says, 'I'm sorry.' No one apologizes. Husbands rape us, the military rape us, anyone can rape us. When men become soldiers here, they turn into animals. They want to kill us; it's how men think." When I asked the men hanging around in the nearby village why this happens, they offered appalling excuses: "Our commanders expect this of us; our women are away in Rwanda; if we don't rape the women, the other men will think we aren't real men."

As the session drew to a close, one woman began to sing, her voice soaring into the treetops. Another woman joined her, then another. The Swahili words of the song meant "Thank you for bringing us together." Soon the entire circle was singing. On the far side of the circle, a woman stood up to dance, then pulled me to my feet to join her. In a moment we were thirty-seven women dancing, singing, rejoicing in one another's company—their experiences of brutality laid to rest for the moment.

With MSF, I drove farther into the province to Nyanzale, where there'd been a sudden increase in mass rape. At the MSF clinic at the top of the hill overlooking the village, a psychologist named Ange Mpala was trying to work miracles with survivors who were anxious, discouraged, and exhausted. She said, "There's physical pain in the back and the stomach when you've been raped. The victims feel dirty and wounded deep inside. They all need treatment within seventy-two hours to avoid pregnancy and sexually transmitted diseases." But shame kept many away—that and the fear of being found out and rejected by their families.

The worst cases that Ange Mpala sees are the women and girls with fistulas. The result of rape so violent that the wall between the anus or the bladder and the vagina is torn, a fistula allows urine and feces to leak into the vagina; such extensive damage to her body also creates a terrible odor that ostracizes the woman from others. Mpala sends those patients to Goma for surgery.

"Together we need to denounce this," she said. "Even if a woman doesn't know who raped her, all the women need to stand up and say, 'In this place there was a rape.' They need to break the silence." Posters declaring "Silence Is Violence" paper the walls of the MSF clinics in Congo. Mpala is one of hundreds of women who have recently called for change: demanding that the UN fulfill its duty to protect by sending in more troops, calling on women everywhere to support the courageous people here seeking change and attempting to persuade Congolese women that stopping violence is a fight they can win.

Such atrocities tend to paralyze the change-makers. No sooner has a law been enacted that makes rape a war crime, and the UN Security Council finally acknowledged that rape is being used as a strategy of war, than it's necessary to immediately confront the fact that some depraved humans will bring misogyny to dreadful new levels, no matter the worldwide condemnation they face.

A cautionary tale was told at the Nobel women's conference about the speed at which the gains women make can be lost. In 1996, a peace agreement brought Guatemala's thirty-six-year civil war to a close. The conflict had caused thousands of civilian deaths, over ninety thousand unsolved disappearances, and more than a hundred thousand cases of sexual violence. After the peace accord was signed, women had become more aware of their rights and some political space had opened for them, says Luz Méndez, vice president of the executive board of the National Union of Guatemalan Women. "Inside the women's movement, we say the peace accords were a marking line. We had more opportunity to speak out, get organized to fight for our rights." But after the war was over, organized crime and narco-traffickers soon moved in. She says, "Now the bandits attack women just because they are women."

The violence that the drug traffickers imported with them altered the landscape outside the home, and the old violence against wives and daughters inside the home resurfaced as well. "Women dare not walk on the street today," Méndez says. "But, worse, the assaults against women have spread like a virus to their own homes." Although the violence at home is affecting all classes of society, the narco-violence is targeting mainly the lower economic classes on the street—the very women who have to venture outside to get to work. Méndez describes an all-too-common occurrence: a bus is hijacked and driven to a dark place, where all the women are taken out and raped. "Every day we hear one of our colleagues has had a problem concerning violence on the street or in the bus. Violence is impacting our lives very much. We changed the legislation; we have pretty good laws protecting our rights. We managed to create institutions. But this social problem of violence against women hinders our possibility to move and hinders our rights as citizens."

Eighty percent of the drug-trafficking from south to north goes through Guatemala. Drug money has corrupted state institutions and imperiled the lives of 15 million people. Security and judicial institutions that have been historically weak are worse now that the drug barons have infiltrated them. Gang members cruise around the towns and cities threatening government officials, attacking and terrifying women. But in Guatemala it's not law enforcement or government institutions seeking ways to keep women safe and defeat the silence and secrecy that causes rape survivors to blame themselves, it's the grassroots women's organizations themselves. Women have learned to be patient, to wear governments down with never-ending petitions, to bowl naysayers over with ironclad data. Their tenacity has led to changes one might never have expected, like the announcement in Pakistan in January 2012 that the country's senate had approved two bills that would better protect women and girls. The bills created harsher punishments for acid attacks on women (more than eighty-five hundred reported in one year alone, according to the Aurat Foundation, a local organization committed to women's empowerment and citizen participation in governance) and criminalized the tribal law called Bad, the trading of young girls to settle tribal disputes. The bills also reversed the inheritance laws that prevented women from inheriting property. It was a good step forward for a country that the activist Farida Shaheed worries is at risk from fundamentalists. Shaheed knows that extremists are close to the government—sometimes part of it. Like women in Guatemala and elsewhere, women in Pakistan need to stay vigilant to protect their gains.

Gender justice is being examined in developed countries as well. Canada, the United States, Scandinavia, Europe, and Australia all made significant strides in equality rights for women in the second half of the twentieth century. But along the way, the rights of Aboriginal women were ignored, just as Aboriginal people themselves were left out of equality equations in nation-building. When Amnesty International accused Canada of overlooking the possible serial killing of Aboriginal women in two reports, one written in 2003 and the next in 2009, they reminded Canadians that violence against Aboriginal women is a long-held and nasty secret. Their plight was the theme of George Ryga's brilliant play, *The Ecstasy of Rita Joe,* first performed at the Vancouver Playhouse in 1967. Later adapted as a ballet and translated into French, the play focused on violence perpetrated against the young Rita Joe at the hands of an entitled white society. When she was killed, nobody paid attention— which rang all too true in Canada.

So in 2003, when Amnesty International released its first report, *Stolen Sisters,* no one was really surprised that it addressed the fact that too many Aboriginal women were missing in western Canada and not enough attention was being paid by the Canadian government. The report opened with the story of a woman whose name had become a symbol of struggle and the miscarriage of justice for the country's Aboriginal women.

Helen Betty Osborne was a nineteen-year-old Cree student from northern Manitoba who dreamed of becoming a teacher. On November 13, 1971, she was abducted by four white men in the town of The Pas and then sexually assaulted and brutally murdered. A provincial inquiry subsequently concluded that Canadian authorities had failed Helen Betty Osborne. The inquiry criticized the sloppy and racially biased police investigation that took more than fifteen years to bring one of the four men to justice. Most disturbingly, the inquiry concluded that police had long been aware of white men sexually preying on Indigenous women and girls in The Pas but "did not feel that the practice necessitated any particular vigilance."

The sixty-seven-page report ended with a pointed demand that the government do something about it.

Canadian officials have a clear and inescapable obligation to ensure the safety of Indigenous women, to bring those responsible for attacks against them to justice, and to address the deeper problems of marginalization, dispossession, and impoverishment that have placed so many Indigenous women in harm's way.

Amnesty International included a petition with the report and encouraged all Canadians to sign it on behalf of the Stolen Sisters. It reads:

> Young Aboriginal women in Canada are at least five times more likely than other women in Canada to die as a result of violence. Not enough is being done to ensure that these crimes are adequately investigated, or to address the discrimination and impoverishment that put so many Aboriginal women in harm's way. We, the undersigned, urge the Government of Canada to work with Aboriginal women and Aboriginal peoples' organizations to develop a national plan of action to stop violence against Indigenous women. Such a plan of action must:
>
> - Recognize the high levels of violence faced by Aboriginal women because they are Aboriginal women.
> - Ensure effective, unbiased police response through appropriate training, resources and coordination.
> - Improve public awareness and accountability through the consistent collection and publication of comprehensive national statistics on violent crime against Aboriginal women.
> - Reduce the risk to Aboriginal women by closing the economic and social gap between Aboriginal and non-Aboriginal people in Canada.

The petition got plenty of signatures. But successive governments failed to take action, instead obfuscating, delaying, and basically ignoring the issue. For instance, when the House of Commons Standing Committee on the Status of Women released its final report on violence against Aboriginal women in December 2011, the Harper government completely ignored the report, as well as the input of the Aboriginal women who had appeared before the committee.

The Native Women's Association of Canada, along with the Canadian Feminist Alliance for International Action, took their complaint to the UN. And the UN, in keeping with the resolutions it has written (and rarely acted on) on violence against women, decided in December 2011 to send a team to conduct an inquiry into the murders and disappearances of hundreds of Aboriginal women and girls in Canada, based on violations of the Convention for the Elimination of Discrimination against Women. (Like most countries, Canada is a signatory to CEDAW and also to the Optional Protocol, which outlines a process for initiating an inquiry when the CEDAW Committee receives "reliable information indicating grave or systemic violations.")

Relying on the Amnesty International reports, the CEDAW committee noted that in 2008 the Canadian government had failed to live up to its obligations, and had failed again in 2010, stating, "The Committee considers that its recommendation [regarding missing and murdered Aboriginal women and girls] has not been implemented and it requests the Canadian authorities to urgently provide further information on measures undertaken to address such concerns." No information was forthcoming. So CEDAW called for its own investigation into a situation that Canada had refused to acknowledge.

When twenty-three independent experts from around the world came to Canada, a country that prides itself on being a defender of human rights, to investigate a national tragedy that the federal government had ignored, it was strong medicine for "the true north." Mary Eberts, who acts as legal counsel for the Native Women's Association of Canada says, "This is the first time CEDAW has done an investigation in a developed country. It's a big black eye for Canada."

The inquiry wasn't a criminal investigation; it was more about asking questions and writing a report for the UN. Although their findings have not been made public, it is already known that Aboriginal women in Canada experience rates of violence three and a half times higher than non-Aboriginal women, and young Aboriginal women are five times more likely to die by violence. Aboriginal women in Australia, New Zealand, and the United States and much of Central America also suffer from increased violence as well as poorer health and more poverty.

Eberts has no hope for government action even when the UN report does come out because "officials are woefully bad at doing due diligence. Nothing happens because of indifference." But that doesn't mean the report won't have an effect, she says. "Women have to stop relying on governments to make change. Politicians love to talk about change; they talk for years about water quality, about Aboriginals, about the environment. But the resistance to change is endemic. CEDAW doesn't have the clout to make Canada do anything. But this report will build awareness with Canadians."

Cindy Blackstock, the executive director of the First Nations Child and Family Caring Society of Canada, is preparing for action. "Within the hierarchy of First Nations, women have one of the most sacred roles—we are the life givers. With every generation there comes a chance to make the world anew. We have the possibility as women to truly shape the future, the future of humanity."

During the past decade, women's rights have shifted from the margins to the center of discourse in international law after a collection of conferences provided the tools for change: the United Nations Decade for Women, the Vienna Declaration on violence against women, and the fourth World Conference on Women, held in Beijing. The sea change today is that women are ready to talk, and everyone knows that if you can talk about it, you can change it.

It takes men and women together to make a healthier, safer, and more prosperous future. From Molly Melching, the woman who invited the religious leaders to help her group lead the way to ending female genital mutilation in Senegal, to Hangama Anwari, the human rights commissioner who enlisted the mullahs in Afghanistan to reform family law, to Cindy Blackstock, the Canadian advocate for Aboriginal women, to the economists and policy-makers who are calling for the recognition of women's beneficial impact on wealth making and well-being: all these people are seeking changes that are not only good for women but for men too. They are calling violence what it is. They are tackling inequality where it is. They are finding the courage to stand up to brutality and say, "Never again."

They are understanding that the ascent of women is good for everyone.

7

The Final Frontier

Women themselves can be the agent of their own change.
—WINNIE KAMAU, LAW PROFESSOR,
UNIVERSITY OF NAIROBI, KENYA

In 1969, twelve women met at a workshop in Boston, Massachusetts, whose topic was "women and their bodies." What eventually came out of that get-together was groundbreaking. The women asked each other such questions as, how come doctors are the arbiters of a woman's body? Why aren't women making their own decisions about their health? Where is the knowledge women need?

The sixties had been a heady decade for Western women, as one group of equality seekers after another challenged the status quo in everything from health, to education, to marriage, to careers. The Boston dozen decided to research and gather the information women needed about their own bodies and ended up coming together in a book collective to publish *Our Bodies, Ourselves,* which soon became not only a blockbuster best seller but a requisite for women, who had long pondered the mysteries of menstruation and acne, pregnancy and birthing, birth control and menopause, yet had accepted that a doctor's opinion and instruction was all they needed. The new generation digging into *Our Bodies, Ourselves* insisted that they'd make their own decisions.

Although much has changed, the final frontier for women is still having control over our own bodies, whether in zones of conflict, in rural villages, on university campuses, or in kitchens. In 2009, Farida Shaheed, the UN expert on culture, did a multicountry research project, "Women's Empowerment in Muslim Contexts: Gender, Poverty and Democratisation from the Inside Out," exploring these truths: "It is clear that women can be empowered in the marketplace but not in the bedroom. You can have this right but not that right. You're allowed to go out to work but not allowed to socialize." Like most researchers in this area today, she feels that the problem won't be solved until men get involved. "This is holistic because you can't change society by changing only half of it."

Comments such as "I only tapped her—you can't call that hitting" and "She's my wife—I have every right to have sex with her whenever I want" are still common responses from men who think they own women's bodies. For women, that lack of control has at times only held us back but at other times has oppressed and brutalized us. In the past five decades, laws have changed, attitudes have altered, misogyny has been exposed. But rape has persisted as a tool of war, a weapon to oppress women, and a power play by men.

Joanna Kerr, who left her job as the director of ActionAid in Johannesburg, South Africa, to become the executive director of Green Place Canada, says that despite the international conventions countries have signed, "It's really local power brokers . . . whether it's fathers, whether it's priests, whether it's moms, whether it's grandmothers . . . who want to determine how girls and women dress, when they will marry, have children, how they will space their children. Having control over our own bodies is the final frontier for us."

The publication of *Our Bodies, Ourselves* launched the conversation in North America in the seventies, but in much of the world there's been a taboo against discussing related topics—marriage, sex, and the right to self-determination when it comes to reproduction. Some of the most merciless acts of violence have been committed against women who simply had no recourse when someone else decided whom they would marry and when the marriage would take place. Abuse is also a result of a presumption of ownership once a woman is betrothed. And there is a long-accepted view that the violence used against women in the home is a private matter. But now women in Asia, Africa, the Middle East, and elsewhere are engaged in a conversation they dared not have before. They're challenging laws and cultural norms and religious doctrine in order to strip away the misogyny and take control of their bodies.

It is savvy young girls and feisty women who are setting an example in places that still follow ancient traditions; their courage and tenacity are leading to changes most people thought impossible.

Having the right to choose your own husband and the age at which you will get married is an important piece of the final frontier for women and girls. But being regarded as the equal of your husband after you are married—in particular, having the right to refuse to have sex with your husband—is another.

This was the frontier I was researching when I traveled to Kenya in 2010 to write a story about the first project of the Equality Effect. I started this book by describing their unprecedented initiative to help 160 girls in Kenya sue the government for failing to protect them from being raped. The girls scored a precedent-setting victory in court. But before it began, the Equality Effect had launched its first groundbreaking program in Africa, called Three to Be Free.

In the past three decades, while human rights have become the new standard in much of the world, even in Afghanistan, the rights of women in many African countries haven't budged. African women are treated as chattel and are vulnerable to ghastly forms of violence. Since women have no right to say no to sex, they have become the face of HIV/AIDS. Family violence hasn't been curbed even a little, and marital rape is legal. All of which means that sexual assault is state-endorsed violence and a form of social punishment for married women.

That's why an intrepid collection of women human rights lawyers from Canada, Kenya, Malawi, and Ghana were bivouacked in a hotel room in Nairobi when I caught up with them in 2009, putting the finishing touches on a plan that would criminalize marital rape. The Three to Be Free program targeted three countries, Kenya, Malawi, and Ghana, with three strategies—litigation, policy reform, and legal education—over three years to establish a woman's equality rights and in particular her right to refuse to have sex with her husband.

When the African women in the room wondered if the model used in Canada in the early eighties to reform the law on sexual assault—which relied on rewriting the statute, educating the judiciary, and raising awareness with the public—could work in Africa, Fiona Sampson, executive director of the Equality Effect, an organization that uses human rights law to transform the lives of women and girls, told them that it could indeed work, and very well, in fact. She'd connected with the women lawyers in Kenya, Malawi, and Ghana, as well as with women across Canada, who were willing to work pro bono on this potentially precedent-setting initiative. Now they'd gathered to advance their ambitious agenda. They knew it would take at least two to three years to litigate an issue like marital rape through the courts and that test cases could only be mounted once they had lobbied to change the law and had built public awareness to support it.

Most people predicted a ferocious backlash to any new law that said women could refuse to have sex. When on that same trip I traveled "up-country" to Kanjuu in the district of Kirinyaga, ninety minutes northeast of Nairobi, and asked men there how they felt about the proposed new law that would criminalize marital rape, I got an earful. "I own her. The dowry I paid for her means she's my property," said Linus Kariuki, forty, a usually soft-spoken man who sits on the town council in Kanjuu, a village of about five hundred families. He believed that the controversial proposal to make marital rape a crime in Kenya was not in keeping with African tradition. "If my wife refuses to have sex with me, I will rape her. And then I'll beat her because she didn't obey me." His fury on that February day in 2009 when we met was being fueled by the meeting in Nairobi that I had just come from.

So I asked the women of Kanjuu how they felt about the proposed law. "Women need to have the right to say no, but men here have the authority, and women have no power at all," said Jedidah Wanjiku, twenty-nine. Six women had gathered inside her home to meet with me, not just to escape the blistering noonday sun but also because they wanted to voice their approval for the new law safe from their husbands' scrutiny. They told me that the consequences for refusing sex were harsh and immediate.

"He'll kick you out of the house, send you to the bush to spend the whole night outside with the kids; he'll burn your clothes, kill your chickens and eat them, and sell your goats," Wanjiku said, and also confided that she was the only woman in the room whose husband didn't follow these old traditions: he worked as a photographer in Nairobi and believed in women's emancipation. Her friend Ann Wanjiku, thirty-four, said, "When you come back to the house, he [a husband] will beat you for disobeying him. After a man marries you, he owns you completely. He can do whatever he wants to you. That's the way it is here."

Getting rid of the dowry and therefore the sense of ownership a man has over a woman would seem a place to start, but the lawyers thought it would be easier to change the law than to tackle ancient customs. They also thought that the criminalization of marital rape would have a trickle-down effect. "Women will achieve increased equality under the law and will be recognized as persons rather than property," said Sampson. "Furthermore, it will establish a culture of accountability for women's human rights and improve the physical safety and security of women."

Building public awareness was a critically important step, as evidenced by the brouhaha in the villages before the law was even written. Everyone knew the change in the law was coming eventually; there were regular radio broadcasts alerting citizens all over Kenya. But the men, for the most part, pretended it was not happening. Jedidah Wanjiku said, "We need a delegation to come from Nairobi and tell the people here to change the way we behave. They need to say that women have feelings, that a bully in the house is not good and women are the same as men. The men in the village will listen to people who come from outside." So far, no one had come.

The sticking point for these women, as well as the reformers in Nairobi, is customary law. All three countries operate with two distinct sets of laws—the formal laws of the state, and customary laws that aren't codified, aren't written down, and are determined by men. The customary law regarding marital rape is that neither wife nor husband can deny sex to the other unless one is "sick, menstruating, in childbirth, or attending a funeral." The chiefs enforce these customary laws, and most villagers, as well as the lawyers discussing the laws, agreed that they worked against the rights of women, either out of ignorance or in collusion with men.

Ngeyi Kanyongolo, a law professor at the University of Malawi, told me, "Customary law is what we live with. It defines a woman's identity, how she relates to others, and it is the most accessible form of dispute resolution." Because it regulates marriage, divorce, inheritance, and property, because it's patriarchal, biased, and goes against gender equality, women pay a mighty price for obeying its rules. Elizabeth Archampong of the faculty of law at Kwame Nkrumah University said, "When you get married, there's the presumption you will give yourself up, any time, every time, and all the time for sex." And Seodi White, a lawyer from Malawi, said that violence is often a part of the marital bargain and gave me some graphic examples: a man jamming a broken piece of furniture into his wife's vagina, another applying a python to her vagina because a witch doctor told him it would spit out coins after he did so, still another cutting off his wife's labia majora and selling it as a charm—all these terrible acts considered legal as she is his property. In Ghana, Marceline Kabir, a nurse, told me, "When a woman tries to run away from her husband, other villagers will catch her and bring her back. Even a child of a forced marriage or a woman with wounds from female genital mutilation will be sent back to her husband. And even if he's drunk and abusive, the woman has no say." She told a story about a woman in her village who ran for her life when her husband was beating her. She was caught, trussed up like a goat, and brought back to her husband. What's more, if a woman reported the rape or the abuse, she was likely to suffer more grief from the other villagers. One woman walked around for more than a year with a dislocated shoulder because she didn't dare ask for help for fear that her husband would throw her out of the house to fend for herself if she exposed the fact that he had beaten her.

Customary law is seen as the personal law of all citizens, so no one can opt out of it. Kanyongolo gave me another example. "A man killed his wife because she refused to have sex with him. He was arrested by the state and charged with murder. But since a woman has no right to say no, the customary law court declared her behavior provocative and found her husband guilty only of manslaughter."

Malawi, Ghana, and Kenya reformed some of their laws around sexual violence in 2006 and 2007, and marital rape was part of the package, but in each jurisdiction the parliamentarians on the review committee said, "Get rid of the marital rape section. It will never pass—our men will never allow it." The reformers in all three countries succumbed, and the reforms went through without mention of marital rape.

The Canadian women on the Three to Be Free team had faced a similar resistance back home in Canada. Jennifer Koshan, a professor of law at the University of Calgary, told her African colleagues the story of how many male members of Canada's House of Commons had burst out laughing, joking to each other across the floor about beating their wives, when MP Margaret Mitchell presented the sexual-assault law-reform package in the House in 1982. "Before 1983 there was immunity for men who raped their wives in Canada for the same reasons African women are struggling with now: women were assumed to be property once married and there was implied consent because of marriage vows," she said. Even today some judges rely on old adages like "When a woman says no, she means yes."

Mary Eberts, who has spent most of her career pursuing cases that promote equality in Canadian law, says, "Marital rape is one of the toughest barriers to the full equality of women, conceptually at least, since it is a remaining incident of married women's inferior, or nonexistent, legal position. I do not, though, see that it is the only keystone to change. Each barrier will still have to be taken, one by one." Eberts, too, believes that it's often easier to change the jurisprudence first, because there you are dealing with educated elites who have less allegiance to "the way it was" in many areas than do the people who hold "custom" dear. "They also know in their heart of hearts that changing the jurisprudence gives them the best of both worlds: they can look progressive without necessarily affecting real change, because changing the jurisprudence is not the whole story. There remain enforcement issues. I.e., maybe the law will be changed on the books but won't be enforced with vigor. But for those to whom symbolism is important, it seems like a victory."

In Nairobi that February, just four years ago, the women sat like a posse around the long meeting table, creating their strategy to change the law, sharing the stories of rape and domestic violence that brought authenticity to the project, poised to pounce when the time is ripe. They debated the wording of the new statute, parsing every sentence, trying out the vocabulary. Were the language and interpretation broad enough? What about consent—was the definition precise enough?

Effie Owuor, a recently retired judge who is a driving force for women's rights in Kenya, blazed the trail as the first woman magistrate (officiating in a lower court), then as the first woman judge. She was currently the chair of her country's task force on sexual offenses. She said, "It'll be difficult for a judge in Kenya to convict on marital rape in view of the clear omission of marital rape in the code." She suggested it might be better to charge the person with assault rather than try to make a charge of sexual violence stick.

Other women at the table asked this icon of women's progress questions such as, "How would you deal with marital rape when it's a child in a forced marriage?" The no-nonsense judge replied, "I would put it under the Children's Act and say 'customary law is in conflict with written law. This is a child. I argue for the child. I don't want to hear any other argument.' That's all I would say."

And if it was an adult rather than a child?

"I'd use the 'person' argument. Move away from the issue of marriage. Tell them, 'She didn't consent to a beating through marriage. It is nonsense to say there's consent here.' I'd go with that until I convict."

The judge said she'd already seen the signs of change. "It used to be that a woman's role was to read the closing prayer at the village meeting. Not anymore. Change isn't coming from on high down. It's coming from the grassroots up." The discussion at that table was history in the making. A lawyer from each country described the existing laws in Ghana, Malawi, and Kenya, as well as in Canada. Then together they dissected each one. They thrashed out the details—where to delete a section or add an amendment. Judge Owuor reminded them, "We need to remove certain sections of the penal code such as 'this does not apply to married women.'" Then she advised that they sneak the marital rape law into the middle of the code and presume that most MPs wouldn't read the whole thing. "Or wait for a day when the members who are against it are not in the parliament."

Some felt that they needed to tread softly with language, dressing up the law with phrases acceptable to villagers—for example, positioning it from a perspective of caring about and protecting women rather than using words like *marital rape,* and using phrases seen to be free of violence rather than to be equal. "Play on humanity," suggested Seodi White. "Use nonpoliticized language such as 'a man who loves his wife wouldn't beat her.'"

That approach didn't get much support at the table.

Together these women underscored the consequences for a woman who reports violence: she may have to get up at four o'clock in the morning and pay bus fare out of scant resources to get to the court in the city. She gets home at eight at night, after waiting her turn in the court and catching a bus back to the village; her children are hungry, and it's too dark to plant the fields, which is the work she needs to do to grow food for the family. Her case gets postponed over and over again.

"No wonder she gives up," said Judge Owuor. "When you go to court, the social worker is there collecting your children because you aren't at home taking care of them and your man is next door carrying on." They all agreed that a woman can't have access to justice without looking at these issues. "Sexual assault and abuse affect us physically, but also socially and emotionally; it affects families, jobs, the entire country," said Judge Owuor.

Her views were backed up by Kenyan member of parliament Millie Odhiambo, who said, "This new law being proposed will not be very well received. They'll say it's not African style." But she also said, "Domestic violence used to be a topic no one would talk about; now people are being prosecuted left, right, and center." Seodi White summed up the conundrum. "The issue is about a law that gets into the blankets, the bedroom. We're not criminalizing all men. We're criminalizing the act—and the bad men. It's doable. It's a process we need to negotiate with the general public, hear their views, give a little, take a little. Somewhere along the line, we'll get it right."

When I asked Fiona Sampson in August 2013 how the reform process was going, she said, "We have been researching the treatment of consent in sexual assault law and discovered a sticking point relating to the legal treatment of marital rape, i.e., wives are understood to have consented to any/all sex upon marriage." They have scheduled another strategy workshop to vet the research completed to date, and to decide whether next steps will be more public legal education and awareness-building, a formal request for marital rape to be written into the penal code, or litigation, which, if successful, could force the hand of the court.

They have also been asked to make a case for girls in Malawi who had been raped just as they acted for the 160 girls in Kenya. The struggle in Malawi and many other countries is a result of old laws that don't respect the rights of women; laws that were never reformed or removed from the books. For example, in Malawi the traditional English common law requirement that the testimony of a sexual offense complainant must be corroborated by other independent evidence forms part of Malawi's colonial legacy and continues to be enforced today. The reasons given by English judges to explain why convicting on uncorroborated evidence in sexual offense cases would be "dangerous" were based on discriminatory stereotypes about women being inherently prone to fabricating false stories about rape. The oft-cited quote of Salmon LJ in *R v. Henry and Manning* (1968) 53 Cr App R 150, 153 is as follows:

> What the judge has to do is to use clear and simple language that will without any doubt convey to the jury that in cases of alleged sexual offences it is really dangerous to convict on the evidence of the woman or girl alone. This is dangerous because human experience has shown that in these cases girls and women do sometimes tell an entirely false story which is very easy to fabricate, but extremely difficult to refute. Such stories are fabricated for all sorts of reasons, which I need not enumerate, and sometimes for no reason at all.

As extraordinary as that bizarre thinking is to people today, the Malawian courts have cited the same discriminatory rationales in their adoption and application of the corroboration requirement in sexual offenses.

Accordingly, the police will refuse to investigate sexual assault and defilement cases in Malawi, and will refuse to refer cases for prosecution, relying on the need for corroboration. Sampson and her legal strategists want to eliminate the legal violence perpetuated by the corroboration requirement, and ensure that defilement victims are treated the same as any other witness, in any other crime. Then they can proceed with bringing the Kenyan case of police treatment of raped girls to the courts in Malawi.

My bet is that they'll win in Malawi just as they did in Kenya mostly because the people are on their side. While touring the villages in the district of Kirinyaga in Kenya, I talked to three groups of men: men over seventy, who were so horrified by discussing the topic with me that they suggested we meet in the woods out of the view of the other villagers; forty-something men; and men under thirty. The older men were outraged with the suggestion that women should have the right to say no to sex, but they admitted that sex was no longer a big part of their lives, so if the law was passed, it wouldn't really matter to them. The men in their forties said that they'd fight the passing of the law, they'd go to Nairobi en masse, they'd march in front of the legislature. But if they lost, they'd obey. The twenty-somethings? Well, they couldn't imagine what the fuss was about. Said one, "The young men sleep with their girlfriends. The women do as they wish. They all go to work. It's not an issue with them."

At a public meeting to air opinion on the proposed law, John Chigiti, a Nairobi lawyer, described the discussion of the topic as a potential win-win situation for everyone. "We need to create a critical mass that can rally around this issue. Discussions like this are the way to do that." When a member of the public asked about backlash, Melanie Randall, a law professor from the University of

Western Ontario, replied, "They'll say the law has no place in the bedroom; that this law breaks up families and attacks men; that it doesn't value children. Don't let that deter you. The strength of the backlash shows the efficacy of your work." Her advice: "Diffuse it or ignore it."

At the end of the event, the facilitator, Judy Thongori, a family lawyer in Nairobi, spoke for everyone in the room when she said, "Ten years from now people will look back at this meeting and say, 'I was in the room that day; the end of marital rape started right here.'"

8

The Anatomy of Change

At Tahrir Square, we broke the barrier of fear. Once that barrier is down, the people can do anything. —HODA ELSADDA, PROFESSOR, UNIVERSITY OF CAIRO

Change is one part nerve, two parts knowledge, and three parts tenacity. The new revolutionaries know that you have to speak your truth and use the law of the land to hold the state accountable for changing the status quo and then be prepared to wait out the naysayers. But the process begins with finding the nerve to conquer fear. That's what happened on Egypt's Tahrir Square during eighteen remarkable days in January and February 2011 that transformed both the Egyptians who rose up during that raucous, dangerous, joyful revolution and Egypt itself.

While the outcome remains tenuous, there is no doubt that Egypt has become a bellwether for change in the entire region. And as much as the convulsions have affected governments, institutions, and families, no group has seized the opportunity of change more steadfastly than the women of the Arab Spring.

Egypt is a country that traces its history back eight thousand years; it's where the pyramids that were built about forty-five hundred years ago still stand watch, evidence of a rich and storied past. Characters like Alexander the Great and Mark Anthony and

Cleopatra and Julius Caesar left their impressive marks on this place. Its ancient history also boasts equality among the sexes: women could own and sell property, make their own contracts, marry and divorce, receive inheritances, and pursue legal disputes in court. Some, like Hatshepsut and Cleopatra VII, among others, became pharaohs. Contemporary Egypt is a contradictory place that has embraced equal wages for women and maternity leave but also enforces draconian personal status laws that favor men over women in marriage, divorce, and inheritance.

The women in Egypt, Tunisia, and elsewhere want change in their personal lives, but first they needed to knock out the dictators. Hoda Elsadda was chair of Arabic studies at Manchester University in England when the first hints of an uprising began in Tunisia. The early rumblings of change rolled into Egypt in October, and as soon as it looked as if the seeds of a similar revolution could germinate there, she took a leave of absence from her job and went home to Cairo. "I had to be here," she told me as we sat in her book-lined office in Cairo exactly one year after the hated Egyptian president Hosni Mubarak was forced to resign. "I couldn't stay away from Egypt when the changes we'd hoped would come for forty years were potentially on the doorstep." By the time Mubarak was ousted, on February 11, 2011, she knew what her own next steps had to be. "I went back to England and resigned from my job, because now was the time to shape the future of Egypt—I wouldn't be anyplace else." She moved to Cairo and took a job as professor of literature at Cairo University.

Elsadda was no stranger to protests, but the ones she'd been in before the Arab Spring were events with five hundred people surrounded by ten thousand police. In Tahrir Square, the protester numbers kept swelling; by the end of the first day, there were more of them than police. "I'm fifty-two years old. I wanted to show my support but was undecided about actually going to Tahrir Square, so I decided I would think about joining the protesters later." In the meantime, her nieces were calling to ask her to go with them to the square. Her brother said to his daughters, in no uncertain terms, "Don't go." She knew of friends who were literally locking up their children so they would not go.

Like others, she was drawn to the protest by activists like Asmaa Mahfouz, twenty-six, who put a message on her Facebook page about a week before the now-famous date of January 25, 2011. It read, "I'm making this video to give you one simple message. We want to go down to Tahrir Square on January 25. If we still have honor and we want to live in dignity on this land, we have to go down on January 25. We'll go down and demand our rights, our fundamental rights. Your presence with us will make a difference, a big difference!" All Egyptians should come, she exhorted, "for freedom, justice, honor, and human dignity." And she added, "Whoever says women shouldn't go to the protests because they will get beaten, let him have some honor and manhood and come with me January 25."

Elsadda decided to go to the square on January 28, three days after the protest began. "We went—all of us together, the whole family—and we stood together for eighteen days. It was a kind of euphoria. I met all my old friends—the usual suspects in the human rights movement, the women's movement, plus people you'd never expect, like my own brother, who became a born-again revolutionary."

It wasn't all fearlessness. She says she awakened every morning with some part of her dreading going to the square. "I had no illusions about the level of violence the state would use. But once there with all the others, I felt totally safe. I felt we were part of history; we were changing Egypt. We were taking a stand. It was very exciting, like an adrenaline high."

She describes the value of being connected by a common cause: "It makes people better than each one was." Although the revolution is now described as the social network revolution and the youth revolution, Elsadda says it was neither. "It was the Egyptian people together who did this." There were young and old people, some who had never seen a cell phone joining hands with Twitter wizards. Women with their faces fully covered worked alongside secular women. "There is normally a huge gap between the rich and the poor in Egypt," says Elsadda, "but this was eighteen days of solidarity. We shared food and water; we were united by a common cause. It tells you a better future is possible."

She says the success was based on a single factor: "We broke the barrier of fear. There used to be so many taboos. Once that barrier is down, the people can do anything."

They got rid of a dictator, but the old regime was still intact a year later when we met. "The objectives of the revolution have not been fulfilled," Elsadda told me. "But now we have to give it time." Justice and equality for all Egyptians is the goal, but women are working on changing the personal status laws, which contribute to such bizarre contradictions in women's circumstances. On the one hand, the laws control the personal affairs of women; for example, a man can divorce his wife simply by saying, "I divorce you." After fifty years of marriage, a woman can find herself out on the street. On the other hand, the country's labor laws are among the best in the world for women, and at state institutions, such as the university where Elsadda works, the percentage of women on the staff reflects the proportion of women in society.

Egypt's personal status laws are derived from Islamic codes that dictate the rules of marriage, divorce, and inheritance. This legal structure is distinct from the rest of the Egyptian legal system, which is based on French civil law. During the past decade, the government has reformed some of the more egregious gender inequities in these laws, but women still face discrimination.

In 2000, when a no-fault divorce law was proposed and passed, a woman had to give up her financial rights, return her dowry, and exempt her husband from any future financial obligation in order to get a divorce. Although a man could have a divorce simply by stating the desire, the so-called reform means a woman has to go to court, and she needs to prove physical harm as a reason for the collapse of the marriage. "You need a broken leg and a witness to the attack, and then you need to wait six to eight years in court," says Elsadda. And the no-fault law contains a provision that was also a setback for women's rights: women no longer have the right to travel abroad without the husband's consent. What's more, Muslim women are prohibited from marrying Christian men, and non-Muslim women who marry Muslim men are subject to Islamic law. The women who marched and shouted and stood in solidarity with the men on Tahrir Square thought that these unfair laws would be negotiable in the new post-Mubarak Egypt. But they were in for a nasty surprise.

It was during the demonstrations that followed the eighteen-day revolution—particularly on March 8, International Women's Day—that women's issues were brought into sharp focus on Tahrir Square. The hostility and violence unleashed against women pro-testers on March 8 shocked everyone. Women were harassed verbally and physically by menacing groups of men who accused them of adopting Western agendas and going against the cultural values of Egypt. Female protesters were dragged from the square and subjected to brutal "virginity tests" by the military—some of them in front of a crowd, others reportedly in a kitchen at the nearby military headquarters.

Samira Ibrahim, twenty-five, had traveled from her small town in Upper Egypt—an eight-hour train ride to Cairo—to attend the protest. When we sat together in a café in Cairo a year later, her emotional scars were still in evidence. Clearly agitated, she fidgeted as we talked, checked her cell phone every few seconds, and spoke at a staccato pace. "They forced me to remove my clothes," she said. "When I struggled, they beat me. They used electric shocks on me, and it was an officer who did the virginity test [using his fingers to find out if her hymen was intact]. I felt like I'd been raped." Sexual violence was the tool men used to silence these female human rights defenders on the front lines.

Ibrahim is a petite woman, barely five feet tall, with cover-girl good looks and wearing model-like makeup. She turned up in jeans, with an animal-print scarf wrapped around her head in the new fashionable "big hijab" style that swirls fabric into a crownlike headdress, and carrying a shoulder bag with a slogan on it that read, "No to emergency laws, no to military rule, no to criminalizing strikes and protests." She was feisty and furious at once. She'd made headlines when she decided to sue the military for the assault on her. And again when she won the civil case she'd brought against them. Although she was told by the military commander in charge of the men who assaulted her that the soldiers would not act that way again, the assurance wasn't enough. According to Ibrahim, the soldiers' description of the assault on her—claiming that a doctor had examined her hymen—wasn't the truth. "It was an officer who sexually assaulted me," she says. "They wanted to humiliate me. I wanted to make sure they don't get to do that to anyone ever again." So she lodged a complaint against the military. "I'm not afraid of them," she said. A month later, the military tribunal pursuing her complaint acquitted the officer accused of administering the virginity test. But Ibrahim isn't through with them yet. She wants justice and says eventually she'll get it by pursuing her case using international law.

The line in the sand that the men drew at Tahrir Square on International Women's Day is something the women protesters, who had stood with them through the revolution, are still coming to terms with.

In late summer and early fall 2013 there was a flurry of activity through women's networks. Street harassment, a longtime problem for women throughout the Middle East, had become brutal sexual assault. Shocking footage depicted boys and men rushing up behind groups of young women, putting their hands on the girls' buttocks, reaching between their legs. This behavior increased during Eid, the holy day that marks the end of Ramadan. It's hard to reconcile—men and boys celebrating the end of a religious holiday by going on a rampage of sexual assault. Like women elsewhere, the Egyptian women had had enough and decided to fight back. One group called Imprint decided to leave their mark by enlisting men and women to form street patrols to stop the assaults and by letting everyone know via Facebook who was committing them. Nihal Saad Zaghloul, the cofounder of the Imprint movement, described what happened on August 9 and 10, 2013, when they launched a campaign called "Eid without Harassment" with seventy volunteers on Talaat Harb Square from four P.M. until ten P.M. "We divided ourselves between three teams: patrolling, awareness, and operations. We spoke and interacted with bystanders on the importance of rejecting this crime and rejecting violence." They figured the ad hoc operation prevented sixty-five individual (verbal and physical) sexual harassment incidents and five mass harassment incidents. HarassMap, which started soon after the revolution and plots sexual assaults online, believes that the most effective way to stop the mob assaults in the long term is to convince bystanders and all of society to stop accepting this behavior, to stop staying silent or joining in, and to intervene to stop it. Sexual assault/harassment is so widespread in the Middle East that the women who work at Imprint and HarassMap have to actually recruit and train volunteers to intervene because normal bystanders don't.

Cyberspace exploded with messages urging women to support these networks. Others joined the discussion online and asked for help in starting up similar networks to stop the assault of women and girls. And Aya Chebbi, a blogger from Tunisia, wrote, "In a country where there is so little respect for women, there are only two ways we can live; as a victim or as a feminist. We should be wary of the new attitudes slowly integrating our culture and refuse to play by the rules of a society that constantly puts our lifestyle and dress under attack. Today more than ever before, I constantly feel that there is always a new thing that is now considered a 'provocation' or 'inappropriate.' Sexual harassment is just a way for men who feel threatened by women's leadership to stop us from living up to our full potential."

Hoda Elsadda says there may be an explanation for the vicious male backlash: "We followed the Western model of modernity in every way except the family. Even in the Nasser regime in 1956, when women could do everything in the public sphere, the private one was not touched. In the seventies, a woman minister in the government was actually stopped from leaving the country at the airport by a husband who felt she should stay at home. Until recently, a woman needed her husband's permission to get a passport."

As for violence against women, Elsadda says the level is about the same in Egypt as it is in most other places. But, she cautions, changing Egyptian attitudes toward women isn't easy. "What I want for Egyptian women is the same thing I want for the country—equality, autonomy, and fair personal status laws," she tells me.

Although most people accuse the military of forsaking their support of the people in Tahrir Square and blame the fundamentalist Islamists for the government's failure to fulfill the objectives of the revolution, there are two things that the revolution has accomplished for women: a sense of empowerment and bringing more women into politics. "History says women are part of the revolution, but once the political pie is divided up, the danger is that women will be excluded," Elsadda warns. After the protests, she joined a political party for the first time in her life. She thinks that the main challenge for women today is guarding against the backlash coming from all sides.

She raises a very interesting and little-known fact about Egyptian politics, which she calls the First Lady Syndrome. "One of the key obstacles that women's rights activists will face in the months and years to come is a prevalent public perception that associates women's rights activists and their activities with the ex–first lady, Suzanne Mubarak."

The fundamentalists argue that Egypt has to deal with the negative consequences of Mubarak's corrupt regime, one of them being the part his wife played in destroying the values of the Egyptian

family. In particular, critics point to her role in endorsing legal mod-
ifications of the personal status law, which undermined the stability
of the family. As head of the National Council for Women (NCW),
Suzanne Mubarak was the one who pushed these laws through parliament. Trying to expunge any sign of the former president's wife's
activism is part of the argument against women's rights going on in
Egypt today.

The laws that were passed or modified since 2000—the divorce
law, the citizenship law, and the guardianship law, as well as setting
a quota that guaranteed women sixty-four seats in parliament—are
now described by fundamentalist men as evidence of Suzanne
Mubarak's anti-family agenda. They claim that "all the laws that
were passed with the backing of Suzanne Mubarak were politically
motivated to serve the interests of the ruling elite," says Elsadda.
"Already, this public perception [from fundamentalists] is being
politically manipulated to rescind laws and legislative procedures
that were passed in the last ten years to improve the legal position
of women, particularly within personal status laws. These laws are
deliberately being discredited as 'Suzanne's laws,' or more pejora-
tively as 'qawanin alhanim' [referring to Mubarak's wife as a woman
with an entourage and part of the ruling elite]." She says the question people need to ask is this: Were these laws politically motivated by a corrupt agenda of a corrupt regime or did they arise out
of years of work by women's rights activists? Can they rightly be
described as "Suzanne's laws"? If the answer is no, as Elsadda
would argue, what's going on? Why does the new regime want to
discredit the work the activists have done?

Women's organizations had begun to worry about the way Suzanne Mubarak was co-opting their issues when she created the
National Council for Women in 1995. She'd been at the fourth World
Conference on Women in Beijing and had come home ashamed of
how far behind Egyptian women were. The activists say she might
have had the best of intentions in establishing the council, but it
soon became a way of controlling what advances women could

make. Elsadda explains, "The NCW competed with existing women's organizations, sought to appropriate women's activism and work, and tried to monopolize the movement by speaking on behalf of all Egyptian women. NCW members were disproportionately represented in local, regional, and international media and forums. Women's rights activism became linked with the projects of the first lady."

This is the conundrum women the world over invariably face—whatever progress they make, there always seems to be some self-appointed organization ready to claw back gains either in the name of God or to "protect family values." Women need to be wily in the ways they make change. Like Hangama Anwari in Afghanistan, who cleverly positioned her survey on polygamy to identify those who are defying Islam rather than being critical of a custom approved by the Quran. And Judge Effie Owuor in Kenya, who cautioned the lawyers on the judicial reform case, advising, "We need to sneak the law into the middle of the code and presume most MPs won't read the whole thing. Or wait for a day when the members who are against it are not in the parliament." The women in Egypt are attempting similar maneuvers to protect the gains they have made in the face of those who want to annul them. They're lobbying the members of parliament, keeping their demands in front of the people, and are fully prepared with research data to take on those who claim the gains they made in recent years are tainted by the old corrupt regime.

There's a new generation of Egyptian women who have come into their own in the sunlit days of the revolution. Women like Mozn Hassan, the executive director of Nazra for Feminist Studies, a women's organization that aims to bring gender equality to Egypt. The mandate at Nazra is to attract young women and a new generation of activists and researchers who can establish and entrench women's rights in Egypt and throughout the Middle East. For them the time for promises is over. They want action and are prepared to do the heavy lifting to get it. Their goal is to examine the obstacles to women's advancement and create nothing less than a societal debate on women's issues.

Before the revolution, Hassan, who received the Charlotte Bunch Human Rights Defender Award from the Global Fund for Women in 2013, says, "The government ran the women's movement. It was for upper-class women. Now we're writing a new history in Egypt and women need to be there in that history." Originally from Saudi Arabia, where she says there are two spaces—the public one for men and the private one for women—Hassan believes women in Cairo have a sense of the street, and their attitudes are different. "Women are changing their traditional role of being nice, modest, married mothers to being involved in the public life of the country." She feels the patriarchy has to be thrown off, and among the new activists of Cairo, there is a lot of support for her views. When I visited the Nazra office, I was surprised to find women and men there in equal numbers. Hassan says the movement needs men as well as women to make change in Egypt, and if they can make effective change, she believes that the sexual equality revolution will spread to Saudi Arabia, Bahrain, and Kuwait as well.

One of the things boosting their work is a new project called the Women and Memory Forum, which researches and documents the role played by women in the region's cultural and intellectual history. Hoda Elsadda is one of the founders of the forum and says the research they do examines historical and cultural data from the Arab world with gender sensitivity. They are carefully constructing a database of women's accomplishments and a library of their work in order to establish a baseline for Arab women to go forward.

Hassan says it helps women today to see how women's rights issues played out in political and ideological struggles in Egypt that go back to the early stages of nation-building in the nineteenth century, when women asserted their views and contributed to Egypt's modernity. In 1899, when Qasim Amin published a seminal text on the history of Egypt, *Tahrir alMar'a* (Liberation of Women), he was stating facts that governments still need to hear today: that the backward status of women was the reason for the backwardness of the country, and that improvement of the status of women was a prerequisite for the modernization and progress of the country.

More than a hundred years later, in 2002, the United Nations issued a report with the same advice. The UN *Arab Human Development Report* was written by a group of distinguished Arab intellectuals and highlighted three "deeply rooted shortcomings which have created major obstacles to human development." These three deficits? The lack of freedom, education, and empowerment of women. The report's authors called for "the complete empowerment of Arab women, taking advantage of all the opportunities to build their capabilities and enable them to exercise those capabilities to the full." The UN *Arab Human Development Report* issued three years later, in 2005, carried the same message: "Gender inequality is generally recognized as one of the main obstacles to development in the Arab region."

Many assumed that the women of the Middle East had broken the ties that have bound them to second-class citizenship when they bravely sallied forth in Tunisia, Yemen, Egypt, and elsewhere. Their slogan was "We will not be quiet." Women such as Tawakkol Karman, who led the protests in Yemen and won the 2011 Nobel Peace Prize for her work; Lina Ben Mhenni from Tunisia, whose blogs in French, English, and Arabic kept the country informed during the uprising; Razan Ghazzawi, a Syrian who tweeted news updates and was detained for two weeks; and Zainab Al-Khawaja, who stood her ground against tanks at Bahrain's Pearl Roundabout, all helped crush the stereotype of the subservient Arab woman and paved the way for reform, insisting that women's rights are human rights belonging to every citizen.

When Karman, who founded an organization called Women Journalists Without Chains, received the Nobel Prize, she delivered a warning with her address: "The democratic world, which has told us a lot about the virtues of democracy and good governance, should not be indifferent to what is happening in Yemen and Syria, and what happened before that in Tunisia, Egypt, and Libya, and happens in every Arab and non-Arab country aspiring for freedom. All of that is just hard labor during the birth of democracy, which requires support and assistance, not fear and caution." Then she tossed a bouquet to her Arab sisters who have struggled to "win their rights in a society dominated by the supremacy of men."

The message is that although women in Saudi Arabia were lashed for driving a car, and on Tahrir Square they were arrested as whores while marching for liberation, and in Iraq they can be stoned to death for being seen with a man they aren't married to, the process of change has started. Women in most of the Arab world are still denied equal status with men, and the fundamentalist politicians on the rise want to keep women down, but the message from experts worldwide that becomes louder with every passing year is that women are the way forward, the route to ending poverty, improving the economy, and stopping conflict.

In Egypt, Hoda Elsadda told me that getting rid of a dictatorial regime was the first step. Now, she says, they need to make sure there is more space for a women's movement and for the participation of women. If all the studies around the world are correct, that will mean a more prosperous Egypt.

Like others, she was perplexed by the number of fundamentalists who won in the first democratic election in her country in fifty years, but she feels that the enormity of the change the revolution has brought to Egyptian society is bound to need a period of time for adjustment, for rethinking the way the society will operate. For that reason, she estimates that it will take at least two or three years to achieve the goals of the revolution.

That said, the changes for women in Egypt and elsewhere have already begun. In Iran, Iraq, Pakistan, and Afghanistan, women's rights are still highly contested, but the movement to alter thinking that is thousands of years old is burgeoning. The extremist mullahs in Afghanistan are being cornered by women reformers and invited to talk. The laws in Pakistan—the hated Hudood Ordinances that called for four male witnesses to prove a woman didn't cause her own rape, for example—have been challenged by women's groups and are slowly but surely being moderated. In Mali, the women used their voting power to elect president Ibrahim Boubacar Keita, who promised reform. In Pakistan, the first women-only jirga (a decision-making council in Pashtun society) was formed and brought justice to the case of a sixteen-year-old girl who'd been the victim of an acid attack and died.

Women are still caught by the tripwires of religion and culture in the villages, but the chiefs and religious leaders are beginning to listen to scholars who claim that the sacred texts do not support the oppression of women. The education and health care of women is a priority in many more villages today than it has ever been before. And it's women themselves who are driving that change. For instance, in Lebanon, women started Jismi.net (*jismi* means "my body" in Arabic), whose aim is to deal with issues related to the body and sexuality that have been considered private matters and taboos that shouldn't be discussed. The launch of that Web site is as significant as the publication of *Our Bodies, Ourselves* in 1970. Forty-three years later, it's a repeat performance in the Arab world, but this time it's for men as well as women. The traffic on the site is extraordinary: young men claiming all they know about sex they learned in porn magazines and women saying the only thing they've been taught about their bodies is how to use sanitary pads.

Isobel Coleman says that in 2010, when her book *Paradise Beneath Her Feet: How Women Are Transforming the Middle East* came out, some people said, "What change? These countries will never change." It seemed to her critics that the thugs in power and the fundamentalists at the gate would forever oppress women.

But when I interviewed Coleman a year later, she said, "There has been revolutionary change, profound demographic change, and women are at the forefront of many of these changes. Across the broader Middle East, women are the majority of college gradu-ates." She cited impressive numbers: 70 percent of graduates in Iran are women. In Saudi Arabia, it's 63 percent and in Egypt, 55 percent. "Even though there are enormous barriers in the workplace, women are determined to make change. Many are members of Islamic move-ments and wear the head scarf, but you can't conflate that with them wanting to return to the traditional private role for women. They're actively promoting change—seeking jobs, engaged in the future of their countries. They'll be a big part of driving change in that part of the world." And that was before all the events of the Arab Spring.

Women have a natural facility with grassroots movements, shared leadership, and collegiality, skills that contribute enormously to the anatomy of change. An example comes from award-winning actor Geena Davis, whose motto for women and girls is "If they can see it, they can be it." The maxim came from her discovery that when it comes to media portrayals, women and girls have been close to in-visible. The penny dropped for Davis immediately after the debut of the iconic 1991 film *Thelma and Louise.* She played Thelma Dickinson, a passive housewife married to a controlling man. "Within a week [of the film's release], *Time* magazine ran a cover story with a photo of me—Geena—and Susan Sarandon and a cover line: 'Why *Thelma and Louise* Strikes a Nerve.' I was being ap-proached on the street by people who wanted to talk about how the movie impacted them. There was an enormous reaction from view-ers. Something had really resonated with women."

For Geena this was an awakening about the power of the media. *Thelma and Louise* was the ultimate chick flick. But it became the change maker for gender roles in the road movie genre. It exposed chauvinism and stereotypical presumptions about male-female re-lationships. Then a year later she played Dottie Hinson in *A League of Their Own.* "This movie was a celebration of women's power and success and of working together. Thirteen-year-old girls were telling me, 'I play sports because of that movie.'"

Davis had an almost instant realization that the way women

and girls are portrayed in the media is directly related to the way people treat women and girls. In the movies as well as on TV, she says, women and girls are seen as eye candy or the girlfriends of baseball players rather than the baseball players. It was when her own daughter, Alizeh, was two years old, in 2002, that she decided to open the Geena Davis Institute on Gender in Media. "I'd been watching TV with my daughter and realized entertainment for little kids had serious problems with gender identification. There were far fewer female characters, and the ones there were had fewer speaking parts." The long slow climb out of movie and TV obscurity for women and girls was about to begin. The research her institute produced showed the ratio of men to women or boys to girls on TV was 3 to 1. Even crowd scenes were only 17 percent female. And behind the camera, there were four males for every female.

The executive director of the Geena Davis Institute, Madeline Di Nonno, says, "This doesn't come from some evil conspiracy; it's from an unconscious bias." And that is what the institute is trying to change. A study shows that if there are 17 percent women in a room, men think there is a balance. If it's 30 percent, men think there are too many women. Through evidence-based research, it is known that the media influences our behavior and beliefs. But Davis's goal wasn't to start a public awareness program. Instead she wanted to influence the people who make the content decisions in the industry she works in. "We present our research to them and they're floored at how the world they are creating is 17 percent female. Eighty percent of the world's media is made in America—so just look at what we are exporting to the world. What we're doing is training children to see women and girls as less important than men and boys."

The research done at the institute also shows that the more hours a girl watches TV, the more limited her life will be. The more hours boys watch, the more sexist he becomes. But Davis is encouraged as she sees the needle moving; writers are changing their scripts. "Sixty-eight to seventy-eight percent of the incoming students in forensic science at universities are female. And about 78 percent of the young actors playing forensic scientists on TV are women." That's why she's convinced that change is coming and that "if they can see it, they can be it."

An example is the reaction to the TV show called *Commander in Chief* (2005–2006) in which she played U.S. president Mackenzie Allen. The Kaplan Thaler Group advertising agency claimed that the ABC drama reshaped America's political landscape, that millions of TV viewers changed their minds about voting for a female presidential candidate. Their research showed that of the 76 percent of the viewers familiar with the show *Commander in Chief*, 58 percent were now more likely to take seriously the idea of a female president. Data like this spurred the institute to start a program called See Jane. It's sassy and hip and uses research, education, and advocacy to engage the entertainment industry and recognize the need for gender balance and varied portrayals of female and male characters in movies, TV, and other media aimed at children eleven years and under. Says Madeline Di Nonno, "Our aim is to inspire and sensitize the next generation of content creators to focus on gender equality and reduce stereotypes in children's media."

Davis, now the fifty-seven-year-old mother of three, is still stopped on the street by young teens who tell her how the roles she has played in movies and on TV have affected their lives. She thinks women are at a tipping point. "This is the time when change can happen, and one of the ways we can make sure it happens is by paying attention to the way we depict girls and women in the media. We haven't had momentum ever—now it has started."

As much as women prepare the research, deliver the documents, and demand change, there continue to be obstacles to equality, some of them from unexpected places, such as the United Nations. The UN is supposed to be the epitome of change-making institutions, responding to the needs of the people and holding meetings among nations. At the fifty-sixth meeting of the UN Commission on the Status of Women, held in February and March 2012, the opposite was true. The pathetic report filed after the meeting ended in failure sends two clear messages: the UN has serious problems, and women are still easily betrayed.

The focus of the 2012 meeting was to find ways to ensure that rural women would be fully empowered to reach their potential. Rural women make up one-quarter of the world's population and are vital economic agents who, if empowered, could unleash improvements to reduce poverty and boost food security, so ameliorating their situation was the goal of this conference.

Typical for conferences of this nature, the participants had already met through e-mail exchanges and had shared research and decided which measures they wanted the meeting to endorse. But to their immense surprise and disappointment, none of the agreed-on reforms were approved. The session ended without a conclusion. Why? Because the meeting got derailed by delegates unnerved by the subtext of many reforms, which was about women having control over their own sexuality: the promotion of reproductive and sexual health, family planning and reproductive rights, and the elimination of harmful practices such as early and forced child marriage. Some of the delegations had decided to repudiate the terms that had already been agreed on and ignore the legal reforms and services that had been prepared in advance, in spite of the colossal expenses incurred to house and feed the delegates for nineteen days in New York City.

Then executive director of UN Women Michelle Bachelet said the delegations were unable to overcome "a disappointing inability to reach consensus." The chair of the conference, Marjon Kamara from Liberia, put it more bluntly: "I will not hide my great disappointment that we have found ourselves in this position. If we really want to tell the truth about it, I'm not sure that we all came with a spirit of compromise."

At the end of the conference, delegations from twenty countries rose to express their regret: the Norwegians spoke for many when their representative said they could not accept the use of religious, cultural, and moral concerns to block negotiations on documents that would protect women's rights and, in some cases, save thousands of lives every year.

But in no document, on no Web site, in no press release does the commission state who opposed what or why the meeting ended in failure. The debacle brings new impetus to the need for women to make changes themselves. Indeed, education allows women to know what the law says and doesn't say, and as illiteracy rates drop in countries such as Afghanistan and Pakistan and in much of Africa, where women's rights are still challenged, new knowledge is giving women the power to speak out. As for Iran, a country that boasts a high literacy rate but draconian measures to keep women subservient, its homegrown Nobel laureate Shirin Ebadi says, "Iranian women may very well be the force that brings down the oppressive regime that controls Iran." And the world watches with bated breath each time Iranians go to the barricades, hoping that this will be the time they break through.

At the Nobel Women's Initiative conference held in Montebello, Quebec, in May 2011, Ebadi told a story about dealing with the authorities in Iran that likens the change process to catching flies with honey. "The legal status of women is very discriminatory, and this has been the result of bad laws that were passed against women after the revolution." The slightest criticism of the law or practice of government in an Islamic country is considered critical of Islam and labeled heresy by the government. Anyone who fights for human rights, especially women's rights, is caught in that heresy trap. "You cannot speak of logic with Islamic fundamentalists," Ebadi says. "Their prejudice won't permit it. So I bypassed religion and found common ground with the government. My strategy is this: I ask the government to perform the obligation it accepted when it acceded to the UN conventions on human rights and to enforce them. When I tried to defend women's rights, they said, 'Get out of here, you feminist, you liberal, you defender of human rights.' So I started with the Rights of the Child—a document the government had signed and had to go along with. By the time the government knew I had tricked them, it was too late." She reminds the women from Islamic lands to choose their words carefully, to avoid any terms that could be found insulting to Islam, and to never, ever suggest that Islamic laws are bad. "Don't talk in a way that Islamists won't accept you or will call you a non-Muslim or nonbeliever. It weakens your struggle. The fundamentalist Muslim women were against me when I started. Sometimes I thought I was alone. But thirty-two years later, the women who opposed me are on my side— sometimes they are even more radical."

A lot has changed. Gloria Steinem cites a classic example of lost opportunity due to gender blindness. "One of the great debacles during the Vietnam War came about because when the peace talks began in Paris, the U.S. government thought the Vietnamese weren't taking the negotiations seriously because they sent a woman." Twenty years ago, rape wasn't a war crime; violence against women wasn't on the development agenda. Now it's included in the planning of every government and NGO intending to offer humanitarian aid.

What the world is also making inroads in today is improving the welfare and education of girl children. That new emphasis was sparked a dozen years ago when NGOs such as World Vision hosted events that brought girls together to dream bigger dreams and plan better plans. Now the girl has become the poster child for turning around the economy in the village. Consider this: based on World Bank research and UNESCO education statistics, the estimated economic cost to sixty-five low- and middle-income and transitional countries of failing to educate girls to the same standard as boys is a staggering $92 billion each year.

Numbers like that speak volumes. And they have become the

basis for marketing programs that aim to alter the lives of girls. Plan International's Because I Am a Girl initiative has become a social movement to unleash the power of girls in the developing world. It has attracted a host of well-known supporters, and the money is flowing in to the projects for education and health care as never before. Why? Because according to Plan International, when a girl is educated, nourished, and protected, she shares her knowledge and skills with her family and community. But more than that, she builds a powerful sense of self-esteem and self-confidence, which can change the status of a nation.

Another outside-the-box campaign is Walk a Mile in Her Shoes: The International Men's March to Stop Rape, Sexual Assault, and Gender Violence. The popular marches in Canada and the United States are most often led by men wearing red stilettos. Though its organizers were criticized initially for mimicking the way women dress, the march was soon seen for what it was: an opportunity to bring attention to a topic most people don't want to talk about— gender relations and sexual violence. Actors and journalists, radio and TV personalities, sports heroes and firefighters lead the marches and invariably tell hilarious stories about walking a mile in four-inch heels but also deadly serious stories about stopping violence against women. As the organization's motto says, "First you walk the walk, then you talk the talk." The march also sends the message that it's time men as well as women talked about sexual violence. Some people still don't want to know it exists. Others say the statistics are rigged. Still others—the victims—often want to hide from the memory. The marches are doing what women's groups have tried to do for decades: shine a hot light on the problem and get the community talking about it. Watching six-foot-four-inch male broadcasters stumbling down the streets of Toronto wearing red stilettos has a way of doing precisely that. The organizers also hand out pamphlets for preventive education and community services available for anyone who needs help.

Marketing savvy is playing an increasingly important role in the lives of game-changers, who can now mobilize and communicate with lightning speed, as they did during the Arab Spring. Experience has taught them to spot an absurdity at a thousand paces and react to it before the press conference is over, as they did in Afghanistan when President Karzai "pardoned" a woman who was in jail because she had been raped.

In February 2012, the mother of all David and Goliath stories was splashed across the newspapers and broadcast almost incessantly on radio and TV in the United States when the Susan G. Komen for the Cure Foundation dumped its annual donation to Planned Parenthood. The brouhaha blew up because the juggernaut that is the Komen Foundation, which initiated the pink ribbon campaign to cure breast cancer and has raised more than $1.9 billion since its inception in 1982, was beating up on Planned Parenthood, an organization that received grant money from Komen to provide mammograms for poor women in the United States.

Here's what happened. On January 31, 2012, the Komen Foundation announced that it was cutting its funding to Planned Parenthood. According to its own press release, the foundation said it was because Planned Parenthood was under investigation by Florida representative Cliff Stearns, the staunch anti-abortion campaigner who runs an aggressive propaganda machine to annul *Roe v. Wade,* the court case that secured abortion rights for women in the United States and established a woman's right to control her own body. Stearns claimed that he was trying to find out if Planned Parenthood was using public money to fund abortions. Some thought he was in cahoots with a newly hired member of the Komen Foundation who had similar views about abortion rights. The truth is that although Planned Parenthood and their affiliates do fund abortions, the money they have received—$680,000 per year—from the Komen Foundation is used to provide about 170,000 clinical breast exams and 6,400 mammograms mainly to low-income and minority women. The foundation board had recently made a resolution that any organization under investigation could not receive their funding. No one knew why the board of directors had made such a decision or how they thought it applied to Planned Parenthood. But everyone suspected that the funding cut was a direct assault on abortion rights.

Overnight it became a headline story of epic proportions. Critics hurled accusations of political interference. Pro-choice groups denounced what they regarded as more of the same old attacks from anti-abortion groups. Insiders noted that Planned Parenthood was the only grantee among two thousand other organizations whose funding had been cut off because of the new policy. Some foundation board members resigned.

It was a self-inflicted body blow to the organization that had been founded and has operated with the best of intentions. Its Web site tells the story of the woman whose name it bears, Susan Komen, who fought breast cancer with her heart, body, and soul. Throughout her diagnosis, treatments, and endless days in the hospital, she spent her time thinking of ways to make life better for other women battling breast cancer instead of worrying about her own situation. That concern for others continued even as she neared the end of her fight. Moved by her compassion for others and committed to making a difference, her sister, Nancy Brinker, promised Susan that she would do everything in her power to end breast cancer forever. Reading the story of these two sisters, who were devoted to each other and best friends, is heartbreaking in itself. Nancy, whom Susan called Nanny, tells the story of the last time she saw her beloved sister.

> After my sister was released from M.D. Anderson [Cancer Center at the University of Texas in Houston], I tried to come home every other week for a visit. One particular Sunday afternoon on the way back to the airport, Suzy spoke to me again about doing something to help the sick women in the hospital. This practically tore my heart out because here

she was, hardly able to manage a whisper, and she was worrying about other people. I couldn't bear it.

When my father pulled up to the curb, I quickly kissed them both good-bye and jumped out of the car. I was just about inside when I heard a funny sound that sounded like my name. I stopped in my tracks and turned around. There was Suzy, standing up outside the car on wobbly knees, wig slightly askew.

With her arms outstretched, she said gently, "Good-bye, Nanny, I love you." I hugged her so hard I was afraid she might crumble. And then I ran to catch my plane.

I never saw my sister alive again.

Funds of $1.9 billion get attention. So do decisions to drop Planned Parenthood. Controversial decisions often make headlines in the short term, but, as the old Armenian saying goes, "The dogs barked; the caravan passed by," meaning the attention usually quickly dissipates. Not this time. In keeping with the new activism by and about women around the world, American women rose up to protest the bizarre treatment of Planned Parenthood. They appeared at rallies decked out in pink T-shirts that read "Women's Health Matters." They carried placards that said STOP THE WAR ON WOMEN and I STAND WITH PLANNED PARENTHOOD. It was an astonishing show of support.

A who's who of celebrities soon joined the protest. Novelist Judy Blume sent a Twitter message that said, "Susan Komen would not give in to bullying or fear. Too bad the organization bearing her name did." Representative Jackie Speier of California announced, "Komen's decision hurts women—it puts politics before women's health." The comments roared in like a storm. So did the donations to Planned Parenthood. More than $3 million for its breast cancer program was donated in the first forty-eight hours after the news of the Komen cut broke. New York City mayor Michael Bloomberg said he would give $250,000 of his own money and match every dollar that Planned Parenthood raised up to another $250,000. Oil tycoons donated money, and so did indie rock bands.

Rebecca Traister and Joan Walsh wrote in *Salon* magazine, "The overreach by the Komen foundation, while surely intended to strike yet another blow on the side of antiabortion activism, succeeded instead in waking a powerful constituency—armed with precisely the language and emotional heft they [American women] have been lacking for too long."

Facebook exploded with support for Planned Parenthood, and radio stations were inundated with callers demanding a retraction of the foundation's decision. And three days after the announcement of the cut was made, the women of the United States got an apology and a retraction.

On Friday, February 3, Nancy Brinker, the president as well as founder of the organization, said, "We want to apologize to the American public for recent decisions that cast doubt upon our commitment to our mission of saving women's lives. . . . We have been distressed at the presumption that the changes made to our funding criteria were done for political reasons or to specifically penalize Planned Parenthood. They were not.

"Our original desire was to fulfill our fiduciary duty to our donors by not funding grant applications made by organizations under investigation. We will amend the criteria to make clear that disqualifying investigations must be criminal and conclusive in nature and not political. That is what is right and fair."

This kind of protest demonstrates the power that women have to alter their own lives, to gain control over their own bodies. And now there's another tool in the arsenal for protest—the Internet. A call for action can come almost instantly after an incident, via cyberspace, containing all the data you need, including e-mail contacts, phone numbers, and mailing addresses, and even a form letter so you don't have to worry about composing your own.

Here's an example. Women Living Under Muslim Laws, along with a group known as Violence Is Not Our Culture, often instigates calls for action. Sometimes it's because a woman has been jailed without trial or a government has ruled unfairly toward women. Activists are accustomed to receiving such calls on their computer screens and following through with action. When the government of Afghanistan was planning a meeting in Bonn, Germany, to discuss the so-called peace process, an action call went out from WLUML on November 24, 2011, saying:

> In the wake of the exclusion of Afghan women from the "peace process" at the Bonn Conference that is to take place on the 5th of December 2011, WLUML vigorously denounces:
> - the ethical incoherence of States that engaged in a devastating war in Afghanistan under the fallacious pretext to protect "poor oppressed Muslim women living under the burqa," and now prevent them from participating as full-fledged citizens in the peace process in their country, all while engaging with their oppressors
> - the moral responsibility of these States, which are delivering Afghan women, bound and gagged, to the very same Taliban and warlords they pretended to save them from, just a few years ago
> - the political short-sightedness of alliances, such as with Taliban and warlords, which fearfully remind us of other past historical compromises that cost so many lives
> - the fallacy of the so-called "democratic" process taking place in Germany, but without the "untermensch" of the day: Afghan women

They provided e-mail contacts for the government representatives and each of the delegates. Responses poured in from around the world. Before the conference even began, its agenda and delegation list were changed to include women who would speak up about women's rights.

The Stop Stoning Forever Campaign is another case example. Women Living Under Muslim Laws teamed up with Violence Is Not Our Culture and Justice for Iran to announce the release of a new publication, *Mapping Stoning in Muslim Contexts,* a report that named the fourteen countries where the punishment of stoning is still in practice, either through judicial (codified as law) or extrajudicial (outside the law) methods. Mapping reports carry a surprising amount of weight in the form of naming and shaming the countries that still condone stoning.

Historically, stoning has been used in many religious and cultural traditions as a form of community justice or capital punishment. Although there is no mention of stoning in the Quran, the practice has come to be associated with Islam and Muslim cultures. WLUML says laws that rendered stoning a legally sanctioned punishment emerged with the revival of political Islam during the late twentieth and early twenty-first centuries. Sharia law, the Islamic legal system, says that men will be buried to their waists and women to their breasts for the execution and that the stones thrown must not be so large as to kill the person quickly. The death is to be slow and painful. WLUML reports that women are stoned far more often than men. In Afghanistan recently, a twenty-nine-year-old woman called Amina was stoned to death for adultery. The man accused with her was lashed eighty times and freed.

When a woman has been sentenced to be stoned to death, the joint campaign puts out an action call. Women and men around the world respond with letters to the judiciary or government official sent by e-mail and fax. WLUML claims that public pressure has decreased the number of executions and that several punishments have been cancelled or postponed after their calls for action are made public. However, in places like Afghanistan, the sentence is usually carried out without judicial authority and therefore escapes the protests that these women are prepared to stage.

WLUML says stoning poses a serious threat to both women and men living in Muslim societies today. Sexual relationships outside marriage, along with same-sex relations, are criminalized in most codified interpretations of sharia law. Any sexual relationship outside a legal marriage is considered a crime punishable by a hundred lashes if the accused is unmarried and death by stoning if married.

Whether as activist reformers or public policy–makers, women have learned that the quickest way to establish their own space is by running for parliament and occupying the same space as men. Afghan member of parliament Fawzia Koofi, who plans to run for the presidency in the next election, says, "There's pride in being a member of parliament; there's a sense of success. Initially in Afghanistan there was a lot of resistance from men because our arguments were asking for changes in the law. The men tried to stop us by cutting the microphone when one of us was talking in the parliament. They don't do that anymore. We're strong. We won't go back or give up. It's time for them to give up."

Farida Shaheed says there are plenty of encouraging changes in Pakistan too, such as more young professional women making strides in the workplace and more girls getting an education. "On the other hand, a great conservativism is permeating Pakistani society. We need to be vigilant, make sure we are going forward, not moving backward, where everything is determined by superstition and what someone else says." Still, she thinks women have come a long way from feeling their place has been ordained, that they are stuck with their lot in life and simply have to live with it. "Women need to come together so they can be each other's supporters and fight for equality rights. What we discovered in Pakistan is the fewer women who enjoy their rights, the faster the state can take those rights away from you. And it can happen very quickly."

One can't help wondering what it is that stops men from embracing changes that would improve the economy and stop conflict. The thing is, people become habituated to what they have, and having a woman who takes care of you, a woman you can control, a woman who gets nothing in return, feels normal and essential to men who have never known a different life. They are perplexed by the criticism and afraid of what change will do. Some men truly cannot picture that their lives will be better if they treat their daughters, sisters, mothers, and wives as fully human. Establishing rights has historically been a long, slow, and sometimes confusing process.

Activist Joanna Kerr shares an interesting interpretation about the way her own male colleagues in South Africa and elsewhere, who are mostly human rights champions, view the changes in attitudes toward women and girls. "They tell me, 'It's so in our face, in our private space, because we all have mothers or sisters or wives or girlfriends, and the kind of relationships that are being transformed through gender equality come up against our histories, our hearts and minds. It gets inside our skin in such a way, it creates discomfort.'" She says the struggle for women's rights is not the same as the struggle to end racism, or even the fight for gay rights, because somehow gender equality feels different. "All of us have ideas about how women and men and girls and boys should behave. And gender is the most significant identifier of how individuals interact with each other. If you have never met someone before and you didn't quite know whether the person was a male or a female that you were speaking to, you feel uncomfortable because you don't know what social rules to apply. Whereas when we don't know their nationality, their ethnicity, their social class, we still know how to interact. But gender, the rules of gender, are so deeply,

deeply imbued and embedded in all of us that when we start changing the rules, we don't quite know how to behave."

It is a recognizable dilemma. But one that society needs to come to terms with. There are consequences for not taking women seriously, as Gloria Steinem says: "If you leave inequality in the home, you've left the model for racism and class there as well. You can directly measure the degree of democracy in society by the degree of democracy in the home. You can predict the degree of violence in the street or foreign policy by the amount in the home because everything is normalized in the home."

History is on the side of women's empowerment, which is one of the great moral imperatives of our time. And now that the international economists have pointed to enhancing women's rights as the ticket to financial heaven, institutional change is likely to speed up. Certainly young women—teenagers and twenty-somethings— are poised to make their demands known and to take action if they aren't met.

One hundred and sixty young girls in Kenya knocked on the door of change and made history by suing their government for failing to protect them from being raped. Young women like Asmaa Mahfouz in Egypt are suggesting that the men join the movement to emancipate women, and so is Mozn Hassan.

In Afghanistan, Noorjahan Akbar and Anita Haidary have launched the most powerful change agent that Afghan women have ever known with their organization Young Women for Change. They have also invited men to join the movement. Gloria Steinem thinks their stories are the art of the possible. She says, "Women are certainly the way forward. Men are also the way forward. Progress lies in the direction we haven't been." If Akbar and Haidary's plan to emancipate the women and girls of Afghanistan and throw off the restrictive aspects of old customs takes flight, they could alter the future for 15 million people.

I told Akbar that the women in Cairo said they had breached the barricade of fear, and I asked her if she had as well. She has a small voice that matches her delicate frame, but she speaks precisely. "I am still afraid very often. I think anyone who has joined YWC has had fear because people who dare to speak out against injustice face backlash, and any new idea is bound to be rejected before being accepted, especially if it challenges societal norms and rules. However, I deeply believe in the equality of humankind, and I know that regardless of how tired, depressed, or afraid I am, I will not give up on myself or the millions of women in Afghanistan who can be equal, who deserve to be treated equally. When we rise for what is right, what is our right, when we have a truth we're willing to stand up for, we have nothing to lose."

From Asia and Africa to the Americas, these women and their sisters and mothers are showing the way forward. They aren't victims, they're victors. Like 3.5 billion beautiful rosebuds, half the world's population is about to bloom into the future.

CONCLUSION

Here Come the Girls

As the summer of 2012 morphed into fall and the fresh start that that season brings, I went back to Afghanistan. I decided to return to that fractious, troubled place because Alaina Podmorow, fifteen, a Canadian girl from the interior of British Columbia who had devoted much of her young life to bettering the lot of girls in Afghanistan, was going to Kabul for the first time, and I wanted to be there to see her meet the kids she'd been helping since she was nine years old. She also planned to try to connect with the cofounders of Young Women for Change, an encounter between young women from two sides of the world that I wanted to witness.

For all the pessimists who claim the women's movement is over and that young people don't care, Alaina Podmorow's story is an injection of hope. I met her in the fall of 2006, when I was in B.C.'s beautiful Okanagan Valley to give a speech sponsored by Canadian Women for Women in Afghanistan about conditions for women in that conflict-ridden country. The auditorium was packed. During the question-and-answer period that followed, I could hear a voice calling out but couldn't match a face to it. I strained my eyes to see over the large crowd and finally spied a pint-size girl on her feet, dwarfed by the adults around her. But the words she spoke made her a giant in the room that September night.

Alaina Podmorow, then only nine years old, had no trouble making her position clear. "Those girls you're talking about—they're my age. This has to stop," she said, with all the indignation a girl child can summon. The audience erupted into applause.

Alaina had held up a pure, clear light in the midst of the renewed darkness that had descended on Afghanistan as the hard-won post-9/11 improvements started slipping away in 2006 in the face of an insurgency that was gaining ground. My adult audience surely cared about the resurgent brutality and hoped for change. But Alaina's reaction came from the unvarnished innocence we each had begun with before we were beaten up by "the way things have always been." Later, when I got to know Alaina, she told me that when she arrived home after the event, pamphlets tucked into her satchel and the girls in Afghanistan on her mind, she couldn't stop thinking about how to help her "sisters" halfway across the world. By the next morning, she had a plan. She would start Little Women for Little Women in Afghanistan (LW4LWA), and together with her classmates and preteen friends she would hold bake sales and bottle drives and car washes to raise enough money to pay teachers in Afghanistan so that kids her age could go to school. "I felt I had a power within me," she said. "I knew I could do something that would make a difference to the girls of Afghanistan." After her first fund-raiser, a silent auction, she had enough money to hire four teachers. "I'd made a difference and felt amazing knowing that. If one girl can make a difference, imagine what would happen if a powerful force of girls got together." She lit a torch in the process, building awareness and spreading the facts about the lives of girls in Afghanistan; she carried it all the way to the prime minister's office and then blazed its light from Kabul to Kandahar.

Alaina at sixteen is the quintessential Canadian girl, her wavy hair in a ponytail one minute and flowing over her shoulders the

next as she flies down a soccer field, focused on the goal with victory in her eyes, or pitches forward on her snowboard, cruising
down the slopes near her home in the B.C. interior. Lainy, as she's
known to her friends, also dances and performs in school musicals
and sings like an angel. Since she was nine, she has started chapters
of LW4LWA across Canada, enlisting dozens of girls who are equally
determined to restore the right to education to girls their age on
the other side of the world. She's done hundreds of interviews,
been featured in a documentary, and won the Me to We award presented annually by Craig and Marc Kielburger and *Canadian Living* magazine to ordinary Canadians making an extraordinary
difference in the world for thinking less about me and more about
we. It comes with a $5,000 donation to the charity of the winner's
choice. And she was the ambassador for Canada to the Day of the
Girl held on the UN's International Girls' Day in New York City
on October 11, 2012. She is equally unfazed whether she is chatting
with Prime Minister Stephen Harper on Parliament Hill or Peter
Mansbridge on CBC TV. She sees the many barriers in the way of
her goal to educate girls in Afghanistan simply as nuisance factors
that need to be overcome. Her slogan is "education = peace," and
she has already spent six years of her life working to make those
words a reality. She's a girl who makes us all feel proud because
somehow she represents the best we can be.

But going to Afghanistan? Until this year, that was a dream she
dared not even hope would come true. Then Alaina received an
invitation that no girl with a sense of adventure and a heart of service could refuse. Lauryn Oates, the projects director for Canadian Women for Women in Afghanistan, was going there to check
out their progress and asked Alaina if she wanted to come to see
the work her own organization was funding. She jumped at the opportunity. Her mom, Jamie, who has been working alongside her
daughter ever since she decided to become a game-changer, said,
"Of course she can go—as long as I go with her." And so the intrepid travelers set out in late August.

I caught up with them in Kabul. Sitting cross-legged on the couch in the room where she was staying in Kabul, Alaina described the preparations she'd made for the voyage. The packing was one thing: baggy clothing, hijab, long shirts that covered her female form. But it was the psychological preparation that got most of her attention. She knew about the Taliban and warlords, of course, and naturally feared that she and her mom might be attacked, injured, or even killed. But the greater fear that kept circling through her young mind was of "seeing something I cannot unsee. I had to look inside myself and realize that what I was about to see would change me."

She wanted to meet the girls her charity was funding—the girls attending school, the children being cared for in a center that her group supports for the dependants of women in jail for crimes such as being raped or running away from an abusive husband. But she also hoped to meet Sahar Gul, the girl who had been forced into an underage marriage and then told by her in-laws that she had to work as a prostitute to bring money to the family, and who was tortured when she refused. Sahar had escaped and was living at a shelter in Kabul.

Alaina also hoped she would meet the cofounders of Young Women for Change, Noorjahan Akbar, only twenty-one, and Anita Haidary, just nineteen. She had followed their campaign to change Afghanistan on Facebook and wanted to know how they were getting along, what they were thinking, and whether, as she suspected, they shared much with her in their approach to changing the world.

She described the power of her arrival in a country she'd been imagining for so long. "Driving from the airport in Kabul, I saw how harmed the city was—smashed streets, children begging, some women still wearing burqas, men sitting around, broken buildings. But then I saw past that—vendors creating their own businesses, women wearing hijabs and very high-heeled shoes, girls going to school, children flying kites. What I saw was the broken beautiful that is Afghanistan." Like Alice in Wonderland, Alaina Podmorow went through the looking glass, and what she saw was confirmation of her formula for change.

Then she met Noorjahan and Anita, and they welcomed her into the global sisterhood and, as young enthusiasts do, talked excitedly with her about the possibilities for the future. After the sixteen years I've spent covering Afghanistan and the twenty-six years writing about women's issues around the world, I was moved to observe this meeting of minds. It spoke of the kind of change that is possible as well as sustainable. Anita swept into the room in a long black dress with a cinch belt, a black hijab, and high heels. Less than five feet tall, she is a woman with presence—one of those people who can stand in the doorway and seem to be in the center of the room. She reminded Alaina that the Taliban had stolen the childhood of the girls of Afghanistan, that girls her age had nothing to look back on. "People here talk about Islam all the time—women should do this and that for Islam. And women are not allowed to do this and that because of Islam. What about the men? For them it's a free pass. No one confronts them and says, 'You do not have the right to harass me in the street, to touch me when I walk past you, no matter what I am wearing.'"

Together they talked about the obstacles facing women in their struggle to change the mind-set of men. Noorjahan, who was wearing a short red dress, also cinched at the waist, with black leggings and flat shoes and a skimpy hijab, said she had a level of pity for the "olders," as she called them, who are "old traumatized people who have their own issues to deal with; they've been through wars, and for many of them refugee camps." But her eye was focused squarely on the future for girls. "This new generation has also been through war, although we never played a part in it except as victims. We have new things to tell and new tools to use. The Internet and social media empower us and let us work to make Afghanistan a better country—one that's not just about war but about promoting a diverse culture, one that tolerates different ideas about women's rights and children's rights, where 87 percent of women don't face violence and 45 percent of children don't face enforced labor. Youth and women are the solution to the dreams of Afghanistan."

The topic that caught fire with the trio was how to end street harassment. The vile things that men and boys say to women and girls walking to school or to the grocery store in Afghanistan usually go unchallenged. Comments such as "I think you are not a virgin. I have a car; come with me." Or, "I'm looking at your dress, at your shoes. What I see is a whore." Young Women for Change has made the stopping of that harassment a priority because they argue that it affects human rights as well as the safety of every girl and woman in the country. Although Alaina had only been in Kabul for a few days, she had already been a target herself, despite her long shirt, pants, and brightly colored hijab. She asked Anita how men get away with it, and Anita explained: "If you are followed on the street, you would never tell your parents because they would say it was your fault, there's something wrong with you—you weren't wearing your scarf properly, you weren't dressed modestly enough. It's always the girls who have done something wrong; it's never the men."

Noorjahan says she screams when men on the street touch her buttocks. "I do that so everyone will know. But the feeling here is you shouldn't create a scene. You should shut up. They make you feel that you have committed a crime by walking on the street." Anita added, "They think women's rights are here to attack the culture and make all women Westernized. Sending girls to school is Western. Giving them their rights is Western. Treating them like human beings is Western. If that's the case, what is Eastern? What's Islamic?"

Alaina was on the same wavelength. "[What can have] the biggest impact on change here is the minds of men," she said. "Some men think women should be educated and have the same opportunities as the men do. Others think women should have a child every year and stay at home. Well, Afghan girls are powering their way through this: for every hundred who stay at home, there's one who can see beyond that and think that she can make a difference. There will be another one and then another one." She had already visited the schools that her group supported. The kids she spoke to all wanted to finish school, go to university, and become doctors and teachers. "There's a powerful movement of women and girls here who will be successful global citizens."

The journey to global citizenship that these young women seek for their sisters isn't an easy one. Alaina knew that YWC had staged several protest marches against street harassment and asked Anita what it was like to defy the status quo so boldly. Anita told her the first march was a big event in the lives of local women and girls. "It was a Sunday. I was nervous. Afghan women don't do things like this, but after hearing people talk about the need for change and the fact that now is the time for change, I felt all powered up and decided I was going to do it. No matter what happens, we have to do it today." When it was over, Anita said, "I felt so powerful, like I owned the street and that I had a voice and a place to claim 'I am doing this.' "

The YWC compound wasn't hidden from view the way buildings occupied by most organizations, including the United Nations, are in bomb-battered Kabul. A large white banner with Young Women for Change in English and Dari stretched across the yellow door-way on busy Darul Aman Road, not far from the parliament buildings. Inside was an oasis of calm—beds of flowering plants, shade trees bent over the mud-brick walls of the courtyard—and a surprising level of bustling activity: an art exhibit here, an Internet café there, with clutches of young women and men discussing the news of the day as tailoring lessons went on in the single schoolroom, where skills for the current job market are taught.

The day I visited YWC with Alaina marked the premiere of Anita's documentary, *My Voice, My Story*, about street harassment. Excitement permeated the meeting room, where about sixty young people, half of them men, were gathered for the screening and subsequent question-and-answer period. The ones I spoke with were all between the ages of sixteen and twenty-three: bright, energetic, incredibly polite in the way they greet a stranger, and enormously enthusiastic about getting their story told to the wider world.

Afterward, a young man asked Anita if the harassment comes from uneducated men. She replied, "Part of it does, but mostly it's a way for men to show that they don't want women on the street. In the Taliban time, men owned the street." Another question, also posed by a young man, followed: "Women and girls aren't prepared to talk about this. Even in my own family women are always told they are not to complain about men. So my question is, how do you inspire the women who are still sitting in their houses thinking they have no right to complain?" You could have heard a pin drop in the room as Anita answered: "You're right. Most women in Afghanistan think they have no right to complain about being harassed or beaten. [But] we [at YWC] have lectures about this. We go to the schools and talk to the girls. I think it's easier to work with the generation rising up right now than to try to fix what happened in the past. If I talk to my mom, her ideas are fixed; she won't listen. But schoolgirls, university students, young women—they'll listen. So we focus on youth and on the media."

Then one of the women in the audience asked the young men what they do when their friends harass women. Several spoke up at once, voices commingling: "I tell them to stop. It happens just as much in the office as it does on the street. Bosses do it as much as colleagues. It's an unfortunate part of the culture that is so deep that men think it is their right to do it, and women think they don't have the right to stop it."

When Anita drew the conversation to a close, she said something that even that first screening had shown to be true: "This documentary was made to give women a voice, to let her start talking about what she goes through when 50 percent of the society tells the other 50 percent to stay in the house."

The next morning, Alaina went to visit Sahar Gul at a secret shelter in Kabul, home to fourteen girls who had been abused. To

Alaina's surprise, another young woman, Mumtaz Bibi, who'd been horribly disfigured when the man she refused to marry threw acid all over her face, came into the visitors' room with Sahar to meet her. Watching the three young women—fifteen-year-old Alaina, fifteen-year-old Sahar, and sixteen-year-old Mumtaz—connect with one another was a remarkable sight. Even with the interruptions of cumbersome translations and the ubiquitous Afghan hospitality that required the serving of nuts and sweets and green tea, the girls managed to make a bond. Alaina conveyed her respect for the courage of these young women and vowed to continue fighting for the equality rights of girls in Afghanistan. The painfully shy Sahar could only glance up at Alaina from under her eyelids, wringing her hands as she spoke in a whisper, but still she flashed a smile as she thanked Alaina for the support she had promised. Mumtaz did the same. Then each of them told Alaina about their plans to get an education. But whatever the future brought, they said they would make time to volunteer at this shelter. Later Alaina told me, "I don't think there are words to describe how raw and emotional that meeting was. They've seen what no child or adult should ever see, but each of them wants to give back to the shelter, to help other girls. They're healing emotionally and physically—they are the light at the end of this tunnel."

Confronting the realities in the lives of girls is the single best way to begin the long, sure process of change, even when that confrontation means attacking old shibboleths. For example, in Afghanistan, the subject of the best-known and best-loved poetry is invariably how wonderful women are and how heaven lies beneath their feet. "Still, 87 percent face violence at home," Noorjahan had explained. "More than four hundred women are in jail for moral crimes such as falling in love or running away from abusive families. Most of this poetry is written by men. I know some of those men—they beat their wives. I want to marry someone who will support me, fight for me, argue with me, not someone who will write poetry about me and keep me at home."

These three young women know the size of the change they have to make and believe that it's the young people under thirty who will do it. The two young Afghan women offered this illustration: if a girl asks her grandfather about marching against street harassment, he'll say, "Don't do it; you'll bring shame on the family." If she asks her father, he'll say the same and add, "Stay at home; the street is too dangerous for you." But if she asks her sister, she'll want to know where and when the march is taking place and join in.

Similar initiatives are happening in Senegal and Swaziland, in India and Pakistan as well as in the Americas. The girls I spoke with all over the world confirm that the first step is acknowledging their plight, and the next step will take them into a better future. They believe in their hearts what experts such as Jeffrey Sachs and Farida Shaheed have recently stated: educating and empowering girls and women is the ticket to an improved economy, reduced poverty, and the end of conflict.

Anita, Noorjahan, and Alaina agreed that even if YWC ceased to exist, the idea would go on because the seed of change had already been planted. In fact, in late September 2012, Noorjahan left YWC to start another organization for the emancipation of women through the arts. The group's ideas and slogans are zipping around the country from one province to another via Facebook and Twitter. In villages without technology, news that change is on the way is passed by word of mouth. There's a new generation at work and new hope in the air. "The elders have made all the decisions for us for a long time," Anita said. "It's enough. It's not their time anymore; it's ours." And Noorjahan added, "Women haven't made war; they aren't as involved in corruption. You don't see 80 percent of the men in this country being beaten by their wives."

"We're the generation of change," Alaina said. "We have the power and a new viewpoint and we're going to change the world—watch us."

Acknowledgments

About eighteen months before I started writing this book I had an epiphany of sorts about the status of the world's women. I'd been covering conflict in various parts of the world for twenty-five years, almost always from the point of view of what happens to women and girls. Now I sensed something was shifting. I couldn't put my finger on it at first, but I knew whatever this shift was, it was benefiting women. Players who normally shrugged their shoulders about women's issues were suddenly paying attention. Women who'd seen their lot in life as preordained began to say, "Not anymore."

For the next year I posed questions I hadn't thought to ask before, gathered data that made me certain this inkling I had was valid. But to actually come out and suggest that women are the way forward, that many of the planet's ills, such as poverty and endemic conflict, can be improved by women, that after all the years of oppression and abuse, times were changing, that women were throwing off the shackles that bound them to second-class citizenship and owning their own voices and spaces? Well, that was a leap in thinking that I needed to test.

I decided to try my thesis out on an audience in Oakville, Ontario, when my friend Bonnie Jackson asked me to address her "Bloomsbury Group" at their monthly meeting. This collection of intellectuals would no doubt let me know if I was on track. When I finished speaking, they voiced their surprise and approval with hearty applause. Soon afterward, I had lunch with Marion Garner, the publisher of Vintage Canada, who is always on the lookout for fresh ideas. I told her about the speech, and she said, "This is a book. Get going."

Then Paul Kennedy, the brilliant host of CBC Radio's *Ideas*, suggested I do a version of the story—describing women as "the new revolutionaries"—for his program. And I was at last on my way.

So the first person I have to thank is Marion, for believing in this concept, and then Paul for road-testing it. Anne Collins at Random House Canada provided her usual meticulous editing in Toronto and took the book to the finish line while Marcia Markland at St. Martin's Press in New York called for revisions and took the book worldwide. I am grateful to copy editors Alison Reid at Random House and Sibylle Kazeroid at St. Martin's Press. And to Kat Brzozowski in New York, who kept the project on time and on track.

But most of all, I owe this work to the women and girls around the world who helped me to create it. The women who gave me shelter in places from which local fundamentalists preferred to banish me. The ones who stuffed bread into my pocket to feed me on my journey out of a country that had basically imprisoned them. The many who suffer at the hands of so-called religious men, yet were willing to share their stories despite the threat of retaliation. And those who had the courage to talk about the cultural contradictions in their lives and what they were doing to change them. Women who have been heroes of mine in Asia, Africa, and the Americas shaped my thinking about the tipping point that women are reaching. What's more, they encouraged me to write this book.

And to the girls who filled my journey with laughter and inspiration, who shed such a clear honest light on the situation they are in and shared their energy and enthusiasm for change—thank you. I cherished our time together. To all the mothers and daughters who opened their worlds to me, I offer my heartfelt thanks, and I hope we meet again.

And of course I owe enormous gratitude to my family and Jonathan Chilvers, who put up with the antics of an author with a deadline, and to my agent, Hilary McMahon: I celebrate the publication of this book and the role you played in getting us all to this place.

Selected Bibliography

BOOKS, REPORTS, ARTICLES, LECTURES

Bunch, Charlotte, and Samantha Frost. "Women's Human Rights: An Introduction." In *Routledge International Encyclopedia of Women: Global Women's Issues and Knowledge,* p. 2. New York: Routledge, 2000.

Charlesworth, Hilary. "What Are 'Women's International Human Rights'?" In *Human Rights of Women: National and International Perspectives,* ed. Rebecca J. Cook, 58–84. Philadelphia: University of Pennsylvania Press, 1994.

Coleman, Isobel. *Paradise Beneath Her Feet: How Women Are Transforming the Middle East.* New York: Random House, 2010.

Cook, Rebecca J. "State Responsibility for Violations of Women's Human Rights." *Harvard Human Rights Journal* 7 (1994): 125–75.

———. "Women's International Human Rights Law: The Way Forward." In Cook, *Human Rights of Women,* 3–36.

———. "Human Rights Law and Safe Motherhood." *European Journal of Health Law* 5 (1998): 357–75.

———. "Fostering Compliance with Women's Rights in the Inter-American System." *Revue Québécoise de Droit International* 11 (1998): 129–142.

———. "International Women's Rights Law." Lecture, University of Toronto Law School, January 6, 2000.

Cook, R. J., and B. M. Dickens. "Ethical and Legal Issues in Reproductive

Health: Ethics, Justice and Women's Health." *International Journal of Gynecology and Obstetrics* 64 (1999): 81–85.

———. "National and International Approaches to Reproductive and Sexual Health Law." Lecture, University of Toronto Law School, September 19, 2000.

Coomaraswamy, Radhika. "To Bellow Like a Cow: Women, Ethnicity, and the Discourse of Rights." In Cook, *Human Rights of Women*, 39–57.

Cressy, David. *Birth, Marriage, and Death: Ritual, Religion, and the LifeCycle in Tudor and Stuart England.* New York: Oxford University Press, 1997.

Dutt, Mallika, Nancy Flowers, and Julie Mertus. *Local Action/Global Change: Learning about the Human Rights of Women and Girls.* New York: UNI-FEM and the Center for Women's Global Leadership, 1999.

Fisher, Elizabeth, and Linda Gray MacKay. *Gender Justice: Women's Rights Are Human Rights.* Cambridge, Mass.: Unitarian Universalist Service Committee, 1996.

Fraser, Arvonnes. "Becoming Human: The Origins and Development of Women's Human Rights." *Human Rights Quarterly* 21 (1999): 853–906.

Girard, Françoise. "Cairo + Five: Reviewing Progress for Women Five Years after the International Conference on Population and Development." *Journal of Women's Health and Law* 1, no. 1 (1999): 1–14.

Hamzic, Vanja, and Ziba Mir-Hosseini. *Control and Sexuality: The Revival of Zina Laws in Muslim Contexts.* London: Women Living Under Muslim Laws, 2010.

Hedgepeth, Sonja, and Rochelle G. Saidel, eds. *Sexual Violence against Jewish Women during the Holocaust.* Waltham, Mass.: Brandeis University Press, 2010.

Holmes, Helen B. "A Feminist Analysis of the Universal Declaration of Human Rights." In *Beyond Discrimination: New Perspectives on Women and Philosophy*, ed. Carol Gould, 250–64. Totowa, N.J.: Rowman & Allanheld, 1983.

Hom, Sharon K. "Commentary: Re-positioning Human Rights Discourse on Asian Perspectives." *Buffalo Journal of International Law* 3, no. 1 (1996): 209–34.

Ingram, Martin. *Church Courts, Sex and Marriage in England, 1570–1640.* Cambridge: Cambridge University Press, 1987.

Ishay, Micheline R. *The Human Rights Reader: Major Political Essays, Speeches, and Documents from the Bible to the Present.* London: Routledge, 1997.

Kerr, Joanna, ed. *Ours by Right: Women's Rights as Human Rights.* London: Zed Books, 1993.

MacCulloch, Diarmaid. *Reformation: Europe's House Divided, 1490–1700.* London: Allen Laner, 2003.

McGuire, Danielle L. *At the Dark End of the Street.* New York: Vintage, 2011.

Metzger, Bruce M., and Roland E. Murphy, eds. *The New Oxford Annotated*

Bible with the Apocryphal/Deuterocanonical Books. New York: Oxford University Press, 1991.

Morsink, Johannes. *The Universal Declaration of Human Rights: Origins, Drafting, and Intent.* Philadelphia: University of Pennsylvania Press, 1999.

Papenek, H. "To Each Less Than She Needs, from Each More Than She Can Do: Allocations, Entitlements, and Value." In *Persistent Inequalities: Women and World Development*, ed. Irene Tinker, 162–84. Oxford: Oxford University Press, 1990.

State of the World Forum, September 4, 2000. Welcoming address by Wally N'Dow, convening chairman, Forum 2000, New York. Accessed September 25, 2001. http://www.world-forum.org.

United Nations, Department of Public Information. The United Nations and the Advancement of Women, 1945–1995. New York: The United Nations Blue Book Series, Vol. VI, 1995.

United Nations High Commissioner for Human Rights: Convention on the Elimination of All Forms of Discrimination against Women. Accessed 2012. www.unhchr.ch/html/menu3/b/e1cedaw. htm,

Van der Gaag, Nikki. *Because I Am a Girl: The State of the World's Girls, 2011, So What about the Boys?* Plan UK, Plan International, Plan Canada, 2011.

WEB SITES

Afghanistan Independent Human Rights Commission: www.aihrc.org.af

Afghan Women's Network: www.afghanwomennetwork.at

AIDS Free World: www.aidsfreeworld.org

Amnesty International: www.amnesty.org

Asia Pacific Economic Conference: http://www.stategov/secretary/rm/2011/09/172605.ht

Association for Women's Rights in Development: www.awid.org

Bat Shalom: www.coalitionofwomen.org/?tag_gat-shalon&rang-en

Brenda Boone Hope Center Foundation: www.brendaboonehopecenter.org

Canadian Women for Women in Afghanistan: www.cw4wafghan.ca

Canadian Women's Foundation: www.canadianwomen.org/

Caribbean Association for Feminist Research and Action: www.cpdengo.org

CEDAW: www.un.org/womenwatch/daw/cedaw

Center for Women's Global Leadership: www.cwgl.rutgers.edu

Coalition Against Trafficking in Women: www.catwinternational.org

Coalition of Women for a Just Peace: www.fire.or.cr/junio01/coalition.htm

Equality Effect: www.theequalityeffect.org

Equality Now: www.equalitynow.org

Feminist Majority: www.feministmajority.org

Forum for Women in Development: www.learningpartnership.org

Geena Davis Institute on Gender in Media: www.seejane.org

Global Fund for Women: www.globalfundforwomen.org

HarassMap: www.harassMap.org

Human Rights Watch: www.hrw.org

Imprint—Egypt: http://www.facebook.com/imprint.movement.eg

Inter-American Commission on Women: www.oas.org/en/cim

The International Alliance for Women: www.tiaw.org

International Center for Research on Women (Washington, D.C.): www.icrw.org

International Planned Parenthood Federation: www.ippf.org

International Women's Rights Watch Asia Pacific: www.iwraw-ap.org

Israel Women's Network: www.iwn.org.il

Jerusalem Center for Women: www.j-c-w.org

Komen Foundation: //ww5.komen.org/

Little Women for Little Women in Afghanistan: www.littlewomenforlittle-women.com

Medica Mondiale: www.medicamondiale.org

Musawah: www.musawah.org

National Federation of Dalit Women: www.womenutc.com/national_federation_of_Daht_women.htm

National Organization for Women: www.now.org

National Union of Guatemalan Women: www.globalfundforwomen.org/what-we-do/civic-a-politcal-participation/92

Native Women's Association of Canada: www.nwac.ca

Nazra for Feminist Studies: www.nazra.org

Nobel Women's Initiative: www.nobelwomensinitiative.org/

One Billion Rising for Justice: www.onebillionrising.org

Plan International: www.plan-international.org

PeopleSense Foundation: www.peoplesensefoundation.org

Population First (India): www.populationfirst.org

Ripples International: www.ripplesintl.or.ke

Shirkat Gah: www.shirkatgah.org

Sisters in Islam: www.sistersinislam.org

The Stephen Lewis Foundation: www.stephenlewisfoundation.org

Stop Street Harassment: www.stopstreetharassment.org

Swaziland for Positive Living: www.swaPol.net

Terres des Femmes: www.frauenrechte.de/online/index.php

Tostan: www.tostan.org

UN Commission on the Status of Women: www.un.org/womenwatch/daw/esw/

UN Women: www.unwomen.org

Urgent Action Fund for Women's Human Rights: www.urgentactionfund.org
V-Day: action.vday.org
Walk a Mile in Her Shoes: www.walkamileinhershoes.org
Women in Black: www.womaninblack.org
Women Living Under Muslim Laws: www.wluml.org
Women Moving Millions www.womenovingmillions.org
Womankind Worldwide: www.womankind.org.uk
Women's Centre for Legal Aid and Counseling: www.wclac.org
Women's Legal Education and Action Fund: www.leaf.ca
The World Bank: worldbank.org
World March of Women: www.marchofwomen.2000org
Young Women for Change: www.youngwomenforchange.org/

MAGAZINE ARTICLES BY SALLY ARMSTRONG

"Eva: Witness for Women." *Homemaker's*, Summer 1993.
"No Way Home: The Tragedy of the Girl Child." *Homemaker's*, October 1994.
"Not My Daughter." *Homemaker's*, November/December 1998.
"Honour's Victims." *Chatelaine*, March 2000.
"Speaking Their Peace." *Chatelaine*, September 2002.
"The Untouchables." *Chatelaine*, July 2004.
"Trouble in Paradise." *Chatelaine*, September 2004.
"Rights of Passage." *Chatelaine*, December 2004.
"Guardians of Hope." *Fifty Plus*, April 2007.
"Hope on the Horizon." *Chatelaine*, March 2010.
"The Go-Go Sisterhood." *Reader's Digest*, January 2011.
"These Girls Are Changing the World." *Chatelaine*, September 2011.

Index